EYEWITNESS

Erwin Weit

EYEWITNESS

The Autobiography of Gomulka's Interpreter

Translated by Mary Schofield

ANDRE DEUTSCH

First published 1973 by
André Deutsch Limited
105 Great Russell Street London WC1

Printed in Great Britain by
Ebenezer Baylis & Son Ltd
The Trinity Press Worcester and London

ISBN 0 233 95701 4

Contents

Introduction

Not quite three years have passed since I left Poland, and since then my life has been completely transformed. I came to the West from a country under communist rule and was able, for the first time since my childhood, to enjoy the freedom which here is taken for granted. Behind me lay thirty years during which I had lived under two dictatorships, first the Nazis and then the communists.

I wrote this book, in which I describe some of the experiences and information I had acquired, in the first few months of 1970. The first edition, in German, was published in the late summer of 1970. In the following year, up to autumn 1971, the book was translated and published in ten different languages in the West. World famous newspapers and magazines, such as *Le Monde* in France and *Der Spiegel* in Germany, printed extracts from it. I appeared in many Western television and radio programmes and was invited to lecture at universities, academic institutions and academic symposia.

In addition to this international success the book provoked a reaction in the Eastern bloc, for the people there heard about it from radio broadcasts and from friends who had visited the West. The first reaction was quicker than might have been expected. When it became known that my book was to be published Ulbricht sent an official note of protest to the Polish Foreign Ministry with a request that it be forwarded to the Polish Central Committee. The note criticized Poland in very strong terms for having let me emigrate to the West after I had been present at so many summit talks. But this was still a private protest. A few months later a press and propaganda campaign was launched which, with little regard for accuracy and a combination of lies and absurdities, tried to convince Polish newspaper readers that I had been a Zionist and Western agent since 1955. Thereafter the campaign escalated.

Naturally this did not surprise me. It had always been the tradition in communist countries to describe any critic of the regime as an agent of the Western imperialists. Stalin perfected this method and his successors followed it faithfully. Leonid Brezhnev also finds it useful. At the twenty-fourth congress of the Soviet Communist Party he described Roger Garaudy, formerly a leading French communist, and Ernst Fischer, formerly a leading Austrian communist, as mouthpieces of bourgeois ideology and propaganda, simply because, after years of political activity, they had realized that the communist world is not so perfect as it is made out to be, and stated their opinions openly. This is a verbal form of the Stalinist show trials to which the entire leadership of many communist parties fell victim. There is no discussion with those whose opinions are different, no other evidence is admitted – they are either silenced or physically destroyed. Whether this is a sign of strength, or of weakness – even of a neurotic fear of the freedom of thought – can easily be decided.

The communist revolution and the attempt to build communism in the Soviet Union and the other East bloc countries was compared by the Polish writer, Viktor Sukiennicki, to a political version of the mistake made by Columbus. Indeed, when Columbus set out to sea from a Spanish port in 1492 he was convinced by scientific calculations that he was going to reach India. But how far from India was the country where he eventually landed. In 1917 Lenin and his comrades set out on the path to socialism and communism, basing themselves on the calculations of Karl Marx. They were making for a world of social justice and brotherhood, of freedom and the good of all humanity. But how far from this political goal were they and their disciples to land . . .

I do not intend to describe the whole history of the communist movement in this introduction. Rather I am concerned to bring my book up to date in view of the latest developments and the present situation in Eastern Europe.

Recently several of the principal figures in my book have been overthrown. Gomulka, together with his closest collaborators, fell from power when the palace revolution which had failed in 1968 was finally put into effect in December 1970. In these chapters I had already described in detail how Gomulka became isolated, how he contributed to his own political suicide in a way that led, inevitably, to his downfall – and I did so at a time when he was still believed to be firmly entrenched in power, in both East and West. I also showed that Ulbricht, involved in the struggles for power within the Kremlin, had aroused the opposition of a section of the Soviet leadership.

Both these leaders have now been deposed, although for very different reasons.

In 1956, and the years immediately after, when Gomulka seemed to want to introduce liberalization inside Poland, he was one of Moscow's most hated men. But since he held real power, in the shape of the support of the overwhelming majority of the Polish people, the Russians respected him. So when he then sided more and more with the Kremlin in both internal and external politics and finally surrendered to them completely, he sealed his own fate. When he had estranged himself from all sections of Polish society and had therefore destroyed his own defences, he was overthrown. The Kremlin respects only men who act fearlessly because they are strong enough to do so. This was no longer the case with Gomulka.

The group opposing Gomulka, led by Moczar, overstepped all conceivable limits. In 1970 the exploitation and suppression of the Polish people reached a new high point. The hungry workers were driven on to greater and greater efforts and, as a final straw, Gomulka was presented with information in December which was intended to make him announce radical increases in the retail prices set by the state, and introduce a new economic policy of which the main feature was a further raising of norms and simultaneous reduction in wages. Gomulka fell into the trap and the absolute crisis point was reached. His enemies waited contemptuously for the moment when their plans would work out.

Then, when the desperate workers in the Polish coastal region went on strike, shots were fired against them. The bloody battle spread from day to day and the spontaneous rising of the workers and the people threatened to develop into a civil war. Now there were only two alternatives: either to escalate the armed retaliation of the state – leading to a civil war with unforeseeable consequences on the western frontier of the Soviet Union; or to carry out a palace revolution with lightning speed so that all the unpopular measures could be immediately blamed on the old leaders and the situation calmed down with high-flown declarations and promises. The third possibility – that of a Soviet military intervention – would present enormous problems. First, the Soviet Union was not prepared to start this kind of action alone, so it would be necessary to involve the other Warsaw Pact countries. Second, the political and military preparations would take time, and this was not available in view of the threat of civil war. And thirdly, Moscow feared the internal and external political and ideological repercussions that would follow such an action – particularly after her experiences in Hungary and Czechoslovakia – and was therefore only willing to take this step as a last resort. The leaders of the Polish conspiracy therefore allied themselves with the Kremlin in overthrowing Gomulka. He was immediately put in a hospital, where he heard the news of his downfall on the television.

The 'new' leadership countermanded the orders to shoot, made public a catalogue of promises, put the whole of the blame on the dismissed politicians, and hoped that this would make them masters of the situation. But this leadership was not new – either in their concept of power, or as individuals – and consisted entirely of leading politicians from the Gomulka regime. They did state that the price increases which had led to the revolt were a mistake, but they did not cancel them; the new economic policy announced by Gomulka was not introduced, but the workers were compelled to work extra shifts without pay 'in honour of the new leadership', and were even made to do unpaid work on Sundays. Inside the country there was no liberalization – on the contrary, the secret police terror was intensified. It was admitted that the unions and their central organizations had been too bureaucratic and had not represented the interests of the workers, because the 'trade union officials were not democratically elected by the workers', but Kruczek, who was well known as the last Stalinist in office in Poland, was then put in sole charge of the unions. Naturally Gomulka and the leaders who fell with him were given no opportunity to defend themselves before public opinion. The whole press was organized to shout '*le roi est mort*, *vive le roi*' even though the old king was still alive.

But this palace revolution and the attempt to present it as something completely new had an unexpected effect. The people had grown more sure of themselves and made use of their new confidence. When they saw that they were to be fobbed off with empty promises, and that the old policies were to be continued and intensified, they declared their veto. During the next few weeks and months there were more strikes in the coastal area, and the strike movement spread to the rest of the country. This was all the more remarkable because the workers had no organization and no press to help them. As the situation threatened to deteriorate into a general strike – and in a communist country this means civil war – the new leadership was gradually forced to grant a few concessions in the area of prices and wages. To improve their image they also allowed a few writers who had previously been banned to publish their work and, to make things look even better, they gave a few of them passports to travel abroad.

This kind of action, which was in opposition to the general political line, reflected the precarious situation within the new Polish leadership. They were working against time. The Soviet Union and the other East bloc countries feared that the sparks of the Polish revolt would spread to their countries, and waited impatiently for 'law and order' to be restored in Poland; meanwhile they even improved social conditions to some extent for their own people, and promised to raise their standard of living. But in Warsaw the battle continued. Moczar began a general attack on Gierek, whom he regarded as a springboard for his own rise to power once Gomulka was overthrown. In this attempt he was supported not only by his secret police but also by a large section of the impatient party apparatus who were now waiting anxiously for the promotions they had been promised. But in view of the highly explosive situation in Poland, Moscow was not prepared to permit any further experiments. Moczar was abandoned – or, in view of the fact that his links with the Kremlin are still intact and many of his collaborators have kept their posts – put on ice. He remained a member of the Central Committee with the function of senior State Controller, and so can be brought back into action any time.

With Ulbricht the position was different. Since the faction within the Kremlin that favours a relaxation in relations with the West now has the upper hand, whereas Ulbricht supported the hard-liners, he was forced to resign from his post. In my book I also showed that Ulbricht had set himself up in opposition against some of the Russian leaders during the sixties, long before his fall from power, and that there were forces in the Kremlin which were critical of him.

There was one common factor in the fall of these two men. Both in Poland and in the GDR the men at the top are much less well known than their predecessors, and know perfectly well that they owe their jobs to the Kremlin. This marked a new departure in relations between Moscow and the Eastern bloc countries. In the first uneasy years after the Second World War one country after another succeeded in escaping from the Soviet sphere of power. First came Jugoslavia, then Albania with China's support, and then Rumania. To halt this process, which would have ended in the complete isolation of the Soviet Union, one of the methods used was a new attempt to realize the aims of the Soviet leadership first in Poland, then in Czechoslovakia, and finally in the GDR. The Kremlin tried to set up two rival groups in the Warsaw Pact countries whenever they managed to get a completely free hand in the personal politics of each separate country. If Moscow can play the role of arbitrator, it can crush any group that is getting too strong and support its rival, thus minimizing the risk of a new Tito, Hoxha, Ceaucescu or Dubcek appearing. And in this way the need to put into practice the Brezhnev doctrine – which by the way, was invented long before Brezhnev – can be avoided.

In Poland Moczar was first built up in order to hold Gomulka in check. But when Gomulka fell from power in December 1970, and the balance was threatened, he was shunted into a siding. Gierek, often mistakenly described in the West as a technocrat or a pragmatist, was presented with his own rival in the shape of Prime Minister Jaroszewicz, a faithful disciple of Moscow.

In Czechoslovakia Husak was appointed by Moscow. But at the same time Moscow supported the claims of Strougal, Indra and others. Naturally, this led to rivalries. The ups and downs of the battles and 'victories' won by both factions during 1969 and 1970 made this obvious. Only because they were disturbed by the events of the Polish December did the Moscow leadership force the rivals into an apparent harmony. The disagreements continue under the surface but the danger of a possible 'Rumanian solution' for Czechoslovakia has been prevented.

Meanwhile, in the GDR Ulbricht finally became too awkward a figure. When the Soviet Union was trying to intensify its attempts to ease tension between East and West, Ulbricht was strong enough to put obstacles in its way. He held up the traffic on the Autobahn to West Berlin, claiming that he was hitting at West Germany, but in reality the red light was directed eastwards. Halt, you doves in the Kremlin! That was the real message of support from Ulbricht to his friends on the hard-liner wing of the Soviet Communist Party. A year before Ulbricht's dismissal I described a conversation between Ponomarev and Gomulka in my book which showed that a section of the Kremlin leadership was against Ulbricht but was afraid that his fall from power would provoke internal struggles for power within the GDR (without the support of Moscow). But by spring 1971 things had gone far enough. In Honecker and Stoph the Soviet leadership believed they had found two men who were strong enough to compete with each other but neither of whom had the power to become another Ulbricht.

Naturally, the next question is what can be the aim of the Soviet Union and her east European satellites in pursuing this policy of *détente*. To understand the foreign policy of the communist countries it is essential to realize its relationship with internal policy; in these countries foreign policy is a function of home policy, a fact that is often overlooked in the West. There are even some who say that the foreign policy of the Eastern bloc varies according to the international political situation. It is not splitting theoretical hairs to oppose these two theses; they represent solid realities.

Internal policy – and no Eastern leader would ever admit the slightest doubt about it – is based on the ideology of 'Marxism-Leninism'. So if foreign policy is a function of internal policy, then one of the declared aims of foreign policy is to bring about world revolution.

On the other hand, if one accepts the theory that 'foreign policy is a result of the international situation', this means that the Eastern bloc can be persuaded by means of various concessions that it is not under any threat and, in this way, liberalizing elements can be encouraged in Soviet foreign and internal policy. But every step taken by the West in granting the concessions demanded by the Eastern bloc helps, whether willingly or not, to support Soviet foreign policy *as a function of internal policy*. The threat from the West, which is a constant factor in propaganda for both domestic and foreign consumption, has not been taken seriously by the Eastern leaders, at least for the last fifteen years, as I was able to see at numerous summit meetings. In private discussions the leaders of the Eastern bloc never attempt to conceal their belief and conviction that the West does not seek any armed confrontation with the East. The so-called 'threat' is used as a means of exerting pressure: You must give in to us, without any significant concessions in return, so that we can have a chance to liberalize ourselves.

The same is true of the policy backed by Eastern bloc propaganda and diplomacy of claiming to favour the maintenance of the status quo. The communist camp is forced, for ideological reasons, to strive to change the *status quo* to its own advantage. The final aim remains world revolution. And the diplomatic tactics and strategy of Marxism-Leninism are subordinated to this goal.

Another fact that confuses many people in the West is the language of the Soviet version of Marxism, which they are unable to translate or which makes them overlook the most important factors in the immense amount of communist propaganda. So many tons of paper have been published in the East about Moscow's declared policy of 'peaceful coexistence' that many people in the West ended up by believing in it. However, in the great flood of words it is sometimes possible to find a true meaning. For example, in October 1970 a *Pravda* leader stated: 'Peaceful coexistence contributes to the development of the class war on a national and *international* level . . . Bourgeois liberals and pacifists have a different idea of the meaning of peaceful coexistence. . . . Peaceful coexistence presupposes mobilization for *active* war . . . and the use of the whole might of socialism.'

The words of one of the creators of Soviet foreign policy under Stalinism and a founder member of the Komintern, Manuilsky, should also not be forgotten. In 1931 he declared, 'War to the death, a war to the knife between communism and capitalism is unavoidable. Naturally we are not yet strong enough to attack at the present time. . . . To achieve victory we need the element of surprise. The bourgeoisie must be lulled into security. Therefore we shall begin by setting up the most dramatic peace movement which has ever existed. There will be exciting and extraordinary concessions made. The capitalist countries, simple and decadent as they are, will collaborate eagerly in bringing about their own destruction. They will fall into the trap of this opportunity for a new friendship, and as soon as their vigilance slackens and their defences are down we shall shatter them with clenched fist.'

Of course, one could say that this declaration is out of date, that the Soviet Union, in speaking of a *détente* at the present time, does not intend to deceive her political opponents and is abandoning the Marxist strategy (world revolution). But Brezhnev himself, forty years later, made this statement on foreign policy at the congress of the Soviet Communist Party held in March/April, 1971: 'The revolutionary slogans which we proclaim to the people are not empty words. Even when whole decades intervene between the sowing and the harvest. . . . The Soviet Communist Party will continue to pursue a policy in international affairs which will lead to the furtherance of the world-wide anti-imperialist struggle. . . . The complete victory of the cause of socialism *throughout the whole world is inevitable.*'

When Krushchev told the Americans years earlier: 'We will bury you', he provoked a flood of protests. But the phrases in communist jargon pronounced by Brezhnev in 1971 are overlooked, even though they follow exactly the same line as Manuilsky and Krushchev.

Since the Soviet leadership is not monolithic, whichever faction is the stronger at any particular time decides the course of foreign policy. Even in Moscow there are opponents of the policy of *détente*. And here is another mistake that is often made in the West. It is thought that the disagreements within the Kremlin are political or ideological in character, although, of course, other factors such as struggles for power between individual leaders are also not without significance. But Soviet tactics and strategy are concerned not with 'if' but only with 'how' world revolution can be realized. The so-called hawks favour a foreign policy which they consider less adventurous. They want to hold and consolidate their present acquisitions and maintain the sphere of influence they have been able to build up. They fear experiments, especially where the industrial countries of the West are concerned, and feel that greater contacts with the West could lead to internal disturbances. They use slogans like 'guarding the frontiers' and 'the threat of social democracy', and want to maintain tight control internally, particularly when they feel that their own position is a strong one: and with a re-Stalinization without Stalin they run no danger of losing their own heads in periodic purges.

So consolidating the frontiers stands for the concept of an isolationist foreign policy, while the accusation of social democracy is aimed at the internal reform movement.

However, the politicians who favour *détente* feel that they are in a stronger position. They want to achieve world revolution in their lifetime, or at least go some way to bringing it about. They aim at a concerted action against the West in which all methods will be employed: political pressure and wooing of western statesmen; blackmail and deliberate indiscretions; hints about the threat from the East (China) while in the West they gain one foothold after another; help for left and extreme left groups in the West accompanied by solemn assurances that they do not aim to 'export' revolution; corrupting Western journalists and using confidence tricks to win the support of uncommitted Westerners; preparing detailed plans for taking advantage of a favourable situation to overrun non-communist countries at a moment's notice and inciting dissatisfaction and insecurity among whole population groups; assurances that they are ready for wide-ranging, comprehensive co-operation but uncompromising attitudes when they are faced with anything concrete; a rejection of freedom for people, opinions and information, but a readiness to take over Western know-how. These are just a few examples. It is a fact that the faction in favour of *détente* have achieved many successes, geo-political, propagandist, diplomatic and military.

If the West does not immediately recognize the true aim of all communist activity and react accordingly, this 'soft-line wing' could become a significant danger for the whole free world. Even if there are setbacks this faction will not be discouraged but will continue to work stubbornly and patiently to realize their aims – and successes will also be used in the internal battle for power to strengthen their own position.

Here are a few examples of the political activity and partially achieved successes of the 'soft-liners'. In present-day circumstances Germany – including West Germany – is, in Soviet eyes, one of the keys to world revolution; this is an old theory which is also well known in the West. By cunning and very effective diplomatic manœuvres the Soviet Union is now in a position to have *a say in who shall be in power in West Germany*, the Social Democratic party or the Christian Social Union. Both parties are roughly of equal strength and therefore depend on the few million floating voters. These votes can, to a great extent, be manipulated by the Kremlin. Willy Brandt's Ostpolitik is a bone of contention in West Germany, so visible successes or failures have an effect on the way these decisive floating voters cast their votes in elections. If the Kremlin tightens the screw before an election, causing an obvious failure for the foreign policy followed by the Social Democrats, then most of these voters will cast their votes for the CDU and CSU. But if, for example, the order to shoot people attempting to cross the Berlin Wall is cancelled just before the election, or it is even suggested that the Wall might be pulled down (measures and promises that have always been countermanded), then this section of the West German electorate sees it as a sign that Brandt's policy of reconciliation is succeeding and is actually making things easier in human terms. This capacity for exerting an influence in the heart of Europe is already a considerable success for Moscow.

Here is another example of Soviet tactics. For several years pressure has been put on the West German government by various Eastern countries to expel Radio Free Europe, an American organization which is popular and influential in the Eastern bloc, from West Germany. This radio station is a real thorn in the flesh of the communist masters, but they work on the assumption that if West Germany agrees to this demand then America will transmit the programmes from another country. So does that mean they would not win a real victory? No, they would win a tactical victory because such a step would inevitably lead to a worsening of West German relations with America and would represent yet another slice in the salami tactics of the Soviet Union.

There is a similar situation in the efforts of the east Europeans to set up a European Security Conference. This is considered as a method of driving America out of Europe and widening the differences between the West European countries. The same is true of the Eastern bloc's suggestion of abolishing both NATO and the Warsaw Pact. The West would keep to the agreement it had signed while the East would not even allow international inspections. Anyone who tries to protect his security from the Soviet Union only by means of treaties is building with paper. The Eastern bloc would like to deal with a divided Europe, not with a monolithic bloc. In theory this represents a policy of *détente*, but in practice it represents the realization of the strategic and tactical aims which should lead on to world revolution. Only *once* has a senior Polish party official declared *publicly* the true purpose of a European Security Conference when he declared that the aim was to create an 'all-European way of thinking'. But not in the sense in which this term is used in the West. The security conference would be a step towards the realization of what the *East bloc leaders* mean by 'an all-European way of thinking'. It would not be a single act, which would begin at the moment of the official opening; rather (as far as developments in Western Europe are concerned) this security conference has already been set in motion. One can only wonder that the official Polish newspaper, *Zycie Warszawy*, allowed this disclosure to be published in 1971. But at private talks between Eastern bloc leaders, which have never been made public, no attempt was made to conceal this strategy.

About forty years ago there was another dictatorship in Europe that was not sparing with assurances about its peaceful intentions, although its plans for aggression had been announced, in veiled terms or quite openly, in its party jargon. At that time many democratic states preferred to believe what they wanted to believe, and learnt the truth too late about the realities hidden behind the fair phrases. The bloodbath of the Second World War was the direct result of this chain of mistakes in foreign policy. Today it is high time to analyse the concrete plans of the Eastern bloc in the areas of politics, military affairs, diplomacy, propaganda, economics and culture, and to draw the right conclusions. Otherwise Europe will find itself on the road to socialism. To a socialism of the Soviet kind, with dictatorship and show trials, with confinement of political offenders in mental institutions, and brutal exploitation of one's own people, with oppression and aggression.

To close let me quote an expert: 'Russian policy is unchangeable. Russia's methods, her tactics, her manœuvres may change; but the Pole Star of Russian policy – mastery of the world – is a fixed star. . . . The Russian Bear will certainly be capable of anything so long as he knows that the other beasts with whom he associates are capable of nothing. . . . There is only one way to deal with a power like Russia, and that is the way of fearlessness. . . . If Europe retreats, then it will not suffer a mere defeat but will, in a manner of speaking, give itself up to the Caudine Forks.' The author wrote these phrases in his reports on Eastern politics of 1853–1856, when he was the London correspondent of the *New York Daily Tribune*. His name was Karl Marx.

Paris, January 1972
ERWIN WEIT

CHAPTER I

Emigration

'Mr Erwin Weit?' The ice-cold voice of the frontier police officer hit me like a thunderbolt from a dark sky. His short, dumpy figure came hurrying in my direction.

'Give me your passport back, please.'

I stood, rooted to the spot, in the queue of airline passengers who had already passed through passport control and were putting their cases and bags on the desk in front of the customs woman. My mouth went dry. I could not get a single word out. Silently I handed him my 'passport', a small piece of blue paper folded like a concertina and printed with the words '*Dokument Podrozy*' (travel document). On the very first page of this official certificate, below the name, date of birth and place of birth in three languages, were printed the words: 'The owner of this travel document is not a Polish citizen.' Strictly speaking, the piece of paper I handed to the frontier police officer represented a clean break with more than thirty years of my life.

But was it really going to be the final break?

'Come with me,' ordered the police officer. He looked me over with an appraising eye. My blood ran cold in my veins and my nerves were on edge. The experiences of the last few years had left their trace on me.

The officer walked quickly in front of me. I could see how his greenish brown uniform was stretched tight across his back. Between the waiting-room and the customs clearance hall was a glass cabin with a narrow entrance beside it and an electrically operated barrier dividing the two rooms. Here we were still in Poland, but the other side was, in a way, already abroad. You can see similar barriers – or turnstiles which will only turn in one direction – in supermarkets or underground stations. You pick up your wire basket or put a coin in the slot and the barrier is raised. Here it was different. My fate depended on this barrier: was it to be freedom or would I be forced to turn back?

'Wait here for a moment,' said the officer. I stood in front of the barrier on the 'abroad' side.

'No, not there, come through to this side,' he told me. A short buzzing tone indicated that I could pass through the barrier. One short step – and I was back in 'Poland'.

In fact I was not completely unprepared for this nerve-racking suspense. I had really expected something of the kind. All too often I had heard of cases where people who wanted to leave the country and had managed to get their long-awaited 'passports' after time-consuming bureaucratic formalities, had been visited by the security police the night before their intended departure and had the vital papers confiscated. These people then found themselves in a terrible position, materially as well as psychologically. In cases like this complaints and appeals were of no use. The regime showed its power and its tyranny by crushing defenceless men. I had also heard of people being brought back at the last moment, when their planes were already on the runway. Why should I fare any better?

These thoughts, with others based on my own experiences, flashed through my mind. It was only fifteen minutes since I had passed through the barrier for the first time. The same police officer had taken my travel document and given me a cursory glance. He had made a note behind the counter which I was not able to see for the desk hid his hand. Then he stamped the blue paper and gave it back to me, pressing the button to raise the barrier. So fifteen minutes ago he could let me go through.

What was he up to now? What did he want from me? Did he only want to make me feel his power over me? Or was there something else behind it? Did he have instructions to act in this way?

I had noticed that he left his desk for a quarter of an hour straight after checking my papers for the first time. All the passengers in the queue behind me had had to wait. This had disconcerted me at the time but I still hoped that I had left all that behind me.

There had been long weeks of anxiety and hope before that day, February 11, 1969. When I decided to apply for permission to emigrate I had to fill in a form with the written declaration that I was a 'Zionist' and wanted to emigrate to Israel. The anti-semitic stand taken by the mass media left me in no doubt of the consequences if my request were refused. Every day the radio, television and press hammered out the message that 'Zionists' were rootless cosmopolitans, traitors and troublemakers, agitators in the pay of international Jewry and of the state of Israel which was allied with the worst of the Nazi war criminals. The Polish people were told that the 'Zionists' were the worst kind of criminal, betrayers of Poland and of the international labour movement. Anyone who wanted to emigrate was forced to brand himself with the mark of Cain, at the demand of the authorities. I had to do so, as did thousands before and after me.

Of course, I was well aware of the effect of my request to emigrate and of the consequences if my request was refused. But it was an unavoidable risk that I had to take.

The last months had been all the more nerve-racking because I belonged to that 'chosen few' who were usually refused a travel document by the authorities. In a way my position was paradoxical. On the one hand my qualifications as an interpreter meant that I was useful and highly valued; in my career I had great prospects of promotion. But on the other hand I was constantly subjected to provocations and attempts at intimidation on the part of the Polish security authorities.

In 1954 I had started to work as an interpreter in addition to my job as a journalist. To begin with I acted as a simultaneous translator at international congresses and, since my professional skill was recognized, I quickly made headway in my new career. The biggest foreign-language state publishing house in Poland, Polonia, offered me a position as head of its German editorial department, and accepted all the conditions I made. At the same time I was asked to act as interpreter at meetings between prominent Polish politicians and German-speaking foreigners. My services as a translator were greatly in demand among leading deputies in the Sejm (the Polish parliament), well-known politicians in the Council of State, the government and the party leadership, not to mention union bosses and scientists. Often I even had to turn down work.

Sometimes the courtesy shown to me by my 'clients' took forms that were almost embarrassing. Well-known personalities from Poland, the German Democratic Republic, Austria and other countries were not sparing with words of recognition and thanks. I was presented with gifts, letters and dedications.

I was present when delegations representing the Socialist Unity Party (the official name of the East German communist party) or the East German government, including Ulbricht, Grotewohl, Stoph and other leading politicians, came to Poland, or when Gomulka,

Cyrankiewicz, Kliszko, Loga-Sowinski and other Polish leaders travelled abroad. This work often permitted me to look behind the scenes and to compare my opinions – which were those of the average man – with the true facts (which, unfortunately, were known only to a small circle). During my work as an interpreter I also got to know not only the leading politicians in Poland and the German Democratic Republic, but also the top men in the Soviet Union, including Krushchev, Mikoyan, Brezhnev, Kosygin, Andropov and Ponomaryev, not to mention Max Reimann, the leader of the banned communist party of West Germany, Gerhard Danelius, the leader of the West Berlin Socialist Unity Party, Klaus, the then Austrian Chancellor, and Maletta, the President of the Austrian parliament, Helmut Schmidt, at that time parliamentary leader of the Social Democrat minority in the West German parliament, and numerous other top politicians in both East and West.

Since I was not a party official I did not have to face the alternative of either bowing and scraping to further my career or keeping my self-respect and running the danger of antagonizing my superiors.

As time went on my reputation grew, and I could even afford to take a few liberties. I well remember the day in autumn 1962 when I was called back urgently from Bulgaria by Stanislaw Trepczynski, the head of the secretariat of the party leader, Gomulka. He told me that I must interrupt my leave immediately and return to Warsaw because a party and government delegation, headed by Gomulka, had been invited to Berlin by the East German leadership. I broke off my holiday, caught the train, and on October 9, 1962, when I was only two hours away from Warsaw, I was involved in the worst train crash in Polish history. The number of dead and injured ran into hundreds. I was lucky to escape with minor injuries and severe shock, but for years I found it impossible to travel by train. When foreign delegations came to Poland and made the customary tour of the country, the junior officials would be furious: if the delegation were to travel by train they would be obliged to provide an alternative form of transport for me – a plane or a car. This often led to complications and made the visit more difficult to organize.

But now I stood at Warsaw Airport on that cold winter day – February 11, 1969 – separated from the frontier police officer by only the glass window of his desk, frightened of betraying myself by my look or my impatient expression. I had arrived at the airport much too early, and had bought a few newspapers in the waiting-room to help pass the time. But the state of my nerves made it impossible for me to read them. I held them folded in my hand the whole time I was waiting. In the end I glanced down at them. Where my hand had gripped them the paper was wet with sweat. *Trybuna Ludu*, the organ of the Polish communist party, February 11, 1969. I looked around me and asked myself, '1969?' The figures began to dance before my eyes and, after February 11, the year seemed to change. Wasn't it 1943? Wasn't I still a fifteen-year-old boy, surrounded by persecutors and tormentors, searching desperately for an escape? Would I end up yet again in Loncki Gaol in Lvov? Was this the notorious Jew murderer, SS *Oberscharführer* Waltke, standing in front of me, or just a Polish frontier policeman?

I pulled myself together and rubbed my eyes to banish this bad dream. Behind me straggled the queue of impatient passengers. They were warmly dressed, for it was a cold day. But I was so hot that I unbuttoned the neck of my shirt and loosened my tie. Was it the air in the airport buildings or the atmosphere in Poland that made it difficult to breathe?

The queue of passengers behind me cut off my escape. I looked quickly round. Indifferent faces. But that could be just a front. Perhaps there was among them someone like me, a companion in fate, who was trying to hide his nervousness behind a mask of indifference – a mask that you meet every day in Poland wherever you go. The seconds passed unbearably slowly. In the last few months I had been made to feel only too often that, as a Jew, I was one of the enemies of the people. So often before I had been refused a passport. Branded on my memory still was the notorious 'Paragraph 4', the reason given in writing for the refusal of a passport: 'The provision of a travel document may be refused when such an action would be contrary to vital national interests.'

In 1963 I had, quite by chance, traced my surviving sister who had disappeared in the war and was now living in the United States. For years I had believed that I was quite alone in the world. She immediately sent me an invitation to visit her, and a return air-ticket. But I was not allowed to go. 'Vital national interests' apparently made it impossible for me to travel to the West. A few years later there was a second refusal.

In 1968 I was offered a holiday by the Polish Journalists' Union in a villa on Lake Balaton in Hungary. The foreign department of the Journalists' Union looked after all the formalities. I wanted to travel in my car. All the other members of the party had already received their passports. Every day the girl in the foreign department tried to reassure me: 'You'll be sure to get your passport tomorrow.' Two days before the date I was to leave she sent for me. I could see how much she hated giving me the news. 'I'm afraid your request for a passport has been refused.'

So I could not even travel to Hungary. No one ever bothered to ask the Polish security authorities what 'vital national interests' prevented me from spending my holidays in another Eastern bloc country.

I did not even trouble to do so myself. What good would it have done? The security authorities were a state within a state – and not the only one. With their unlimited power and arbitrary actions they could play their little games with anyone, and were immune to any complaints. To whom could I have gone to demand my rights?

Thoughts rushed through my mind: Will he let me through or has he already had orders to turn me back? I glanced at a big electric clock. The seconds passed so slowly. I was filled with a helpless rage. 'I must do something,' I thought. Suddenly I determined to fight. Not to give in easily, not to resign myself.

The officer's voice interrupted my thoughts. 'Your address in Warsaw?'

Was it a bad joke? Black humour? Didn't he know that the homes of all Jewish emigrants were confiscated? Not only that – that they were subjected to all kinds of sharp practice, made to pay for their homes to be renovated after their departure, and forced to trail round from one authority to another until they finally got hold of a document stating that they had given up their homes? The formalities and the endless journeys took as much time as the process of acquiring a dwelling which, in Poland, was unbelievably difficult.

What address should I give him? I didn't have one any more. It was four whole days since I had got the authorities to certify that I had given up my home. It had cost a few thousand zlotys for redecorations, more money for the official stamps. There was the commission which had to consider the matter and decide whether they would take over the dwelling, there was the official who sent me right across Warsaw three times to get just one of the six or seven documents which were essential for the surrender of the dwelling: 'Get going, Jewboy. We're not going to make it too easy for you, even if Gomulka *has* said that you can get out.'

'Krakowskie Przedmiescie 53', I answered mechanically.

The officer made a note, handed me my travel document, pressed the button and the way was open.

Half an hour later I sat in the Austrian Airlines plane, the engines roared and the aircraft took off. A new era in my life had begun. The plane circled and then climbed sharply. I looked down through the oval window. Below me was a strange chessboard of fields, dusted with snow and blackish brown. This was the country where three and a half million Jews were living in 1939, and which thirty years later, could not find a place for even twenty thousand.

Some of these twenty thousand people had no Jewish connections left. They had non-Jewish husbands and wives, and their children were not, and did not feel, Jewish. They wanted to forget the terrible persecution which they had suffered, and that was all. They could not have imagined that, for years, the Polish Interior Ministry had had a Bureau for Jewish Affairs which kept files on all Jews, half-Jews and quarter-Jews. Beneath me was the country where I had had wonderful times, and where I had witnessed the most terrible crimes. A country, like certain others, whose most enlightened sons had attained the heights of the human spirit, but which had also known the darkest obscurantism of bestial barbarians. A country which set honour above all other moral values, but also a country of grave robbers. A country which had been enslaved countless times throughout the centuries, but which went on producing men who, in their turn, tried to enslave others. A lovely country, with delightful beauty spots, glorious lakes and mountains, fields where the ripe gold of the corn was scattered with the pale blue of cornflowers and the bright red of poppies. But also a country where every inch of land was soaked in the blood of murdered innocents. One vast cemetery for every regime where, in the past thirty years, the number of people who had suffered violent deaths was nearly as great as those who had died naturally. Poland.

At Schwechat Airport in Vienna I embraced my sister who had flown out from American to Austria to meet me. She was surprised at my odd appearance. My suit was not badly cut but it hung on me as if I were a scarecrow. In the last few months I had lost forty pounds.

CHAPTER 2

The Green Questionnaire

It all began in the summer of 1945. An international architects' congress was due to take place in Warsaw. At that time there were no professional simultaneous translators in Poland, so the organizing committee was desperately trying to find people with a good enough knowledge of foreign languages to act as interpreters. Of course, professional simultaneous translators could have been hired in Switzerland or other West European countries. But very few of them spoke Polish and, besides, they were too expensive and would have expected payment in hard currency.

The result was that the organizing committee invited me, along with many other candidates who spoke several languages, to try my hand at a special test. In the hope of revealing our hidden talents the committee had rigged up a simultaneous translation installation. A text picked from a newspaper was read out and we had to translate it directly into another language. I managed to do this fluently at the first attempt without making any mistakes, so I passed the test and was immediately accepted as a qualified simultaneous translator from Polish into German and German into Polish.

At the time I attached little importance to this 'examination' as far as my future was concerned. I was working as a journalist on the editorial staff of the Warsaw daily, *Trybuna Mazowiecka*. And I thought that I would only be called upon to act as interpreter on this one occasion.

If I had had the faintest idea of the consequences of this brief test – it lasted under fifteen minutes – I am sure I would have been too nervous to get a single word out.

As far as the translating team was concerned, the architects' congress passed without incident. The delegates expressed their appreciation of the interpreters who sat in small cubicles and fluently translated the speeches as they were made in the hall – the congress took place in the Warsaw headquarters of the Polish Council of Ministers.

This was my first experience of an international congress, but in the following weeks and months several other institutes which were planning similar events approached the architects' organizing committee and asked them for their list of translators. In this way our names were passed around, and I soon had more requests to act as interpreter. Of course, each time this happened I had to get permission to be absent from work. At the beginning this was sometimes difficult, although my editor-in-chief always ended up by giving me leave. Influential officials on the organizing committees of the congresses always argued persuasively that Poland could not afford to pay out hard currency for translators. This argument was unanswerable.

So things moved fast. In quick succession I translated at congresses and conferences of trade unionists, teachers, and at a scientific conference on geodesy. And when an East German government delegation led by Otto Grotewohl visited Poland I came into close contact with leading East German and Polish politicians for the first time.

On one occasion I was asked to travel with Klosiewicz, at that time the President of the Polish Trades Union Organization, who was leading a delegation to a Conference of European Workers in Leipzig, and another time I attended the so-called World Festival of Youth and Students in Warsaw. Finally, the Polonia state publishing house in Warsaw offered me a post as head of the German editorial department. This consisted of a team of translators whose task was to translate texts supplied by the central Polish editorial department into the best possible German with maximum speed and accuracy, to prepare them for printing and to correct the proofs.

The first few years of my work as a simultaneous translator were interesting and varied, but they did not give me any special insight into the world around me. But this was soon to change.

In 1958 international political activity was at its height in Poland. With only a short interval two top-level political meetings took place in Warsaw: the visit of a party and state delegation from the German Democratic Republic, led by Walter Ulbricht, and the celebrations marking the fortieth anniversary of the founding of the Polish Communist Party. These celebrations were attended by an East German Socialist Unity Party (i.e. communist party) delegation led by Erich

Honecker, at that time recognized as Ulbricht's successor, a Soviet deputation led by Anastas Mikoyan, and high-ranking members of the Czechoslovak party leadership.

By now I had an established reputation as an interpreter; I was well known to the party leadership and had already attended private talks on several occasions, when I would be given details of previous secret discussions and negotiations so that I, as interpreter, should be familiar with the crucial issues.

Yet, officially, I was an outsider. I did not belong to the hierarchy of party officials, but neither was I one of the boot-licking hangers-on who thought only of their careers, deferred to everyone, and were mainly concerned with organization. Most of these men had to wait outside the door during the negotiations at bilateral or multilateral summit meetings when the leading party and government comrades were speaking their minds. But, as an interpreter, my services were most needed at this very time, and I was able to witness what happened with my own eyes and ears.

My work opened up perspectives which I could not have imagined. I gained an insight into problems and transactions which unrolled behind hermetically sealed doors. I was able to observe high-ranking politicians at times when they did not trouble to assume the carefully studied mask which they liked to present to the public. I shared their everyday life and studied their behaviour, their beliefs, their projects and their arguments. Yet, at the same time, since I was not an official, I had both feet on the ground and could compare the opinions and plans of the party bosses and government leaders with the living conditions of the man in the street. For the purposes of observation my position was ideal – for studying not only the development of a man like Gomulka, but also the conduct of the Camarilla, the little group of officials who flocked round the party leaders.

To begin with these *apparatchiks* were obsequious and servile, but in the course of time they developed into a political force to be reckoned with. Naturally these men realized that the party leader was well disposed towards me and so they thought it advisable to be in my good books. They were generous with compliments and courtesies, and acted quite naturally in my presence. The president of the parliament gave me one of his books with a personal dedication, and Pilatowski, the first secretary of the party organization in the Wroclaw district, wrote inviting me to spend my holidays in

Lower Silesia (an offer which I did not accept). It shows how far some comrades took me into their confidence that a leading official of the Central Committee of the Polish Communist Party once touched me for a loan when I was on holiday in Zakopane.

As time went on I won the trust of the *apparatchiks* without any particular effort on my part. They began to forget that I did not belong to their class, that I was an outsider. In the end they did not even bother to hide dishonest actions from me. Once, when I was accompanying a Polish parliamentary delegation to Austria, I was taken on one side by Wiktor Obolewicz, at that time a high-ranking trade union official who also headed one of the Polish parliamentary committees, and was a member of the Central Committee of the Polish Communist Party. He talked to me in private for quite a while, skirting round the subject, and finally came to the point: 'I've smuggled some zlotys out of Poland. There's bound to be a Polish Jew somewhere in Vienna who would change them into Austrian schillings on the black market. As you know, Comrade Weit, our official allowances are very limited and so I have a favour to ask you: can you help me change the money?' I did not even try to explain to Comrade Obolewicz that he was trying to break a law which he himself had helped to introduce; instead I told him that I had no contacts of that kind, and that time was in any case too short to find someone we could do business with.

Smuggling was – and is – widely practised among senior party officials. And elsewhere in this book I shall have something to say about the private trading activities of Polish diplomats in East Berlin.

Of course, with delegations which are only abroad for short periods things must be organized differently. Illegal activities cannot be organized over a long period of time but must be carried out quickly, in one transaction. But the conditions are particularly favourable. Whether they travel by special plane or by diplomatic train, made up of specially assembled Pullman carriages, customs officials and frontier police have no authority to check the luggage or credentials of members of travelling delegations. All formalities are seen to by the secretary of the delegation or by an official escort. There is no danger of being caught, and the West, with its consumer goods, is very tempting. It is a temptation that few can resist.

To take just one example, in the spring of 1966 I accompanied the two Polish guest delegates, Artur Starewicz,[1] the Central Committee

[1] Appointed Polish ambassador in London in 1971

Secretary, and Stanislas Kociolek,[1] later a member of the Politburo, to West Berlin where they were attending the party congress of the West Berlin Socialist Unity Party headed by Gerhard Danelius. This party was an offshoot of the East German Socialist Unity Party and had been founded with the consent of the Senate and the three Western allies. First they took me along to an East Berlin bank where they could change an unlimited amount of smuggled zlotys into East German marks. They then used this money to shop in East Berlin and later, after visiting a West Berlin exchange office, in the Western Sector. Naturally it did not occur to the two comrades to declare their purchases to the customs officers.

But there was one barrier to my intimacy with these medium and high-ranking *apparatchiks*. I did not – and still do not – drink alcohol, and so I could not take part in the obligatory drinking bouts they all indulged in. Nor did I share their liking for hunting, which was also essential above a certain level in the party hierarchy if one wished to be regarded as socially acceptable. I was not interested in shooting. And I could not even get the hang of bridge, the favourite game of the junior officials.

And yet the comrades were friendly to me because they knew that I had direct access to the party leaders. And, in Polish terms, this was a logical and realistic attitude for them to take, even though I had done nothing to earn it.

Probably to the amazement of my friends and acquaintances, I did not attempt to make use of the advantages and amenities which I could have acquired from my contact with the most powerful men in Poland if I had taken the trouble to win their protection.

I was more interested in using my position behind the scenes in Poland and other communist countries to get a true picture of political realities. This was not just a hobby, but a kind of private necessity. I wanted to know whether a regime which proclaimed the watchwords of socialism was really prepared, either in practice or at least in principle (that is, at least in the intentions of its leaders), to recognize the well-being and development of society as its primary target, and to work towards this end. Not only in theory but in practical politics. Did the leading group really want to put into practice the ideas which they expressed with such fervour, and on which their own claim to power was based, or were they only concerned with consolidating and improving their own positions and the count-

[1] Appointed Polish ambassador to Belgium in 1971

less privileges that went with them? Was the people's freedom of expression suppressed because it would endanger the supreme target, the building of a free and just society, as the party officials always claimed? Was the party leadership really striving to achieve this goal, did they even believe in it, or did they merely use it as an excuse to satisfy their own lust for power? Was the dictatorship in socialist states, which party theoreticians always qualified with the extenuating epithet, 'of the proletariat', only an unavoidable, temporary expedient as described in Marxist theory, which was essential to protect a new and still vulnerable socialist system from the evil and still dangerous class enemy? Or was it all empty phrases, ideological window-dressing?

The communist regime in Poland was not the first dictatorship I had lived through. In 1941 I lived in a little town near Lvov. I was engulfed in the German advance and, for the next three and a half years, I was a victim of Nazi persecution. As a training for life it was dangerous but thorough. When I was captured by the Gestapo in 1943 and shut up in the Loncki Police Prison in Lvov I noticed that the SS guards wore buckles inscribed with the words *Meine Ehre heisst Treue* (my honour is fidelity). Even then, in my cell, I realized that this definition of the word, 'honour', must lead to a complete collapse of morality.

After years of persecution and danger I was liberated by Soviet forces in January 1945 in the little Galician town of Nowy Sacz. I had escaped the gas chambers. At seventeen I had already witnessed barbaric crimes and been the victim of violence and oppression. And on their caps my liberators wore a red star with a hammer and sickle. I was politically inexperienced, I was half-starving, and I had no papers and no money. For me, the red star with the hammer and sickle was the symbol of salvation.

As soon as the fighting had moved on to the west I went to the newly constituted authorities. The official of the people's militia, that is the police, to whom I applied for papers, listened to my story and explained that I would receive an identity card in a few days' time. But since I had no home, no money and no papers I should go to the KP PPR. I had no idea what the letters stood for.

But I went where I was told, and there a man talked to me for half an hour. He too listened to my story and told me that coming to see him was the best thing I could have done. He took me to the canteen and there, for the first time in many months, I was able to eat my fill. Then he went back with me to his office, spoke to me in a very friendly way – it was the first conversation without fear or hatred that I had had for many years – and gave me a little green questionnaire to fill in where I had to note down basic personal details. I filled in the form and signed it. The friendly official took the paper and told me, 'From now on you are one of our members – a member of the Polish Workers' Party.' Only then did I realize that KP PPR were the Polish initials of the District Committee of the Polish Workers' Party. So, without any formalities, and certainly without any political training or convictions, I became a communist.

In the next few months I was to hear and read the propaganda slogans, 'Equality, social justice, the highest form of democracy'. I believed in them and began to study Marxist theory. What I read corresponded to my own ideas about society. Gradually, with constant indoctrination, I became a convinced communist. Yet I could not overcome one private reservation: the party demanded unquestioning obedience from its members. At this phrase a red light would turn on in my brain and I would remember the slogan on the buckles of the SS guards in Loncki jail, *Meine Ehre heisst Treue*. I resolved never to accept any ideology unreservedly but to keep my own critical judgment. My honour, I promised myself, would never be unquestioning fidelity. It may sound paradoxical but it was an SS slogan that helped me, in this negative sense, to build up an inner independence which I have managed to preserve ever since.

I had many different kinds of jobs and finally ended up as a journalist. In the next few years I observed many practices in the exercise of power by the communist regime which I could not reconcile with my idea of communism, socialism and people's democracy. The sharp division between theory and practice, between ideas and facts, threw me into a crisis of conscience although, to begin with, I still tried to defend the communist party, of which I was myself now a member, against my own arguments.

My thirst for knowledge led me to seek out any book published before the war, any political publication from the West, wherever I could find them. And as I read more, as my horizons expanded, my doubts about the party grew. Finally, a complete mental break with the 'great mother of all workers' became unavoidable.

Ten years after joining the Polish Workers' party I had, like many other communists, come to a conclusion which can be formulated as follows: communism is a fine ideal, perhaps the finest and most human of all. But – it is being perverted by narrow-minded, brutal and stubborn politicians jockeying for power. Many of the old communists with whom I would often discuss this subject right through the night would refuse to draw any further conclusions from this realization. These men who, before the war, had fought and been imprisoned for their beliefs, who had risked their lives in the Spanish Civil War and in the resistance against the Nazis, had the feeling they were standing on the edge of a spiritual abyss. Perhaps they were instinctively afraid that they might break down psychologically if they could no longer cling to the thought that, in spite of everything, their struggle had been justified. Or perhaps it was the irresistible, self-lacerating, persuasive power of communist ideology which prevented them from drawing the logical conclusion from facts which they realized as well as I.

In private conversations with friends I would often ask the question: Who is the good communist, the executioner or his victim, when both claim to be following their principles? Only a few were prepared to answer.

Many old communists had been tortured and imprisoned for years in Soviet prisons and camps. They had experienced for themselves the darkest side of communist rule. They were often clever and articulate, with a capacity for penetrating analysis, but they were not ready to give up their ideals, their communist convictions. The more brutally they had been treated, the more their political masochism increased.

In 1955 a process of political ferment began in Poland which ended by bringing Gomulka to power in October 1956. Without any reservations I lined myself up with the forces that were fighting for a moral and political renewal of the country, for socialism with a human face. Naturally I knew what the consequences would be for me if this reform movement failed and the orthodox party officials could once again decide the course of events without any restraining influence.

Still, I did not confine myself to private discussions, but used my position as a journalist to criticize the policies of the party and government leadership in public, even at the plenary session of the Polish Journalists' Union. My attacks were published, albeit with some cuts by the censor, in the organ of the Polish Journalists' Union. So I had to face up to the fact that the Stalinists would have an account to settle with me if they ever got back into power.

When Gomulka[1] took over the leadership of the party and headed the reform movement in 1956, Stalinists everywhere – in the government and party apparatus, in industry and the arts – were dismissed from their posts.

Early in 1957, when the liberalization campaign was at its height, my earlier stand was recognized and I was unanimously elected party secretary of the central committee of the Polish Journalists' Union. This was a special mark of confidence in me at a time when the dogmatists were losing power at every level of Polish life. And now I really felt that it was my duty to seek out the truth.

It was during this period of romantic dreams of a better model of socialism that I started my work as an interpreter for the party and government leadership. This meant that I had the opportunity to judge at close quarters whether there were contradictions between the theory and practice of communism and if so, why; whether benevolent despotism can exist in an industrial age and if not, why not; how the much-vaunted fraternal relations between socialist countries worked in practice. Since it was now my job to echo the sentiments expressed at international meetings, I was in a position to find out what were the facts behind the slogans of friendship. I could observe the new national leaders at close quarters and see what lay behind the speeches of these all-powerful figures.

As a kind of side-product of the private discussions I attended, especially when the tongues of the speakers were loosened by alcohol, I came to realize the whole truth about both internal and external policies. After that, there was no going back for me.

By 1963 the political regression towards the Stalinist concept of socialism had gone so far that there was no longer any possibility of working effectively for the renewal of the system. So I gave up my post as party secretary of the central committee of the Polish Journalists' Union and refused to accept re-election. Two years later I stopped attending the meetings of my local cell which were compulsory for all party members. So my break with the party, which was a natural consequence of my spiritual abdication, was complete. The local party leadership left me in peace – they preferred not to tangle with one of Gomulka's interpreters. The party and government leaders knew nothing of all this. With their great task of improving Poland and the world, they had no time to check if I was still dutifully attending meetings. I was a good interpreter, and

[1] Deposed in December 1970

this was enough to win me a place at discussions at the highest level.

During the later years of my life in Poland, when I was doing more translation work, the events I witnessed only strengthened me in my convictions. With my many contacts with statesmen and party leaders I did not need the leading articles in the communist central organs to help me work out my own point of view. These apologias were aimed at the man in the street, for, not content with using his labour, the state also wanted to control his mind. I was in the disagreeable position of an outsider among the initiates who had to look on as events developed and the leaders of the communist states became enmeshed in contradictions that arose from the legitimate requirements of social development. In these cases, decrees and directives were of no help.

A new generation was growing up which was immune to party dogma, both at home and abroad: there were only two alternatives – to give in to them or to sweep them away with an iron fist. Gomulka responded by sending his army into Czechoslovakia and letting his security police loose on students and writers. The same fate met progressive forces in the Soviet Union and in East Germany. Whenever the leaders of these countries met, they would indulge in wishful thinking and reveal that they harboured illusions which could have been dangerous if they had acted upon them. It is always risky for leading politicians and statesmen to take illusions for facts. And that, in my opinion, does not only apply in the Eastern bloc.

One of the basic differences between a Western bourgeois democracy and a people's democracy on the Eastern pattern is that politics in the communist states have none of that openness typical of Western societies. In countries in the socialist bloc the information media of the press, radio, and television, and even the cinema, theatre and literature are subject to strict controls; the appropriate official channel hands out the party line, which may be valid only for the day, and anyone who thinks differently, or has doubts, or wants to criticize, is silenced, even if he is in the Marxist camp. But even when the news is filtered in this way the party leadership is still not satisfied that the mass media will keep absolutely to the official line. So there is another official watchdog to control the mass media – censorship. In Poland this authority is officially called the 'bureau for the control of the press, publications and theatrical performances'. The very existence of such a bureau is contrary to the

Constitution of the People's Republic of Poland, and yet it has unlimited powers. Not only newspapers and books, but all kinds of printed matter, including visiting cards and labels for wine bottles or cans, must be approved by the Censorship Bureau and given an official stamp before they can be printed. Public photostating machines of the kind that are to be found in many department stores or big photographic shops in the West are naturally unthinkable in Poland, as in other socialist countries. Without the censor's official stamp, which consists of a letter and a number, any printed matter is illegal in the People's Republic of Poland, and this is true even of a book of Gomulka's speeches or of the works of Lenin, Stalin or other communist writers. The reasoning behind this muzzling policy is obvious: the people must only be told what the leadership wishes. The leadership alone decides what the public shall hear, what books shall appear, which plays shall be put on.

But, of course, the party officials claim the right to more information; indeed, the higher their position in the hierarchy, the more information they expect to be given. Medium-ranking state and party officials receive daily a special bulletin published by the Polish News Agency, PAP, which is highly confidential. These men are kept informed, at least in extracts, of what, for example, the American President has actually said in a speech the previous day, or are told when there has been a *coup d'état* in a developing country which has not been reported in the press. Certainly, these reports are tendentious and incomplete, but they do give the basic facts. High-ranking officials are also issued with a more complete news review and commentary by PAP. And finally, the party leaders enjoy complete freedom of information, in accordance with the old saying, 'Knowledge is Power' and 'Ignorance is Weakness', although they may, like Gomulka, be surrounded by political rivals who filter news and information in an attempt to control the leader's policies.

One of the demands made in the reform campaign of 1956 was the abolition of censorship and of this system of graded information. But the demand was emphatically rejected by the newly elected 'liberal' Politburo led by Gomulka. The party leader knew perfectly well that if the mass media were to report the news fully and objectively they could not have ignored the subject of the government and party leadership. And it was essential for this area to remain unexplored.

As an interpreter I was now able to cut through these controls at a stroke. My work was certainly very instructive, but it was also disillusioning, not only as regards important world affairs, but also in small matters. For example, in the middle sixties I learnt that a change was to be introduced in the organization of relations between the Polish Communist Party and Western communist parties: whereas previously questions relating to the financing of Western parties had been dealt with by the deputy head of the foreign section of the Central Committee of the Polish Communist Party, a certain Comrade Jaques Kaminski, this task was now to be transferred to the Polish Foreign Trade Ministry. The change was not interesting in itself, but I was in a position to learn at first hand what form the involvement of the Polish Central Committee in these transactions took. And when the Socialist Unity Party delegate taking part in discussions, who was also a deputy head of the foreign section of the Socialist Unity Party Central Committee, expressed his astonishment at the change, it was easy to draw the conclusion that *he* was going to *carry on* looking after these transactions in East Germany.

As for the tight circle of the top leadership, I was also able to learn, for example, that Boleslaw Bierut, who was First Secretary of the Central Committee and State President until 1956, did not die of heart failure in Moscow as the official communique stated, but committed suicide after the Twentieth Party Congress of the Soviet Communist Party when Krushchev condemned Stalin and his methods. Bierut, who headed the Polish delegation to the Congress, was instructed to go back to Poland and, following the Soviet example, to dismantle the now discredited cult of the personality. It was like asking a wolf to turn vegetarian. After Krushchev had refused to receive him for several days, Bierut escaped from the dilemma by ending his own life. And Krushchev managed to find the time to go to Warsaw for his funeral, and took the opportunity to get his own candidate, Edward Ochab, accepted as Bierut's successor at the Sixth Plenum of the Polish Central Committee.

I was also able to observe the human weaknesses and reactions of our leaders at close quarters, their petty jealousies and intrigues. Facts which would normally remain in the background were made very clear to me – whether it was a question of power struggles between different groups, of the establishment of a common foreign policy, or of questions of economic co-operation. I saw how Gomulka who, in 1956, was idolized by the whole Polish people, brought about his own political downfall over the years as he was used by other powerful groups within the Polish leadership, and gradually became the docile tool of his opponents who had managed to insinuate themselves into the circle of his closest collaborators.

At the top there were no secrets about the mutual efforts to exploit other fraternal socialist countries, 'with the Soviet Union at the head' as the slogan had it. Here all the contradictions became apparent. Sometimes there were open quarrels, sometimes disputed matters were swept under the table by referring them back to a joint committee, although everyone knew that this committee would not be able to make any progress in the foreseeable future, because even in economic affairs only lip-service was paid to the 'fraternal solidarity' of the socialist countries.

In the first few years after 1956 Gomulka, Kliszko[1] and their closest collaborators worked out and pioneered a plan for co-operation, co-ordination, specialization and division of labour between socialist countries, based on the example of the EEC. But this plan was frustrated not only by the other countries who all wanted the lion's share of the benefits, but by the Poles themselves because, in all the decisive sectors, they subordinated their own economy completely to the Soviet one.

Plans were worked out down to the last detail to restore the unity of the world communist movement but, to the disappointment of those who worked on them, they were left to moulder away in files. Decisions to act could only be made at this level when one partner was weak and defenceless, as in the case of Czechoslovakia.

Finally I was able to observe one particularly crass example of fraternal co-operation between the People's Republic of Poland and the German Democratic Republic. The Warsaw government was particularly interested, for economic reasons, in trading with West Berlin. But the East German authorities blocked rail transport between the trading partners. The East Berlin leadership wanted to keep West Berlin under pressure. Gomulka complained to Ulbricht about this practice, but he did not relent. For years he used this area of Polish foreign trade as a pawn in an attempt to get the Poles to support his aggressive policy towards West Berlin, and to prevent them from indulging in any independent flirtation with the Federal Republic.

In this area Ulbricht claimed the political prerogative among

[1] Deposed in December 1970

all the Eastern bloc countries, with the exception, to begin with, of the Soviet Union. When, in the period following 1956, Gomulka once suggested that he would, in certain circumstances, be interested in a visit by Herbert Wehner, the leader of the West German Social Democratic Party, to Poland, Ulbricht immediately retorted, 'As far as relations with West Germany are concerned, we are responsible for policy, once and for all. No socialist country can simply follow its own inclinations.'

CHAPTER 3

Ulbricht Teaches Gomulka a Lesson

I met Ulbricht for the first time when he headed the delegation to summit talks with the Polish party and government leadership in Warsaw on December 9, 1958. The other delegates included Hermann Matern, Erich Mückenberger, Dr. Lothar Bolz, at the time Foreign Minister of the German Democratic Republic, Max Sefrin, Deputy Chairman of the Council of Ministers, Dr. Hans Loch, leader of the East German Liberal Democratic Party, Ernst Goldenbaum, leader of the Democratic Peasants' Party, Otto Winzer, Ulbricht's confidant of many years' standing, and, as usual, a few workers and peasants for window-dressing. The Polish delegation taking part in the talks included, among others, Gomulka, Cyrankiewicz, Adam Rapacki, at that time Polish Foreign Minister, Stephen Jedrychowski, later Foreign Minister[1] who was at that time the Polish planning chief with the rank of deputy Prime Minister, Loga-Sowinski,[2] chairman of the Polish Trade Union movement, Jerzy Morawski, member of the Politburo and a Central Committee secretary together with senior government and party officials, and of course Roman Piotrowski, the Polish Ambassador to the German Democratic Republic. It is significant that the Polish side did not bother to include workers and peasants in their delegation, as the East Germans did.

For six days there were discussions at central committee level between the two countries, as well as meetings between the government representatives. Although the delegations were represented as being an integral whole, when the communist party summit talks took place the representatives of the other parties in both delegations naturally did not take part.

The East German delegation made the obligatory tour of Poland, visiting Lodz, Danzig, the brown coal district of Konin and a few

[1] Appointed Finance Minister in December 1971

[2] Appointed Polish ambassador to Turkey in 1971

other towns before returning to Warsaw, where talks took place at the highest level, culminating in the publication of a joint communique.

These talks were my first opportunity to observe the leader of the Socialist Unity Party at close quarters. Naturally I had already heard and read a great deal about Ulbricht from both Eastern and Western sources. I looked forward to meeting him with great interest, and to forming my own opinion of the man who wielded unlimited power over a section of the German people.

Political relations between the Polish people and the German Democratic Republic were then very far removed from the usual public formulas of friendship and fraternal solidarity, and this applied not only to the ordinary people but also to the leadership. The Poles had not forgotten the memory of Ulbricht laying down the law on the line from Berlin when the German Democratic Republic had manifested its opposition, in the clearest possible way, to the reforms introduced by its eastern neighbour in the days of October 1956.

At this time Gomulka was still trying to build up contacts with the West, the Federal Republic not excepted. He was also interested in making contact with various circles in Western social democracies. And he kept constantly in mind a plan which he wanted to realize in every possible sphere: he wanted to build a triangle within the socialist camp, a kind of Warsaw-Berlin-Prague axis which, through close economic, political and cultural co-operation, would eventually form a counterweight to the other countries in the socialist camp.

These plans, and the negative attitude to them of the German Democratic Republic, had been made quite clear to me in the course of many previous meetings. Before the summit talks with Ulbricht there had been discussions between individual Politburo members when the Poles had tried to win acceptance for this plan – or at least to make some progress towards its realization. On the other hand, there had been many occasions when visits by East Germans to Poland had been exploited to attack the new Polish party leadership, directly or indirectly, in the most vigorous terms.

These emissaries from the German Democratic Republic had included such men as Herbert Warnke, the Politburo member, and at a rather lower level Horst Sindermann,[1] and even Günter Kertzscher, the former Nazi who was now toeing the party line in

[1] Appointed to the Politburo of the SUP and Deputy Premier in 1971

the Socialist Unity Party, and who visited the Polish Journalists' Union. This negative attitude on the part of the East Germans was also forcibly expressed on many other occasions. For example, there was the secret visit paid by the then head of the East German Bureau for National Reserves, Karl Stoph – brother of the present East German Prime Minister – to his Polish opposite number, Mr Katz. Once in Warsaw, Stoph showered him with reproaches about the political reforms in Poland. During a break in the discussions I suddenly noticed, standing opposite me, a man who had spread fear and horror in Poland for ten whole years, Stanislaw Radkiewicz. He was the former Polish Security Minister and, between 1944 and 1954, he had been a member of the Politburo and one of the most powerful men in Poland. In 1954 he vanished suddenly from the political scene; only a very small circle of top party officials can have known his fate. And now I saw him in a corridor at the Polish Bureau for National Reserves where he was working as head of a department.

Among the visitors who brought their warnings and reproaches to Warsaw was Kurt Blecha, who for many years was head of the East German press bureau and who was attending discussions with representatives of the Polish journalists in Warsaw. This former member of the Nazi party was now trying to teach Polish communists their business.

There was really only one thing that made me thoughtful: at the preparatory conferences it was always understood that Ulbricht would be accompanied on his Polish visit by the then Prime Minister of the German Democratic Republic, Otto Grotewohl. In the end, however, the East German side stated officially that, on medical advice, the head of government had decided to call off his proposed visit to the People's Republic of Poland. At that time, in the fifties, it was unheard of for a single word about the health of one of the top leaders of a socialist country to be made public, so it seemed to me that this sudden backing-down by Grotewohl must have political causes or must be a result of party in-fighting. These seemed all the more likely since Grotewohl was said to be suffering from the after-effects of a cold which must have lasted several days, if not weeks. And yet the fact that Grotewohl would not be included in the party was only announced in East Berlin on the day set for the departure of the East German leaders.

Naturally the delegation was received in Warsaw with all the usual pomp and 'popular enthusiasm' which is always organized in such cases. Vast numbers of adults and children, who had been specially sent by their factories or schools, lined the road where the visitors were to pass, and waved paper flags as the East German delegation drove from the station to the residence in Ladowa Street which had been put at their disposition.

The first summit talks at party and government level showed clearly that the differences between Ulbricht and the Gomulka leadership, which had already existed for two years – since the 'Polish October' – had not been overcome.

Right from the start Ulbricht, with his stiff vocabulary, set himself up as the mentor, whereas Gomulka and the other Polish delegates were more concerned, international questions apart, to resolve the differences in order to win over the German Democratic Republic to the plan for an 'iron triangle'.

However, during the party and government talks there was some tough discussion between Ulbricht and Gomulka. At the same time, the Poles avoided any kind of provocation, and confined themselves during these high-level talks to, for example, raising the question of the Polish journalist, Janiurek, who, in spite of many applications, had not been granted a visa to visit the German Democratic Republic.

But Ulbricht was well informed on Gomulka's attempts to set up discussions with Western and West German Social Democrats, and took the opportunity during private talks to demand that the Poles should on no account take independent action. The Poles tried to mollify their guests by giving unconditional support to proposals Ulbricht was making at that time for a confederation of the two German states, and by repeatedly emphasizing that the German Democratic Republic was the first German state to be truly democratic and freedom-loving.

During both the party and government negotiations Ulbricht took every opportunity to rouse Polish hostility to West Germany with the argument, which I was to hear on countless other occasions, that the West German militarists were planning an attack on the German Democratic Republic in the very near future. Ulbricht constantly used formulas which sounded suspect to Polish ears, such as 'under the leadership of the Soviet Union' or 'with the Soviet Union at our head', but he carefully avoided making any open, direct attack against Poland in general, or against the new Polish leadership and the reforms which had begun in October 1956, and which, at this time, had still not been completely rescinded.

After all the sharp criticism of the Polish leadership and the reform programme which had been made by previous Socialist Unity Party and East German delegations, I was anxious to see if and when Ulbricht, who always wore two blood-red stars on his lapel, would make a frontal attack on Gomulka, Poland, and Polish ideas.

However, Ulbricht had to take into account the political, or at least propaganda, effects of his Polish visit in the German Democratic Republic – at that time Gomulka was seen as an honoured and valued national leader in other socialist countries. But he would certainly regard it as a useful bonus if he could expound his own ideas of government in Poland and follow this up by getting them published in all the East German mass media on his return home.

The first two days were taken up with talks in Warsaw, wreath-laying ceremonies, and other formal duties. Then the East German delegation was divided into two groups which made separate tours of Poland. The group headed by Ulbricht went to Lodz, where they visited a district central heating plant and a newly built sports building, followed by a tour of the Julian Marlewski textile works. Then in the evening they joined up with the second group for a reception held in the Grand Hotel, Lodz, in honour of the German guests. The second group, headed by Hermann Matern, visited Danzig and the brown coal processing plant in Konin.

It was already apparent from meetings with factory workers and discussions held during this trip that the Socialist Unity Party officials, with the exception of Ulbricht, used a very different language from that which they spoke during the party and government talks in Warsaw.

Ulbricht did, of course, emphasize at every possible opportunity that the socialist camp could only flourish and develop 'under the leadership of the Soviet Union' and 'with the Soviet Union at our head', but on public occasions he did not go beyond these formulas.

He left the more specific declarations to his subordinates, like Hermann Matern, then the second-in-command in East Germany or his fellow delegate, Horst Schmidt, who was boss of a crane construction factory in Eberswalde and who informed his Polish listeners at an information briefing that the building of socialism in the German Democratic Republic and in Poland could be finally accomplished 'only through the selfless assistance of the Soviet Union'.

In the meantime a committee was working diligently in Warsaw on the wording of the final joint communique which was to be signed before the departure of the East German delegation. There were many points which were the subject of dispute, and these had to be settled before both sides could declare their willingness to sign the communique. The Poles could not accept East German demands to stress the position of the Soviet Union in the vanguard of the communist movement, to back the collectivization of agriculture in both countries, to make a strong attack on the church, or to include a passage in the communique stating that West Germany was planning an attack on the German Democratic Republic in the near future. But the Polish members of the committee declared their willingness, in order to smooth things over, to include various phrases about the building of socialism in the German Democratic Republic, Polish support for East German plans for the reunification of Germany based on a confederation of the two states, etc.

I myself was on tenterhooks to see how things would turn out. Ulbricht could not dissociate himself from all the emissaries whom he had sent to Poland previously, and back-pedal on his general attack on policy, even if the Polish side was making every effort to take avoiding action and give him no opportunity to make such an attack.

My curiosity to see how Ulbricht would find a way out of this situation was only too quickly satisfied.

When the two delegations returned from their tours of Poland a visit to the Rosa Luxemburg Works in Warsaw was planned to take place between the continuing top-level government talks.

Ulbricht insisted on having me as interpreter for his visit to the Rosa Luxemburg electric light works in Warsaw. He told me so well before the visit, although there were no plans for him to make a speech. The man who was intended to speak on behalf of the guests was Max Sefrin, who was deputy Prime Minister in addition to his party functions in the Christian Democratic Union, and also deputy Chairman of the Council of Ministers and Minister of Health for East Germany. According to Polish information, which was distributed to everyone involved in the visit during the preparatory conference before the arrival in Warsaw of the East

German delegation, Max Sefrin was a former officer in the Luftwaffe. At that time – and indeed, both before and since – the holding of a senior rank in the wartime German army was regarded in both East German and Polish propaganda as an indication of the survival of the Nazi past, so it seemed strange that Ulbricht should pick Sefrin to speak during this visit.

The day before the engagement Ulbricht asked his Polish hosts if there were any plans for questions to be put to the delegation in this factory. He added that he, Ulbricht, would be most willing to answer questions. The next day he repeated the same question several times before arriving at the Rosa Luxemburg Works. So it was obvious that he wanted to say something to the factory staff apart from the formal speeches which had been planned.

When we arrived at the factory and were received in the club room by the management, the party committee of the factory trade union organization and the workers' council, Ulbricht turned to me once again with the request to translate a question for the party secretary of the factory.

Because of the broad hints made in the last twenty-four hours the management and staff of the Rosa Luxemburg Works had already been tipped off that questions should be put to the East German delegation, so the party secretary replied that the factory staff would probably have some questions, and that all the workers would be very interested to hear the answers made by the German comrades.

Ulbricht was still not satisfied. When we took our places on the platform of the specially arranged club room and, after a short introduction, Sefrin began to read his speech, Ulbricht, who was sitting next to me, told me to go across to the rostrum and tell Sefrin to ask the audience to put questions to the German delegation.

I whispered back that it might be rather tactless if I were to go to the rostrum and interrupt the speaker by whispering in his ear. But Ulbricht insisted. All right, I thought to myself. After all, Walter Ulbricht is Sefrin's boss. So I went over to the rostrum and tugged Sefrin by the sleeve. He broke off in the middle of a sentence, turned round to me in surprise and listened to what I had to tell him.

Then, instead of making the request for questions to the factory staff at the end of his speech, he followed Ulbricht's instructions like a good boy and declared straightaway, before continuing with his speech, that the East German delegation would be very happy to answer any questions at the end of his address.

When Sefrin had finished his speech a few dozen questions on pieces of paper were handed up to the platform. Since all the questions were, of course, in Polish, I translated them for Ulbricht. He went to the rostrum and took advantage of the situation to give an unprepared ninety-minute speech. I stood beside him and translated, phrase by phrase. Until then, nobody on the Polish side had understood why Ulbricht had been so anxious to speak at this factory. Only when we heard how he was answering these perfectly ordinary and insignificant questions did it become clear what he was aiming at. This was the public attack on Gomulka's 'revisionist' policies.

Ulbricht was transformed. During the last few days I had already become accustomed to translating for him and, in this respect, we got along well. I found it even easier to translate when he was speaking impromptu than when he spoke in the long sentences, full of communist cliches, which he used on other occasions. Now, in this room, full of tobacco smoke, I saw an Ulbricht who was no longer cool and collected, droning out his arguments. Instead he was an inspired political agitator.

In theory foreign journalists were not permitted to attend this meeting between the East German delegation and the staff of the Rosa Luxemburg Works, but both Western and West German journalists managed to get past the guarded factory gates.

The advantage for Ulbricht was that, in theory, he was not giving a speech on this occasion, but only answering questions. So there was no need for a prepared text which, out of courtesy, he would have had to show to the Polish side in advance. This meant that Ulbricht was free to speak frankly.

Ulbricht held nothing back.

As I have said, the questions were innocuous. They asked how socialism was being built in the German Democratic Republic, how the German Democratic Republic was developing in other spheres, and so on. But Ulbricht disregarded this. Now came his formal attack on the Polish attitude to the Soviet Union, the new Polish agricultural policies, Polish policy towards the church, the excessive freedom which was permitted to the arts and the mass media in Poland.

Ulbricht began by pointing out that Rosa Luxemburg, after whom the factory was named, was a champion in the fight against reformism and revisionism. This allusion provoked no reaction, since most of the audience were not particularly well versed in Marxist theory, and did not understand the implications. Even when Ulbricht went on to get in a dig at the Poles by saying that Rosa Luxemburg, who was of Polish extraction, had not completely understood the role of the party, and that any underestimate of the leading role of the party must lead to revisionist and anti-Marxist errors, it was obvious that the audience was not paying much attention. Then Ulbricht attacked Bonn, covering Adenauer, West German policies and, of course, Poland. He spoke like a clever agitator, using humour to get his points across.

Dealing with the question of how he intended to beat the Federal Republic in economic competition, Ulbricht eagerly began to lecture his audience about the people's army and the armed workers whose task was not confined to defending the Republic. He talked about the Oder-Neisse Line which, according to him, Strauss intended to invade, and painted a vivid and frightening picture of a new war in Europe.

But this was not the main point of his speech.

Ulbricht was a master of the art of ignoring a question and answering something completely different. So now he began to make a vehement attack on Gomulka, though naturally without mentioning him by name. In reply to a question asking how culture and art were developing in the German Democratic Republic Ulbricht replied more or less as follows: 'Well, comrades, we too have had out problems with our artists, with our writers, painters, and sculptors. But it is not so very difficult to overcome these problems if you go about it in the right way. Whenever our artists seemed to be developing in the wrong direction and were no longer capable of creating the kind of works which the working class expected of them, we packed them off to a factory for a year or two, to a mine where they could work underground themselves and come into closer contact with the workers. You can hardly imagine,' said Ulbricht, 'what marvellous results this treatment has. After a while we bring the artists back from the factories and they create really exceptional works, filled with the spirit of socialist realism. If, after a year, any of them still show signs of an insufficiently developed consciousness, we simply send him back to the mines for a while until he understands what a socialist country expects of its artists.' This was Ulbricht's attack on Polish cultural policy.

In his answers to a few more questions, including one about East German agriculture, Ulbricht also made an indirect attack on Poland's new agricultural policy. He heaped praises on the achievements and experience of the Soviet Union in this field, and then went into the question of collectivization in the German Democratic Republic. But here he was nearly driven into a corner by an interruption from a worker in the audience:

'Is collectivized agriculture in the German Democratic Republic successful economically or not?' he wanted to know.

Ulbricht was not at a loss for an answer. 'As for profitability', he said, 'this is the responsibility of every worker in his own particular job. And I am sure this is also the case in your factory, Comrade,' he added in an aside to the worker. 'As for our agriculture, it is obvious that the socialist transformation of a village can lead to a temporary falling-off in output. But,' said Ulbricht, 'when you want to build socialism you must be prepared to pay the price.'

This was one of Ulbricht's favourite phrases.

Ulbricht's speech dragged on. Now I had the answer to my own question – if and when he would make his general attack on policy. Using the pretext of answering questions, he attacked, one by one, all the reforms which had been introduced by the Polish party leadership in the last two years since Gomulka had come to power.

On the last day of the visit the joint communique was signed. This time Ulbricht gave in to the Polish demand to include a mention of the achievements of the People's Republic of China in the communique immediately after the achievements of the Soviet Union and before the achievements of the other socialist states. There was another ceremonial reception in the Polish Palace of Culture, and one more at the official residence of the Polish Prime Minister, and then the party was accompanied to the railway station and, at long last, the East German delegation left for Berlin.

It is true that Ulbricht did not manage to effect any basic change in the opinions of the Polish party and government leaders during his stay. But, unlike the Poles, he had managed to notch up a few pluses from the visit.

A few days after this visit a new series of summit talks was due to take place in Poland; this time to mark the fortieth anniversary of the founding of the Polish Communist Party. Leaders from three countries: Krushchev from the Soviet Union, the First Secretary of the Central Committee from Czechoslovakia, and Ulbricht from the German Democratic Republic were to meet in Warsaw. Since Ulbricht was at that time probably not particularly keen on a quadripartite meeting of this kind, he made a successful bid to sabotage the talks. He excused himself on the grounds of various duties and appointments and declared that it would not be possible for him to lead the East German delegation at the celebrations.

Since the unwritten protocol governing communist meetings lays down that each delegation must be headed by leaders of equal rank, Krushchev was forced, whether he liked it or not, to call off his own proposed visit to Poland and to send Mikoyan in his place. The East German delegation was led by Erich Honecker.[1]

[1] Appointed First Secretary of the Central Committee of the SUP in 1971

CHAPTER 4

Two Visitors from the West

In the summer of 1966 Helmut Schmidt, who was at that time parliamentary leader of the Social Democrat minority in the West German Bundestag, and is now the West German Defence Minister, paid an unofficial visit to Warsaw. The head of the West German Trade Mission in Poland informed the Polish side of the visit.

As far as I could judge, Helmut Schmidt was travelling partly as a private citizen and partly as a politician through Czechoslovakia, Poland and the Soviet Union. Naturally he was interested in meeting leading politicians in these three countries. But I had no idea of the basic motives for his visit. So I was very interested to see how the competent Polish officials prepared the discussions with him and how they acted during his visit.

Schmidt may have had the idea of sounding out the possibility of bridge-building between the Federal Republic and Poland in light of the Western policy of relaxing tensions between East and West. Or he may have wanted to win approval for Bonn policies. But, in any case, any such attempt would be condemned in advance to failure. The zig-zag political course which Gomulka had steered all his life was now once more based on hostility to the West. He seemed to have almost forgotten his attempts of a few years earlier to make contacts with the West, and even to be ashamed of them.

In talks with Ulbricht he dissociated himself specifically from the meetings between the Polish Prime Minister Cyrankiewicz[1] with Berthold Beitz, the head of Krupps, even though they could not have taken place without his approval; he set his whole propaganda apparatus on an anti-Western tack.

But there was another reason why Schmidt's mission to Poland was bound to fail. As a result of struggles for power between different factions within the leadership, the group led by Moczar,[2]

[1] Deposed in 1971

[2] His power was neutralized for the time being in 1971

which was opposed to Gomulka, had already succeeded in isolating the party leader and using him as they wanted. To consolidate his internal position even more, Moczar was now concerned to find allies among the dogmatists in other communist parties and to point out to them that he had considerable power in Poland, and with the help of his apparatus, was in a position to sabotage any deviationist plans on the part of Gomulka, even if their only aim was to overtake the West, politically or economically.

Whatever motives Gomulka may have had at that time, he still showed some interest in making contact with Schmidt, which he intimated through his close friend and collaborator, Kliszko. The events of this visit showed me how deception and confidence tricks can be used to influence policy at the highest level and, not to mince words, can outwit both friend and 'enemy'.

As is usual on such occasions, a few days before the arrival of the Social Democratic leader in Warsaw a preparatory conference was held in the Sejm, the Polish parliament. I was asked to act as interpreter at this session, which was attended by prominent deputies and senior officials of the Foreign Ministry, the Foreign Trade Ministry, the Central Committee, the PAX Movement and the Institute for International Affairs. First, all those present were given a *curriculum vitae* of Helmut Schmidt which had been prepared by the Foreign Ministry so that they could make themselves familiar with his personal background, at least in outline. An official from the Foreign Ministry commented on this paper and expressed the opinion that Helmut Schmidt was a rising star and the heir apparent of the SPD.

Things were getting interesting. I remembered the many attempts made by Gomulka since 1956 to arrange talks with the Federal Republic. A few years earlier Herbert Wehner[1] was due to come to Poland, but this plan foundered on the vehement protests of Ulbricht. But now Helmut Schmidt was coming. The Polish leadership, we were told at the conference, was not quite clear about Helmut Schmidt's exact purpose in visiting Warsaw. But since he had previously stopped in Prague it was decided to ask the Czechoslovak comrades for information about his attitude and the subjects which he had raised there. We were told that Zenon Kliszko, one of Gomulka's closest collaborators who, among other functions, was responsible for foreign policy in the Politburo,

[1] Chairman of the Social Democratic parliamentary party since 1969

would, in certain circumstances, be prepared to receive Helmut Schmidt. Of course, protocol laid down that he would not be able to do so as a Member of the Politburo or as a Secretary of the Central Committee, but only in his capacity as Vice-President of the Polish Parliament and leader of the Parliamentary Communist Party in the Sejm. All the details, including the composition of the Polish delegation, would be decided shortly before the arrival of the visitor. Nor did we learn anything about the political line which the Polish side would adopt at the meeting.

A few days later, I believe it was on a Sunday, when Schmidt had already arrived in Warsaw, he was due to be received in the Sejm at midday. The Polish participants in the ceremony, together with me as interpreter, were requested to arrive at the Parliament building two hours earlier. For this was the time for us to be briefed about all the details.

I arrived punctually and was immediately taken to a small, tastefully decorated room on the first floor, where a parliamentary committee usually sat. A few of those due to take part in the meeting had already arrived, including Kruczkowski, at that time head of the Institute for International Affairs. This man, a sworn opponent of Gomulka, was to be spokesman at the discussions with Helmut Schmidt. The son of a Polish writer best known for his play, '*Niemcy*' (The Germans) he was typical of the young, rising *apparatchiks* who were cold and pragmatic in their efforts to further their careers, and did not concern themselves with ideological principles. In this respect he showed particular talent. His patron, Moczar, who was the leader and manipulator of the opposition to Gomulka within the party, appointed him deputy Foreign Minister in 1968.

A few minutes later the other participants arrived. The composition of the Polish group was not very impressive, for apart from Kruczkowski there was only a single deputy from Warsaw, Henryk Korotynski.[1] The other deputies were from the provinces – rather narrow and simple types whom I had met previously on various occasions. They were in no way qualified to take part in a serious political discussion. Among those present only Henryk Korotynski, the editor-in-chief of the Warsaw daily paper, *Zycie Warszawy*, had any intellectual training. But he was well known

[1] Released from his post as editor-in-chief of *Zycie Warszawy* in January 1972 and appointed to the chairmanship of the so-called United National Front

as a careerist, a man without any political or moral backbone, a stiff-necked official who tried to compensate for his anti-communist past before the war by zealously following even the most senseless directives and instructions from the party. Among Warsaw journalists Korotynski was regarded with a mixture of irony and contempt. On several occasions the party leadership had picked him out as a suitable member for the Central Committee. But even in the not very democratic elections at lower level party congresses he always failed to be selected, which made him something of a laughing stock.

Among those chosen to talk to Helmut Schmidt was a deputy named Dubiel, of the United Peasants' Party, who had not succeeded in the years since 1945 in clearing himself of frequent accusations that he had collaborated with the Nazis during the war.

In his introduction Kruczkowski explained to us that he had telephoned Prague. In Czechoslovakia Helmut Schmidt had been received by Koucky, the Central Committee Secretary with responsibility for foreign political affairs. The visitor from Bonn had tried to defend the policies of the Federal Republic and to take the first steps towards establishing a *détente*. Schmidt had also expressed an interest, continued Kruczkowski, in meeting Kliszko. 'But we shall not give him that pleasure. His request was passed on to us by the head of the German Trade Mission and Kliszko is prepared to take part in such a meeting. But I suggest that we act as follows: we explain to Schmidt right at the beginning of the discussions that *we* are a group of deputies who have been instructed by the leadership of the Sejm to take part in talks with him. Schmidt is a good enough politician to understand that this means that Kliszko is declining a meeting with him, and he will probably not repeat his request. But if he does, Kliszko is prepared to meet him. He has asked me to pass on any such request by telephone during our conversation with Schmidt. But,' added Kruczkowski sarcastically, 'I doubt if it will come to that . . .

'Our correspondent in Bonn, Marian Podkowinski, a reliable comrade who is not badly informed about German questions, has been detailed to assist Schmidt. He is speaking with him at this moment to determine any particular wishes our guest may have. Podkowinski will be keeping us informed about this. Among other things, Schmidt is interested in attending the military parade due to take place on July 22 as a spectator. We will explain to him that all the invitations have already been taken up. After all, there is no need for us to show our newest and most modern weapons to a visitor from West Germany. Especially since Schmidt is an expert in this field. He is the SPD spokesman for military affairs. There are enough Western spies among the foreign diplomats who have seats on the reviewing platform in the normal way without us making things any easier for Herr Schmidt. . . . The basic theme of our conversations with Schmidt must be a vigorous attack on the Federal Republic and the SPD so that he will completely lose his taste for bridge-building. What's more, we will stick to the three principles of our official foreign policy. We will demand that West Germany give official recognition to the Oder-Neisse frontier, renounce nuclear weapons, and establish normal diplomatic relations with the German Democratic Republic. And if he still hasn't had enough we can inform Herr Schmidt that the Federal Republic must give up West Berlin and introduce various internal measures before we can think of holding talks with them. Of course, that doesn't mean that we want to interfere in German internal affairs – we must emphasize that,' added Kruczkowski with a smile.

'. . . I would also like to request Comrades Dubiel and Koraszewski, if the conversation takes an unfavourable turn, to talk at length and in detail about Nazi crimes in Poland. It's true that this is nothing to do with our basic theme, but after all, even in the American Congress there are filibusterers who make speeches lasting twenty-four hours just to wear out their listeners. I doubt if Herr Schmidt will have so much patience. And finally we have one more weapon in reserve. We can suggest to Schmidt that we show him over the Sejm building, the main auditorium, the rooms of the State Council, the deputies' quarters etc. He will soon see that it's useless to go on talking to us.'

Only one thing really surprised me in this programme: Schmidt wanted to have serious discussions with Zenon Kliszko, and according to Kruczkowski, Kliszko was also willing. Did these subordinate *apparatchiks* now feel themselves strong enough to sabotage such a meeting? It was not until two hours later that this question was clarified – after the meeting with Helmut Schmidt.

At midday the visitor from Bonn arrived, accompanied by his secretary. He was courteously received, taken to our room and offered brandy, confectionery, fruit and cigarettes. Then he was asked what he wished to do.

Schmidt explained that he was making a private visit to three socialist countries, but he wanted to take advantage of the opportunity to hold talks with competent parliamentary representatives in these countries on a serious basis. He would be very happy to have this opportunity in Poland too.

Naturally Schmidt was not aware that he had been outwitted in the simplest way, that one word from him would have been enough to win him a meeting with Kliszko. The *apparatchiks* had calculated correctly.

The SPD parliamentary leader explained to his hosts that the Federal Republic wished to contribute towards a *détente* in Europe. But for this to come about it was essential for both sides to be genuinely interested in peaceful coexistence. Neither the Federal Republic nor the Federal Government had any military designs on socialist countries, Poland included. But there was no doubt that barriers of misunderstanding and mistrust existed. Both sides must take on the task of breaking down this mistrust through mutual contacts. The visitor then spoke on the question of disarmament and explained SPD attitudes to various questions of internal and external politics.

Hardly had Helmut Schmidt finished his final sentence than Kruczkowski put his plan into action and began heaping him with reproaches. He said that there was no doubt that the Federal Government wanted to acquire nuclear weapons and that the Poles found it incomprehensible that the SPD should support them in this. A policy document recently published by the SPD, added Kruczkowski, put the Social Democrats on the same level as the Nazi generals and militarists since it demanded the right for the Federal Republic to have a finger on the nuclear trigger. There was more in the same vein. Schmidt immediately replied that this was certainly a misunderstanding. Perhaps there had been an error in the translation of the policy document. He could assure his listeners that neither the Federal Republic nor the SPD wished to possess nuclear weapons. And to adapt the same metaphor, the SPD wanted a finger not on the trigger but on the safety catch. Naturally misunderstandings were unavoidable if there was confusion between 'trigger' and 'safety catch'. But there was a very basic difference, even if it was not completely obvious at first sight. For this reason, explained Helmut Schmidt, he wanted to explain in more detail exactly what it meant. A finger on the nuclear trigger meant the right to decide when nuclear weapons should be used in a hypothetical conflict between

East and West. But if the SPD claimed the right to a finger on the safety catch, this meant that not only did it reject the possession of nuclear weapons by the Federal Republic, but also that it claimed the right for Bonn, as a member of NATO, to exercise a power of veto against the use of nuclear weapons in a crisis. Once again the SPD leader emphasized that there must have been an error in the translation of this passage. Then he expressed the opinion that it would be helpful if he could report back in West Germany that the Polish authorities had assured him that Poland was also willing to renounce the possession or stationing of nuclear weapons on its territory, or that no such weapons existed in Poland. This was certainly an allusion to the question of whether Poland, as a member of the Warsaw Pact, still backed the Rapacki Plan.

At this point Korotynski went into the attack. He declared that the Polish participants in the talks were deputies, and not sufficiently informed about military matters. At the same moment Kruczkowski gave a meaningful glance at the others and they all began playing their prearranged roles.

Dubiel talked about his experiences in a concentration camp. Koraszewski described the suffering of the Polish people during the German occupation and so on. The talk continued for a while and time slipped by. Helmut Schmidt realized that his hosts were not ready to take part in a serious political discussion. The two sides took leave of each other.

I remained in the room. Kruczkowski said: 'Kliszko is expecting the results of our talks. We must draft a short report for him straight away. We managed the whole affair very well. You all saw that Schmidt did not want to meet Kliszko or he would have addressed his request to us, since we were competent to deal with it. Also, he will certainly meet Podkowinski again and then we will learn what opinion about our talks he is taking away with him.'

A shorthand-typist was already waiting in the next room. Kruczkowski and the others sat at a round table in our room, and he took a piece of paper and began to draft the report. As he wrote he read out each sentence aloud so that any of those present could correct it, factually or stylistically. He began with the statement that Helmut Schmidt had arrived at the Sejm at 12 o'clock, accompanied by his secretary. He had taken part in talks with Deputies So-and-so and So-and-so. Then Kruczkowski described the political content of the talks. As he wrote, he read out: 'In answer to our reproach that the SPD was in favour of the Federal Republic acquiring nuclear weapons, Schmidt declared that the SPD wanted to have a finger on the nuclear safety-catch. Schmidt went on to say that Poland should abandon all military armaments . . .'

I was astounded. Had the comrades not understood Schmidt's words? Since I had been allowed to stay in my role as interpreter so that I could help to correct any errors in the report, I interrupted immediately: 'Excuse me, but Helmut Schmidt took care to point out that this kind of terminology can lead to misunderstandings. In fact he explained at some length the exact difference between the desire to acquire nuclear weapons and the phrase, "a finger on the nuclear safety-catch".'

But Kruczkowski was not to be dissuaded from falsifying the report on the talks with Schmidt. The friendly expression was wiped from his face. He got up, came over to me and said, coldly: 'My friend, today is a holiday and I am sure you have some private plans. We won't detain you any longer. Good-bye!'

The visit to Poland of another eminent Western politician a few years earlier had passed very differently. Franz Olah was at that time President of the Austrian Federation of Trade Unions, and also played a leading role in the socialist party in his country. He visited Poland in 1961.

In the first few years after the 'Polish October' in 1956, the Gomulka leadership showed the greatest interest in making contacts with the West at every level. At that time Poland, like all the other 'fraternal states', had had a decade of close dependence on Moscow, and had been largely isolated from the West. But there were now both political and economic reasons for breaking through this isolation, at least to some degree. At this time Gomulka and his closest collaborators were still clinging to their wishful thinking about building up an 'iron triangle' – Warsaw, Prague, East Berlin, which would form an economically and politically viable counterweight to the rest of the Eastern bloc. He was obsessed by the geographical position of the three countries, and fascinated by his vision of the interlocking and complementary economic potential of these states. Gomulka also expected that, in the future, Kadar's Hungary would seek to join the triangle.

This vision of a 'new order' in Eastern Europe, a socialist bloc of countries that would eventually reach from Jugoslavia to the

Baltic, with all the political and strategic implications which that involved, was so powerful that it made him lose sight of the real facts: it was not geographical frontiers but internal political barriers between the leaders of these countries that would be decisive. As part of this global plan the Poles first tried to make contacts with the West in the fields of art and science, then through various mass organizations, and finally, with great caution and prudence, on a political level. They wanted to break down the mistrust and reserve felt in the West and to show, convincingly, that the communists – at least the Polish variety – were not bloodthirsty barbarians. In short, Gomulka and his collaborators wanted to make Poland socially acceptable on an international level and also to clear the way for wide-ranging co-operation with the West. This was not easy, for on one hand the party leadership wanted – and was obliged – to stay true to its ideological and political principles, and on the other it had to seek to win confidence in international public opinion without coming into conflict with its own apparatus or the 'fraternal parties'. Gomulka had to act cautiously, for not only the party leadership in the Soviet Union was opposed to his plans. The Stalinists in the German Democratic Republic and in Czechoslovakia also regarded his policy with suspicion. This was frequently shown during private talks.

One day in 1961 I was summoned by telephone to the Central Council of the Polish Trade Unions. This organization was headed by Ignacy Loga-Sowinski, a close collaborator and friend of Gomulka since the time of the German occupation. I was told in an information briefing that relations between the Polish and Austrian Trades Unions were to be improved. It was intended to invite Franz Olah, the President of the Austrian Federation of Trade Unions, to visit Warsaw. The Austrian side had declared its willingness to send a delegation to Poland to prepare the visit. This deputation duly arrived, headed by Olah's deputy, Hillegeist.

The Polish trade union officials were as helpful as possible, anticipating every wish of the Austrian delegation and trying to give them the best possible impression. In talks with Hillegeist, Loga-Sowinski spoke quite frankly and even criticized the Socialist Unity Party in strong terms: 'We regard it as a misfortune,' he said, 'that the Socialist Unity Party is hampered by bad Prussian traditions which, since it is not in a position to overcome them, are causing considerable harm to the cause of socialism in Germany.'

I was amazed at such frankness. If any Polish journalist had published this kind of idea in his newspaper he would have had the toughest measures taken against him. Even at that time the agreement made in 1958 between Ulbricht and Gomulka was in force – differences of opinion between the German Democratic Republic and Poland could only be discussed between the two principals, never in public or with third parties.

Loga-Sowinski's frank speaking also seemed to have an effect on the Austrians. They promised to present an exact report of the proceedings in Vienna, and Olah's visit was agreed. When he arrived in Warsaw, self-confident and friendly, together with Gertrude Wondrack, Kurt Blümel and Johann Mayer, all eminent trade union officials, I was again asked to act as interpreter.

Naturally the Poles were aware that in the early Fifties Olah had been the trade union leader responsible for putting down an attempted communist coup in Austria. And although he made it quite clear that his delegation included representatives of all political groupings in the Federation of Austrian Trade Unions, with the exception of the communists, he was received with the greatest friendliness. To show their willingness to make concessions, the party leadership even had an account of Olah's life published in the central organ of the trades union organization which omitted any reference to the attempted communist coup in Austria. Instead, the article described the way Olah was persecuted before the war, the years he spent in a Nazi concentration camp, and his political career since the liberation of Austria which had taken him into the Parliament and into the highest posts in the Austrian Socialist Party and the trade union movement.

The talks with Olah were by no means restricted to trade union subjects. But even in this area a basic difference emerged. For example, Olah explained that the Austrian trade unions had no intention of achieving a steady increase in wages by encouraging the workers to overfulfil their norms. For the Polish trade unionists this attitude was incomprehensible. For in Poland, as in the other socialist countries, the basic principle was to pay a one hundred per cent wage if the norm was fulfilled one hundred per cent. The more the norm was exceeded, the more, in proportion, the wage was increased. It was some time before Olah could make his hosts understand that the Austrian trade unions represented the interests of the workers, not of the employers, and therefore tried to push basic wages as high as possible without encouraging any kind of Stakhanovism. 'The worker must receive a good wage for his labour, but he should not be forced to work like a slave so that he goes home dead tired with no time for his family or to enjoy some cultural activity,' explained Olah.

One of the reasons why the Polish side was interested in making contact with the Austrian Federation of Trade Unions was that they also wanted to set up links with the International Federation of Free Trade Unions. Since the various national trade union organizations belonging to the IFFTU were mostly allied to the social democratic parties in their countries, it followed that this would also mean an approach to the Western social democratic parties. So Olah was intended to act as a middleman for discussions with Western socialists.

The Poles did everything to achieve this goal. They entertained their guest royally and put a Pullman carriage at his disposal for the obligatory tour of the country. In the policy talks the Polish trade union officials acted in a most receptive way, and overstepped marks which they themselves had previously established. In their excess of zeal they also committed an embarrassing solecism.

In Eastern bloc countries it is customary to present official guests with a considerable amount of pocket money on their arrival. Olah, of course, came from neutral Austria, but on the first day of his visit he too received a sealed, blank envelope. He took it, clearly unaware of its contents, and found there were Polish banknotes in it. Immediately his face went bright red and he tried to hand the envelope straight back. The Polish officials were startled. No one wanted to take the envelope back. Olah began to tremble with rage: 'I won't be given anything of this kind.' But the offending envelope was only removed when I whispered to one of the Polish assistants to take it back immediately, for the love of heaven, or there would be real trouble, for Olah obviously thought it was an attempt to bribe him, and an insult. He was in a bad humour for some time after the incident.

Olah met many leading party and government politicians, including Zenon Kliszko. During the talks with him the visitor from Vienna spoke more or less as follows: 'I am also of the opinion that in spite of all the political and social differences that divide our two countries there is certainly a possibility of closer relations. But I should also like to say, quite frankly, that there are some things I don't approve of . . .' Since I was making a simultaneous translation

Kliszko thought he knew what Olah was going to say. He interrupted, 'There are plenty of things in Austria that I don't approve of.' But before I could translate this sentence into German, Olah completed his phrase with an ironic smile: 'to be found in Austria.' Silence is sometimes golden, at least until your interlocutor has finished his sentence.

During the tour of Poland the Austrian delegation was accompanied by Wit Hanke, a senior Polish trade union official, who was also a deputy in the Sejm, a member of the Central Committee and a close friend of Loga-Sowinski. Later the two friends fell out for both personal and political reasons. During the 'Polish October' Hanke, as leader of the Miners' Union, had played an important role – he had mobilized the Silesian miners in support of Gomulka. Then, a few years later, he was demoted. Now, since he knew what was at stake, he avoided all political topics during the whole of the tour. When a rather pushing junior trade union official tried to join in the conversation, expressing his political opinions with great chauvinism, Hanke retorted sharply: 'Stop interfering in important policy questions. Even I don't do that!'

But the visitors did not restrict themselves to minor questions, and so Hanke frequently found himself in a difficult position. He tried to avoid answering fundamental questions with as much skill as he could muster, but since he was dealing with a man who knew exactly what he wanted this was not always easy. So frequently he had to take refuge in propaganda. When Olah suggested to him that freedom of the press was an integral part of democracy, and asked him how such things were ordered in Poland, Hanke explained: 'In Poland freedom of the press is very highly developed because all the press is put at the service of the labouring masses and the whole people. So it goes without saying that we do not give freedom of the press to reactionary elements and people who want to attack our achievements.' But it was obvious that Hanke was not happy with his reply for he quickly changed the subject and started to go into great detail about the dangers to humanity inherent in the development of anti-matter.

Although Olah was uncompromising on basic principles, he appeared fairly flexible in other matters and was very friendly, as indeed were all the members of the two Austrian delegations. Their attitude to Poland and its problems impressed even the most conformist officials.

As Olah was travelling in his train through Warsaw, together with his host, Loga-Sowinski, he mentioned the increasing number of road accidents in the West. He asked Loga-Sowinski if safety belts were used in Poland, and then promised to send safety belts for him and for Gomulka from Austria. And, as I saw from later correspondence between the Polish and Austrian trade unions, he kept his promise.

Olah showed great interest in Gomulka. At a reception held in his honour at the Polish trade union headquarters, he said quite openly that he would like to invite Gomulka to make an unofficial visit to Austria. He would be able to relax and they would show him all the beauties of the Austrian countryside. This casual phrase had an electrifying effect on Loga-Sowinski. It was obvious that this invitation had fulfilled a secret political hope of the Polish leadership. Loga-Sowinski could hardly hide his excitement and immediately informed Gomulka. However, as far as I know the Polish communist leader did not, in the event, take the proposed political holiday. For Gomulka such a visit would certainly have been useful, for he would have been able to see conditions in the West for himself instead of relying on official reports.

These very modest attempts by the Polish leadership to build up contacts with social democratic parties in the West were immediately attacked by the dogmatists in Poland and in other socialist countries. Delegations from the German Democratic Republic warned their Polish counterparts of these 'agents of capitalism and imperialism' whose only intention was to break the unity of the socialist countries. Poland must on no account be allowed to make closer links with these criminals. But warnings were not enough.

Shortly after Olah's visit a delegation of the Austrian Communist Party appeared on the scene, led by Friedl Fürnberg, at that time General Secretary. Officially this visit was to discuss co-operation between the Austrian and Polish communist parties. But from the beginning it was clear what the real reason was behind this not very welcome visit. On the very first day Fürnberg asked me, in private, if I had also acted as interpreter in the talks with Olah. When I answered in the affirmative he immediately tried to interrogate me. But I answered him in monosyllables, telling him I could not remember the exact course the conversations had taken.

Olah's visit must have really disturbed the communist party

leadership in Vienna, for the visitors kept returning to this subject. Finally Fürnberg even made an official protest to Edward Ochab who at that time was a member of the Politburo and a Secretary of the Central Committee. The Polish comrades, claimed Fürnberg, had gone behind the backs of the Austrian Communist Party without informing or consulting them, to make contacts with the Social Democrats, the very reactionary forces that the Austrian Communist Party were most concerned to overcome. Moreover, the Polish party leadership had not even informed the Austrian comrades of the results of their talks. Such behaviour amounted to a harmful and unfriendly act towards the Austrian Communist Party. Ochab promised 'to go into the matter and examine the facts'.

CHAPTER 5

'We decide who is a Nazi . . .'

In Eastern bloc countries the 'continuing war' against Nazi criminals has been a constant theme of official propaganda for twenty-five years. It also serves as an excuse for many initiatives in foreign policy. As an interpreter I frequently had the opportunity to learn the real facts and motivations from my position behind the scenes.

In June 1961 I attended the central meeting of the International Auschwitz Committee, which took place in the Rudnjew Hall in the Warsaw Palace of Culture.

I had made myself available as a simultaneous translator for this conference without any clear idea of the work of this committee. I felt that I was in close sympathy with the aims of this organization because I had myself suffered from Nazi persecution. Shortly before the first session the leader of the Polish delegation explained to the interpreters what this general meeting was to consider. This was essential, he told us, because it was not impossible that the discussion might become heated. In these conditions errors in translation must be avoided at all costs. I was shocked by what we were told: the aim of the conference was to unseat the General Secretary of the International Auschwitz Committee, Hermann Langbein[1] of Vienna.

We were told that he had been a communist but the Austrian Communist Party had expelled him because he would not follow the official party line after the Hungarian rising of 1956 and had given his moral support to the rebels. What was more, he had committed the cardinal sin of backing the oppressed Hungarians in a press interview or an article. But at first none dared suggest that he had neglected his duties as General Secretary of the Committee.

Describing his character the Polish delegates also told us that

[1] Herman Langbein is now secretary of the International Camps Committee based in Vienna

Langbein was an incorrigible visionary, a man who, ever since he had survived the concentration camps, had looked on tracking down Nazi war criminals as his whole life's work.

I permitted myself to make the comment that this was not, after all, such a reprehensible activity. But I was immediately told that the effective tracking down of Nazi war criminals and, even more important, the prevention of similar horrors in the future, was only possible in the framework of comprehensive political action by the progressive and communist powers at an international level. I should look at this problem from a dialectical point of view and should not evaluate separate phenomena in isolation. So much for theory.

From conversations during intervals between the sessions I gathered that Langbein would be dismissed as painlessly as possible. The Polish Prime Minister, Cyrankiewicz, himself a former prisoner at Auschwitz whose life had been saved by Langbein, was said to have suggested that he should be paid a pension or a lump sum to compensate him to some extent for the unsavoury manœuvring. But Langbein had turned down the offer.

His most implacable opponents were members of the Austrian Communist Party. The Austrian party leadership were stubbornly insistent on his dismissal from the General Secretaryship. But it soon appeared that this demand would not be easy to achieve. Some delegations, for example a section of the Austrian, Dutch and English delegates, were of the opinion that the criticisms made of Langbein had nothing to do with the activities of the International Auschwitz Committee and therefore they were by no means ready to let him be dismissed without a fight. On the contrary, in view of his years of experience and the many successes which he could claim, these delegations were not inclined to allow a crisis to develop on the Auschwitz Committee which had clearly been hatched up for political motives. They saw the work of the organization in danger.

Gradually two opposing factions were revealed. The Poles, Czechs, Hungarians, East Germans, Soviets and French – the latter mostly communists – came out openly against Langbein. But they did not attack him directly; instead they tried to give the impression that they were only concerned with facts, and with the effectiveness of the committee.

In an interval I learnt that the plan of battle had only been altered to the extent that they were now trying for a unanimous vote in favour of Langbein's dismissal. Any delegates who could not be won over by political intrigue would have to be convinced in argument that Langbein was no longer the right man to be General Secretary.

His opponents now criticized him on the grounds that he was doing little or nothing for former inmates of Auschwitz, that the finances of his General Secretariat were not in order and, finally, he was even accused of interfering in the prosecution of Nazi war criminals by the West German courts. This was really the height of absurdity.

As I sat in my cubicle and translated all this, my thoughts turned to the past. I imagined Langbein, now awaiting judgement from his former comrades, as he must have been when they all wore striped concentration camp uniforms and he was doing all he could to fight for them and the other prisoners. He must have saved the lives of many of them, and of countless others besides. Now he was the accused. Now he had to defend himself, to justify his actions. The 'visionary who wanted to go on fighting Nazi war criminals, but who did not understand enough about dialectics'.

As I had often remarked before, two conferences were really taking place within the same conference. At this meeting too, the action was taking place at two different levels. The function of one conference, the general meeting, was to act as a rubber stamp and approve all the plans and suggestions. But it was during the intervals that the other, really decisive, talks took place – a kind of second conference in which only the initiates took part. The Eastern bloc delegations met for internal consultations, analysed developments in the conference, and decided what was to be done. They were still aiming at getting a unanimous vote in favour of dismissing Langbein. An open disagreement was to be avoided. But whatever happened, they were determined to unseat him. The comrades were completely unconcerned about the effects their action might have on the Auschwitz Committee.

I had already seen on several previous occasions that the Eastern bloc countries were concerned, for propaganda reasons, to play up their role as the consistent avengers of all the crimes committed by the Nazis during the Second World War. Their agents continually claimed that in the West, and particularly in West Germany, Nazis were treated with kid gloves, whereas 'We communists have always been the only true enemies of Hitler and his henchmen'.

This propaganda had two aims: first to rouse the masses against the West and second, and more important, to win the support of the people. Since most of the measures taken by the Eastern bloc regimes were not exactly greeted with popular enthusiasm, they sought symbols which could be used to persuade the people to identify themselves with the regime. One of these symbols was the swastika. If Tito was public enemy number one, every cartoon would show him decorated with this emblem, in spite of the historical facts. In support of the slogan, 'Forward in the struggle against the USA,' the American President would be shown in a uniform which Goering might have envied. Sometimes the better-off peasants would be Nazis, sometimes the Jews or Radio Free Europe. This tastelessness went so far that the world-famous Nazi-hunter, Simon Wiesenthal, was labelled a Nazi in the Polish press. When show trials were being prepared in Poland even a Gomulka or a Spychalski would be shown complete with swastikas in the national satirical press.

Spychalski, who later became Marshal of Poland and President,[1] even confessed at a trial of a group of Polish officers in 1951, in the presence of press and news cameras, that *during the war he had worked with the Gestapo and had given them lists of resistance fighters.* He made his 'confession', which was enough to condemn several of the accused, when he was brought from prison to act as a witness. The 'strength of character' he showed at that time still makes the Poles feel some uneasiness about their Head of State.

But all this did not prevent him, Gomulka, and the other Polish leaders from using the same methods after 1965 against their real or imagined enemies. They decide who is a Nazi, and when. And so the swastika has become a travelling symbol. This propaganda in the press, on television and radio, and in films and literature, has not been altogether unsuccessful. Many people, especially in the younger generation, were gradually convinced that, in this respect at least, the communists had clean hands.

It is true that after the war many Nazis, large and small, were lined up and shot with few formalities. Indeed, there was so much zeal that some innocent people suffered too. But what did it matter? The old saying that you can't make omelettes without breaking

[1] Spychalski was deposed in 1971

eggs was raised to the level of a slogan in the communist movement. Stalin in person used it to 'justify' a few isolated rehabilitations after his great purges. On the other hand, many of the top Nazis were treated more leniently if a new use could be found for them.

I remember, in this connection, the visit of a young West German intellectual to Konstancin, a town near Warsaw. This was Thomas Harlan, the son of the film star of the Nazi period who gained a world-wide reputation through his part in 'Jew Süss'. The young man wanted to come to terms with his country's – or his father's – past. He was invited to Poland. He was given materials, documents, factual reports and translators and secretarial staff were put at his disposal. But it soon appeared that Thomas Harlan had a will of his own and had no intention of letting his hosts control him. He was not ready to confine himself to attacking the Nazis in the Federal Republic and to overlook those living in other countries. So he was packed off home without ceremony.

There was a postscript to this story. All the people who had supported Harlan's invitation to Poland were harassed by the security authorities. I myself was not one of them, for, knowing the real plans they had in store for him, I had declined the suggestion that I work with Harlan. I got to know him only briefly during his stay in Poland when an acquaintance, naively believing that he was helping the fight against Nazism, offered to act as adviser and translator for Harlan for a while. He took me with him to Konstancin and introduced me to him. Since the few hours I spent in the town were in the nature of a private visit I was naturally not included in the files of 'Harlan's associates'.

Another eloquent example that illustrated what the Polish regime was capable of when dealing with real Nazi war criminals was the Eichmann trial.

When Eichmann was tracked down in South America and taken to Israel to be put on trial his abduction was examined by the United Nations Security Council. Israel's action looked likely to be condemned. But since the voting showed that the Western representatives were not inclined to pillory Israel, the Polish delegation abstained. Shortly afterwards I acted as interpreter at a summit meeting between the Polish and East German party leaders and heard Kliszko actually boasting about this. A significant example, but not the only one. In its reports of the Eichmann trial, which was attended by journalists who worked in close collaboration with the Security Ministry, the Polish press even tried to give the absurd impression that Israel was only putting Eichmann on trial in order to protect other Nazis.

Shortly after the Eichmann trial a Polish weekly magazine began to serialize his forged memoirs. Only when many Polish progressives and intellectuals protested against this indirect Nazi propaganda – and at a time when valuable literary works were not being published because, it was claimed, there was a severe shortage of paper – did the magazine stop publishing the series. And when the former Gauleiter Koch who was responsible for the deaths of many Poles and many Germans too, was surrendered to the Polish authorities, he was put on trial but, on instructions from the highest level, the death sentence was never carried out. Yet this did not prevent the Polish authorities from condemning and executing economic offenders during the same period.

The Polish communist party paper, *Trybuna Ludu*, would often publish short reports describing how, for example, a Nazi war criminal had been put on trial in Hamburg and condemned to a prison sentence, with the comment that, of course, the West German authorities were very lenient in these cases: 'So many murders – and only a few years in prison.' Only someone like myself who understood German and could listen to West German radio stations could learn from news broadcasts that such a war criminal might have been captured shortly after the war and *surrendered to the Polish or Soviet authorities* who condemned him to death or to life imprisonment only to *release* him in the Fifties and send him back to the Federal Republic. I shall quote just one example of this – the notorious Kaduk who helped to run Auschwitz.

Was the Langbein case only one link in a whole political chain, or was it an exception? The witchhunt against the General Secretary of the International Auschwitz Committee lasted several days. Langbein defended himself by refuting the slanders with facts. He must have realized what awaited him before leaving Vienna and he had brought many documents with him to Warsaw. He not only rejected all the trumped-up accusations but was able to prove the opposite in every case.

When he was accused of interfering with the affairs of the West German courts he took out a file and read out letters that he had sent to various East European countries. These were requests for the immediate dispatch of any evidence against Nazi war criminals whom he had tracked down in West Germany. Since West Germany was a country where the rule of law was paramount, it would be impossible to put these men on trial without such evidence. To all these letters Langbein had received either no reply at all, or refusals.

The Eastern bloc regimes were clearly not interested in punishing these criminals because it was much more useful politically for them to be living in freedom in the Federal Republic – a few Nazi war criminals at liberty made marvellous propaganda.

Naturally Poland, like the other socialist countries, was forced to co-operate to some extent in uncovering Nazi crimes. Sometimes the authorities even permitted West German judges and lawyers to visit Poland to examine and collect evidence.

But in the cellars of the Polish Ministry of Justice in Ujazdowskie Avenue in Warsaw were many sealed boxes full of original documents relating to the time of the occupation. Twenty years after the war this material had not even been examined, supposedly because of shortage of staff. Naturally nothing of this was allowed to reach the public.

I discovered this when a delegation of the Socialist Unity Party Central Committee was sent to Warsaw, headed by an official named Rehan, to meet the Polish Public Prosecutor, as well as Witaszewski, the Central Committee member in charge of Security, and Gumkowski, the president of the Commission investigating Nazi war crimes. The subject of the meeting was the evidence against Krüger, at that time a West German Federal Minister, and against Dr. Heinrich Lübke, the West German President. The East German delegates tried to persuade the Poles to publish material said to have been discovered in the German Democratic Republic, with a note stating that it had originated in Poland.

A few years later Gumkowski was dismissed from his post. The Warsaw Government designated as his successor a certain Dr. Pilichowski who was known to be a faithful henchman of Moczar. Almost his first act in office was to declare that, under his leadership, the Commission would in future examine a subject which had until now been left completely unexplored: *the collaboration of the Jews with the Gestapo in the extermination of the Polish people.* Naturally he put the emphasis on the 'Jews' for at that time Poland was undergoing a bout of anti-semitism. The sealed boxes in his own cellars were of no interest to Dr Pilichowski.

After a few days it became apparent at the general meeting of the Auschwitz Commission that Langbein was not willing to resign and that it would not be possible to get a unanimous decision against him. So the conference organizers decided to hold a debate and put the matter to the vote. The result was a foregone conclusion, for his opponents controlled the majority of the votes. So Langbein had to step down. In his place was appointed Tadeuz Holuj, the Wendish communist writer.

A few years earlier a congress of the communist-backed World Federation of Trade Unions had taken place in Warsaw. During a reception Louis Saillant, the General Secretary of the WFTU made a cynical remark to his audience – '*In our propaganda even corpses have a job to do.*' It was only later that I understood his true meaning.

Indeed, not much remained of the loudly proclaimed reverence paid to the victims of Nazism when the real facts were examined.

All top-level delegations from abroad would pay a visit to the museum of the Auschwitz concentration camp during their tour of Poland. They would be shown a few blocks of the former camp, the remains of the gas chambers and crematoria. What they were not shown was a very different scene: scarcely a hundred yards from the approach to the neighbouring camp of Birkenau, cows from the surrounding farms are grazing round a small pond. If you pick up a handful of earth it is full of countless tiny splinters of human bone. But the cows don't mind – and neither do the Polish party and government leadership, even though they take every possible opportunity to make the dead of Auschwitz *do a propaganda job for them.*

Naturally most of the suffering of the Polish people in the last war was caused by the Nazis. This fact is exploited for all sorts of political purposes at home and abroad. Past experience has given rise to a national concern with the future. The Polish people cannot make transactions with murderers. Guarantees are demanded to ensure that they will not become too influential. Is this genuine or is it just one more confidence trick?

Murderers are murderers, and mass murderers are mass murderers whichever country they come from and wherever they live now. But Gomulka's accusing finger points in only one direction – West Germany. If former Nazis have installed themselves in a neighbouring Eastern country and are taken under the protective wing of the government there, this fact is passed over in silence.

In Poland there are many books and illustrated albums in which every place where a crime was committed against the Polish people is marked and described in precise geographical terms.

In Warsaw and in other Polish cities there are annual ceremonies of remembrance which are stage-managed in such a way as to have the maximum effect on mass psychology. The Defence Minister or his deputy stands on a platform in the night air, picked out by spotlights and surrounded by guards of honour, torchbearers and vast crowds of people. The drama begins: The minister calls the roll-call of the fallen soldiers and officers from every major battlefield. After each place name the list is interrupted with a deep roll on the drums. And the list includes not only battlefields but also every place where Polish prisoners of war were executed. As soon as the ceremony is over everyone goes home.

However, there is always a small error in the production which, even after a quarter of a century has not been put right by the party and state leadership. One place where about four thousand five hundred Polish officers were murdered is never mentioned: Katyn.

Shortly after the end of the war, reports by Soviet Commissions, eyewitnesses and doctors were published in Poland, proving 'clearly and incontestably' that it was the Germans who had carried out the Katyn massacre, not the Russians. Why then, should there be this reserve on the part of the Poles? Is the fact that the Katyn massacre is mentioned neither in ceremonies of remembrance nor in the countless pamphlets about Nazi crimes in Poland an unintentional admission that the Russians were the true murderers, or is it an indication of the degree of credibility of Polish propaganda? The four thousand five hundred victims of Katyn are the forgotten dead.

But not quite. Even with such an explosive issue there is a man who, against the strictest instructions of the party leadership, to which he himself belongs, makes political capital out of the victims of Katyn. This is Mieczyslaw Moczar, who became security boss of several regions after the war and, on the orders of Gomulka, his boss at that time, was responsible for the deaths of many victims from the ranks of the former Home Army (AK) and the old Peasants' party (PSL). Now this man exploits these forgotten dead for his own political ends. In order to win popularity he spreads the story through the Polish Veterans' Organization (ZBOWiD) which he heads, that if he came to power one of his first acts would be to unmask the real perpetrators of Katyn, the Russians, and set up a fund in Poland to put up a memorial on the site of the massacre. The fact that Katyn now lies within the frontiers of the Soviet Union does not discourage him in the least. He embellishes his fairytale with all sorts of details. For example, according to Moczar, Krushchev had wanted to tell the truth about Katyn at the Twentieth Congress of the Soviet Communist Party in 1956, but Gomulka had opposed him, saying that this would put an additional strain on the already tense relations between Poland and the Soviet Union. Only Moczar, the story goes, had supported Krushchev against Gomulka. What Moczar does not say is how all this could possibly have happened. For at the time he was still only a local party boss in a Polish province and Gomulka was still outlawed. But the main thing, as far as he is concerned, is that his propaganda should be effective. And even dead men can be useful for propaganda.

CHAPTER 6

The War Against the Catholic Church

It was just before Christmas in 1965. Buyers filled the shops. The first Christmas trees were on sale in the markets. Typically, it was in these weeks leading up to the most solemn of Christian festivals that the war between the Communist State and the Catholic Church once more broke out in full force. It was a kind of Christmas present from the atheist party leadership to the believing people.

All the mass media – press, radio and television – spoke with one voice: 'The Catholic Church is the people's Enemy Number One and, what's more, a traitor to the country. It wants to forge links with the Nazis, the murderers of the Polish people.'

All levels of the apparatus were drawn into the fight; the party leadership summoned up its whole army of officialdom, from the Politburo member to the village party worker, against the Catholic hierarchy. Meetings were called in every factory and office. The audiences were called upon to pass resolutions against the Catholic Church. The principal theme in all this propaganda was a letter which the Polish bishops had sent from the Vatican Council to the West German episcopate.

I had often had the opportunity as an interpreter to observe the war against the Polish Church from behind the scenes. But this frontal attack at the end of 1965 included an amalgam of all the methods previously employed, and provided a perfect example of the factional struggles within the party leadership. And since many of the details and motives behind this battle are still not known even to many of the main participants, I should like to examine this event more closely. At all events, the consistent attitude of the Polish episcopate forced the state to beat a retreat. The party leadership had to admit their error and quietly drop the whole campaign.

But first a brief summary of the events leading up to it: during the Vatican Council the Polish bishops sent a message to their

'German brothers in Christ', of which the substance was that in the future, they should strive for a reconciliation between the Polish and German peoples. In their message the Polish bishops did consistently support the national interests of their people without any suggestion of compromise, but they doubtless wished the Church to make a contribution to the building of a bridge between East and West. In fact, the Polish party and state leadership should have been very happy with this letter since it was completely in accordance with the principle of peaceful coexistence which had been backed by the communists for several years; it fitted very well with the attempts made by the Soviet Union and other socialist countries at that time to improve relations with the Vatican; and, in conclusion, the message was bound to increase the moral prestige of Poland and her communist regime, and raise her international standing.

This wide-ranging document awakened a world-wide response and caused a sensation, not only in the European and American press, but also in the Australian, Far Eastern and African newspapers. In all it comprised more than three thousand words.

It began with a brief announcement of the thousandth anniversary of Christianity in Poland, and an invitation to the German bishops to take part in the anniversary celebrations. The remainder of the document was clearly intended by the writers to act as an historical and contemporary commentary with the aim of setting up a dialogue and trying to establish closer contacts between the German and Polish peoples.

The first part of the description of the thousand years of Polish civilization, with special reference to relations between Poland and Germany, covered the historical foundations of Christian Poland. Then followed many examples of German-Polish co-operation in religion and culture. The letter contained a very strongly worded assessment of the Teutonic Knights, the so-called Crusaders 'who used fire and the sword to convert the original inhabitants of the Slavic North and the Prussian and Baltic countries, and have become a terrible and most compromising burden for European Christianity, and its symbol, the cross, and also for the Church. . . .'

Then followed an account of the suffering of the Polish people at the hands of the Prussians, who managed to 'bring everything German into discredit in the Polish lands', leading finally to 'Hitler as the culmination' and to the 'dark night of the German occupation'. 'The country was strewn with concentration camps. . . . More than six million Polish citizens, of whom the majority were of Jewish origin, lost their lives during the occupation period. The leaders of the Polish intelligentsia were simply swept away. . . . A quarter of all the bishops were killed in the camps.'

The Polish bishops went on to say that they were not repeating all this 'to reopen wounds which have still not healed' but 'so that we may to some extent understand each other today. . . .' The bishops then mentioned the 'basic need for security' of the Poles, and the mistrust with which the Polish people 'still regards its closest neighbour in the West'.

On the question of the Oder-Neisse line the Polish bishops took up an uncompromising stand. 'For our country . . . this is a question of very existence (not a question of *Lebensraum*!).'

After words of sympathy for large sections of the German people and the crises of conscience and terrible spiritual need which they suffered during the Nazi period, there followed an appeal 'Let us try to forget! No polemics, no more Cold War, but the start of a dialogue, such as is striven for everywhere today by the Council and by Pope Paul VI.'

The end of the letter reads: 'We beg you, Catholic shepherds of the German people; try to celebrate our Thousand Years of Christianity with us in your own way, either through prayer or with a special day of remembrance. We shall be grateful to you for any gesture of this kind. Convey our greetings and thanks also, we beg you, to the German Evangelical brothers who are striving with us and with you to find solutions for our difficulties.

'In this most Christian and, at the same time, very human spirit, we reach out our hands to you in your place on the benches of this Council, now soon to end, and we grant forgiveness and ask for forgiveness. And only if you, German bishops and Council Fathers, take the hands which we reach out in brotherhood, can we return to Poland with a clear conscience to celebrate our Thousandth Anniversary in a fully Christian way. And so we invite you most heartily to come to Poland.

'May it please our merciful Saviour and the Virgin Mary, the Queen of Poland, the *Regina Mundi et Mater Ecclesiae*.'

The whole tenor of the letter shows clearly that it is not a political document. The Polish bishops sent similar letters to the bishops of fifty-six countries. Each of these letters invited prayers on the occasion of the Polish millenary celebrations and emphasized the ties linking Poland to each respective country.

So what was the reason for the attacks? They began only eleven days after the publication of the letter, on December 10. Was it only by chance that this was the same time that Gomulka's deputy, Kliszko, came back from Moscow? And was it only by chance that similar attacks were published simultaneously in other communist countries, from Prague to Sofia?

There is a certain irony, or perhaps a deeper significance, in the fact that on the same day that the newspapers *Zycie Warszawy* and *Slowo Powszeche* and the Polish radio began their attacks, the well-known (right-wing) *National und Soldatenzeitung* of West Germany published a denunciation of the Polish bishops.

Then there was calm for eleven days. Not a single word on the subject was published. A second, unrestrained campaign, full of lies and misrepresentations, began only when it was known that the bishops were on their way back to Poland. The Politburo knew that once the church dignitaries had returned they would have no means of refuting the falsifications in the press and radio.

The bishops were accused of high treason, of bartering the national interests of their own people, and of going over the heads of a peace-loving neighbour, the German Democratic Republic, especially in the question of the Oder-Neisse line.

The party leadership did not hesitate to use the bishops' message as a weapon in their internal political struggle with the Catholic Church. They used tried and tested methods: lies, slander and provocations. But at the height of the campaign against the church around the New Year of 1966, I still had no idea that a few weeks later I was to be used as a pawn in the battle the party was staging.

The propaganda campaign started with a harsh criticism of the Catholic bishops in the Polish Communist Party newspaper, *Trybuna Ludu*. The paper accused the Polish bishops of betraying the national interests of the country.

After this first shot the avalanche was unleashed. Every paper, radio and television station published interminable commentaries and 'resolutions' from the people protesting against the Polish church leaders and referring to 'quotations' from the message. Just before Christmas a special session of the Sejm, the Polish parliament, was held when the party was also able to sit in judgement on the

Catholic Church. Jerzy Zawieyski, the Catholic writer who was at that time still a deputy in the Sejm and a deputy president of the State Council, protested vigorously against the attacks, but without success. He was shouted down. The all-powerful press censors did not allow the text of his speech to be published. The next challenge from the party was not long in coming. The Security Ministry refused a passport for a visit to Rome to Cardinal Wyszynski, the leader of the Polish Catholics. On January 9, 1966, this decision was also reported in detail in all the newspapers.

About a week later the National Front Committee for all Poland held a session during which Gomulka and the leading party and government officials came out strongly against the Catholic Church. Together with his underlings the party leader accused the bishops of being a clique of traitors, again using 'quotations' from the letter to the German bishops.

Believers of all kinds – manual and white collar workers, women, youth groups, scientists, representatives of every part of the population, were put under moral pressure at mass meetings to pass resolutions expressing their indignation at the 'scandalous action' of their Church.

This was a well-tried method used by the party to give the impression that the whole people was behind them. In the Central Committee the heads of the various sections had only to press a button to put the whole propaganda machine into action. Nor did the party lack hirelings who would write letters to the newspapers on demand. The deputy Minister for Culture and Art, Kazimierz Rusinek, distinguished himself particularly in this area. This was a man who had helped to organize a Nazi concentration camp during the war and who later became notorious on a world-wide scale when he accused the Israelis of having a thousand Nazi war criminals advising their army after the Six Days War. When Radio Free Europe challenged him to name a single one of these advisers he remained silent.

The people drew their own conclusions from the campaign against the Church. Experience had taught them only too well that the party was using this smokescreen to hide some doubtful dealings of its own. Some people set their unshakeable faith against all the persecution and reprisals to which the Church was subjected, others adopted a satirical approach and thought up pointed jokes, others simply shrugged their shoulders.

When the flood of propaganda released by the communist party organizers had reached its height the Church leaders started to defend themselves. Cardinal Wyszinski and other Catholic dignitaries appealed from the pulpit to their congregations not to believe the slanderous assertions made by the party – as I learnt later from the Central Committee, many secret agents of the Security Police joined the congregations, taking their miniature tape-recorders with them. The central arguments expressed in these sermons spread through the people like wildfire. Whereupon the party leadership decided to publish the bishops' letter to the German Catholics – which had still not been made public in Poland – in a journal named *Forum* which was subsidized by the party. In a short preface the editor of *Forum* stated that the Polish party and government leadership possessed only a single copy of the text of the letter released by the West German news agency, DPA, which had been translated word for word into Polish. The print order of this issue of the magazine was increased so that everyone would have the opportunity to see that the Church was lying and the official propaganda machine was telling the truth.

But Cardinal Wyszynski would not be intimidated. He explained in another sermon that this publication contained distortions. The communist party leadership in Warsaw could naturally not leave this accusation unanswered. They issued a communique stating that neither the Polish government nor the Polish press had been sent the text of the letter by the bishops, but that they had supplied a copy to the DPA news agency. So only this text issued by the DPA was available in Poland and this had been translated, word for word, in *Forum*.

Relations between the party and government leadership and the Church had now worsened to such an extent that the Politburo and the Secretariat of the Central Committee of the communist party were now concerned almost exclusively with this question. Gomulka himself poured oil on the fire when he gave a speech on radio and television supporting the accusations against the Church and quoting from the text of the letter as published in *Forum*.

But the Church leaders continued to take every opportunity to claim that this text contained lies, distortions and falsifications. It was one side's word against the other's. This public mutual denunciation had gone so far that it was impossible for either side to retreat. On one side were the public declarations of the First Secretary of the Central Committee of the Polish United Workers' Party, Wladyslaw Gomulka, on the other the public sermons of the Primate of the Polish Church, Cardinal Wyszynski. One of them must have been lying.

It was then that the party leadership expressed the wish that I should give evidence as independent expert and chief witness for the prosecution.

I was summoned to the Central Committee and received by three responsible officials from the press section.

'Comrade Weit', said Stefan Olszowski,[1] the head of the section, 'you must have been following the dispute between the party and the Church in the press.'

'Yes, of course.'

'We have the following request to make to you in this matter: Since Wyszynski persists in claiming that there are certain distortions in the text published in *Forum* we should like you, in your capacity as top linguistic expert, to compare the *Forum* text with the DPA text.' Olszowski paused for a moment, looked at me coldly with his watery eyes and added: 'In our opinion there are no distortions and nothing has been falsified.' Then he left the room. But as he went out of the door he turned round and repeated: 'In our opinion there are no distortions.'

The menacing undertone in this phrase was unmistakable. His two deputies, Adamiak and Weber, stayed with me. We were in a room on the third floor of the Central Committee.

'Since, as you know, this is a highly important matter of policy,' Weber explained, 'we will stay and help you in your work.'

The two comrades spread out a copy of *Forum* in front of me and then handed me a yard-long roll of paper with the teleprinted text in German.

'Now, Comrade Weit, our job is to compare both texts as carefully as possible and to establish that Wyszynski and the Church are lying.' So the aims of my work were made clear. Only later did I learn from a senior party official that Gomulka was disturbed by Wyszynski's steadfastness, and had asked several times if the *Forum* text really did correspond word for word with the DPA text. The translation had been checked by a few official bodies, for example, the Polish News Agency, PAP, the Security Ministry under

[1] Appointed Polish foreign minister and made a member of the Politburo of the Polish Communist Party in 1971

Moczar, the Interior Minister and a group of the so-called 'Polish Movement of Progressive Catholics' (PAX) under Boleslaw Piasecki. I do not know the results of these examinations but it is certain that analyses were sent to the Politburo stating that the texts were identical in meaning. Now I was being brought in as an independent assessor by the party leadership; as 'assistants' I was given two senior party officials so that I could furnish the final proof that the liars were on the Church side.

The two comrades Adamiak and Weber were very friendly. They plied me with coffee, cigarettes, and brandy; they showed me reports from the security services and made no secret of the fact that secret agents had gone to the churches and made tape-recordings of the sermons preached by top Catholic dignitaries. They repeated continually that this would be an easy job for me and half an hour would be enough to prove that the *Forum* text was accurate.

In the end we began our task. I already knew the *Forum* version for I had bought a copy. But the DPA text was new to me: this roll of paper was a highly important piece of political evidence on which top government and party leaders had based public speeches.

I unrolled the paper to examine the text, but immediately Adamiak and Weber warned me that I must handle the document very carefully because it was a most important piece of evidence. And, what is more, evidence from a Western source so that no one could claim it had been produced for communist propaganda.

As I carefully unfolded the paper and started to examine its contents I immediately noticed a few linguistic howlers which a German news agency could never have sent out over its teleprinter – unless the reporter responsible for them was drunk. I read further and came to a place where the text broke off in the middle of a sentence. The next line began with a new sentence. I was more and more puzzled, and asked my two 'assistants' if this really was the authentic DPA text.

'Of course, and all our actions in the last few weeks have been based on it.'

Very well then, I thought. If the DPA wants to send out such shockingly bad material, that is their affair.

I checked a sentence at random. The DPA text used the word 'priest', whereas the Polish translation of the same phrase used the word 'princes'. In the very next sentence the Polish version omitted the words 'in Poland', distorting the whole sense. Then I immediately came across another error. The Polish translation spoke of 'Polish convictions', whereas the German text spoke of 'The general attitude of mind in Poland'. After a few more errors in translation I came to the sentence in Polish: 'From this association there arose also the Polish religious style in which, from the very beginning, both positive and negative aspects of this problem were apparent.' Period. The corresponding passage in the German text, on the other hand, read as follows: 'From this also arose the Polish style of religion in which, from the very beginning, *the religious was closely linked with the national and developed together with it*, with all the positive and negative aspects of this problem.'

I glanced through more of the text. Here and there a word or a phrase was missed out in the Polish as, for example, when the priest, Maximilian Kolbe, was mentioned. The comment that he 'of his own free will, gave up his life for his brethren in the Auschwitz concentration camp' was missing in the Polish text. When a reference was made in the German text to a newly constructed church I looked in vain for the words 'newly constructed' in the Polish translation.

I also came across errors in translation that were clearly tendentious. Where the German text spoke of 'refugees' the Polish text used the word 'emigrants'; when the Polish bishops admitted in the German version, 'we were all powerless' during the occupation, the Polish text used the word 'irresolute' (*bezradni*) or 'perplexed'. In a few places the translators had left certain tendentious words out of the Polish version, elsewhere they had inserted words that were not in the German text.

I think both Weber and Adamiak were taken aback, if not shocked, at the results of my spot-checks. They had obviously not expected that the two texts would have discrepancies of this kind. I told them it would not be easy to check all the material, and it would probably be a time-consuming task since the many errors I had found in sentences picked at random suggested that the remaining text had also not been as accurately translated as had been claimed.

One of the two officials left the room and did not return for a good half-hour, then he said we could finish work for the day. He requested me to come back to the press section of the Central Committee on the following morning.

I was eager to see how things would develop. No doubt my two 'assistants' had sent me away and told me to come back the next day so that they would have time to discuss the matter with their superiors. The affair had had such repercussions that all the foreign press had reported on it. Could the party leadership afford to admit publicly, in Poland and abroad, that they had allowed the sense of the document to be changed?

As soon as I arrived in the press section on the following morning it was clear what course it had been decided to follow. The DPA text and the *Forum* version lay on a desk. The three Central Committee officials who had received me in such a friendly way the day before now greeted me with cold reserve.

'My friend', began the head of the press section, Olszowski, 'we have studied the remarks you made yesterday in detail and established that, basically, there are no real differences between the DPA text and the version that was printed in *Forum*. It is not our job to split hairs; naturally every sentence can be translated in several ways into another language, but this does not concern us. In our opinion, as we told you yesterday, there are no essential differences between the two texts. Will you please go through both texts with Comrades Weber and Adamiak. Naturally you may find a few stylistic differences or variations in linguistic nuances.'

So this was the result of the discussions which had taken place on the previous afternoon. The *apparatchiks* would never admit that the document on which the First Secretary of the Central Committee, Wladyslaw Gomulka, and the Prime Minister, Jozef Cyrankiewicz, had based their arguments was in fact a forgery. And in my capacity as translator I was to provide linguistic evidence in their support.

I knew that there was already a fierce struggle for power within the party leadership. The so-called 'partisan group' led by Mieczyslaw Moczar had been working away assiduously for years to compromise Gomulka and his closest collaborators with the public so as to make it easier to achieve their eventual downfall from power. The conspirators had already won the support of many officials in the party and government apparatus. I pondered: was the mistranslation merely the result of carelessness or was it a cold calculation by experienced political intriguers?

I had little doubt that the partisan group had seized the opportunity to discredit the leading members of the Politburo in the eyes of the people. They had calculated rightly. When Gomulka was shown the falsified document with the assurance that it was absolutely authentic, he fell into the trap and quoted the distorted passages to the whole world.

The plotters were not concerned by the possibility of the whole affair eventually coming into the open – if that happened they could use a member of the *Forum* editorial staff, a reporter from the PAP agency or the translator as a scapegoat without exposing themselves. And they knew Gomulka well enough to realize what bait would attract him. The Polish Communist Party boss never made a secret of his hatred for the Church, which possibly resulted from an inner conviction that they had the better arguments on their side.

Since Poland had been converted to Christianity a thousand years earlier the Church had often enough been the moving spirit behind social changes. Throughout the many vicissitudes of Polish history the Church had always established itself at the head of the national liberation movement. And when the Germans occupied the country in the last war the Church, with a few exceptions, refused to collaborate in any way with the Nazis. Thousands of Catholic priests paid for this steadfastness with their lives in the concentration camps. The whole Polish people was, and is, convinced that, as a result, the Catholic Church has the right to speak for the national interests of Poland.

But Gomulka claimed to be the heir and representative of all the progressive and noble traditions of Polish history, on behalf of the party and doubtless on his own account too. So now he was taking the opportunity to give free rein to his envy and hatred. Naturally he felt that men who had joined together of their own free will to serve God according to their consciences, represented a challenge to the control of their subjects by the communist State. In 1956, when he had once more joined the leadership of the Polish Communist Party, Gomulka had declared the principle that the trust of the people can only be won by men who themselves believe in the truth of what they are proclaiming. But by 1965 he had abandoned this principle for many years.

But to return to the Polish bishops' letter. I was in a dilemma. Either I had to 'certify' that the *Forum* text was not distorted – in which case I would become an indirect accomplice of the plotters of this political intrigue. Or I must oppose the interests of the all-powerful party apparatus and prove that, wittingly or unwittingly, Gomulka and his whole propaganda machine had been lying. The risk this decision would involve was clear. Sooner or later an influential group within the party might try to make me a scapegoat. Nevertheless, I chose the second alternative.

Adamiak, Weber and I set to work. Systematically, we began with the first sentence. As I looked at the teleprinted DPA text I found another discrepancy. At the left-hand side of the top of the page where normal agency reports show a combination of letters and numbers which only the initiated can decipher I saw three significant words: 'Bonn, PAP, Roszkowski'. Then the text began immediately below. Nowhere was there a word to indicate that this really was a DPA report. I drew my colleagues' attention to this fact for it confirmed the doubts which I had expressed on the previous day about whether the text actually had come from the DPA.

Adamiak and Weber were obviously nervous. One of them leaped to the telephone, called the central editorial department of the Polish Press Agency, PAP and demanded excitedly where the report had originated. When he was told that it was the text of the Polish bishops' letter released by the DPA he ordered the head of PAP to come to the Central Committee immediately. After a few hours of animated telephone calls, including one to Roszkowski, the PAP correspondent in Bonn, it turned out that even the text given out as the DPA report was not genuine. In spite of the communique and Gomulka's statements the authorities did not even have a copy of the actual DPA text.

It appeared that Roszkowski,[1] the PAP correspondent, had sent out the teleprinted report that had aroused my suspicions from a teleprinter in a public post office back to Warsaw. He had used the original DPA text as his basic material. So more carefully assembled propaganda arguments were collapsing like a house of cards. Neither Weber nor Adamiak hid their consternation at this state of affairs. They immediately ordered the genuine DPA text to be sent to Warsaw by air. Then my two 'assistants' once more left me alone.

I had to wait there for several hours, imagining what a turmoil had been let loose in the highest echelons of the Central Committee. For now the party would have to give in and admit that they did not even possess a copy of the DPA text which they had officially quoted. The PAP teleprinted report from Bonn had become a worthless piece of paper.

[1] Appointed head of the Polish state news agency, PAP, by the Polish Prime Minister in January 1972

A good two hours later Weber and Adamiak came back and told me that the genuine DPA report would probably arrive in Warsaw by air on the following day. But in order not to lose any time we should continue with our analysis of the text using, for the moment, the PAP teleprinted report from Bonn. As soon as the DPA text was available we could compare the two and correct any further errors and distortions.

A quarter of an hour later Olszowski, the head of the press section, arrived looking red in the face and asked me if I had found any further differences between the DPA text and the *Forum* version. When I pointed out that I did not have a copy of the DPA text he pointed at the table and said curtly, 'That is the DPA text.'

'How do you mean – we don't have a copy yet. This is the text from PAP in Bonn. We established that two hours ago.'

Olszowski threw a furious glance at his two deputies and said: 'Yes, of course, but that is quite unimportant. It is the same text as the DPA report, and we shall have a copy of that tomorrow.' Before leaving us he repeated yet again: 'Well, comrades, compare the DPA text *which you have in front of you* with the version which was printed in *Forum*.'

This was an open provocation, not only to the Church but also to the party leadership. For weeks the competent officials had claimed that they were in possession of the DPA text and they could not back down now. Who would have the courage to confess to the party leadership that they had been misled?

My position was now really delicate. I would have preferred to withdraw from the whole affair but my attempt to do so failed straight away. When I said that I had some very urgent work to complete in my publishing house Weber immediately picked up the telephone, rang them and explained categorically that I would be working at the Central Committee for an indefinite period. We worked through a few more paragraphs of the PAP text, wrote the corrections in on the *Forum* translation, and then agreed to meet again on the following day when the DPA report would be available. And, indeed, the genuine DPA text did in fact arrive.

From a conversation between the two officials I gathered that the Central Committee Secretariat was determined to publish a new version of the letter from the Polish bishops in book form with a suitable commentary. The tactics behind this decision were clear: the *Forum* report would be suppressed. At the same time, the party leadership had been assured that there were no essential differences between the *Forum* text and the authentic DPA report.

There now began a battle over every sentence which lasted several days. I established that the *Forum* text contained in all some 201 errors and distortions. This was already scandalous enough. Naturally not all the discrepancies were of fundamental significance, but a few dozen of the errors changed the sense of the message to the German bishops and many involved really tendentious distortions. All these 201 corrections could only be made after a long struggle with Weber and Adamiak. This laborious business lasted a whole week. If I wanted to make a correction my 'assistants' would immediately begin to argue with me. Each time they would claim that there was no fundamental difference in sense, and certainly no element of distortion. After five minutes of fruitless argument I would correct the mistake. And when they still attempted to persuade me to strike out the correction I would finally lose my temper: 'Excuse me, Comrades, but will you tell me what exactly I'm supposed to be doing? Do you want me to check the text or not? I've checked it and made an amendment. If you don't agree then cross out the correction yourselves.'

'You're a stubborn character, Comrade Weit. You know we can't cross anything out because our German isn't as good as yours.'

'Then take on someone else and release me from a job that I find as unpleasant as you.'

'That is out of the question. We must finish the work. It was decided at the highest level that you should be the one to help us.'

Previous experience had taught me only too well what this 'highest level' expected of me. The party leadership was determined to attack the Church, but at the same time they wanted to give the impression that they were conducting their campaign on the basis of legality. In a heated press campaign the party functionaries were accusing the Church of all the sins for which they were themselves responsible. The bishops, they claimed, had broken the agreements concerning the separation of Church and State affairs. But to anyone familiar with the facts it was ovbious that, in this instance, the State was interfering with Church affairs. Indeed, the Church leaders had no opportunity to exert the slightest influence on State affairs. Gomulka himself had made the accusation, in a public speech on January 14, 1966, that the Polish episcopate and, in particular, Cardinal Wyszynski, had tried to use the thousandth anniversary of Polish Christianity to demonstrate Poland's thousand-year-old links with the West. But the truth was that the party was trying to use the celebrations as an excuse to unleash a wide-ranging conflict with the Church. In the spring of 1965 a secretary of the Central Committee and member of the Politburo of the Polish Communist Party had declared quite openly in talks with a visitor from the German Democratic Republic that the party leadership intended to exploit the thousandth anniversary celebrations to make a frontal attack on the Church.

How did they do this? The party falsified the bishops' letter and then had the nerve to accuse the Church '. . . in their attempts (to justify themselves) before public opinion, of indulging in insinuations that their message as published in *Forum* contained distortions and omissions.' The party leadership accused the bishop of extending forgiveness to Nazi war criminals in their letter to the German episcopate. But it was true then, and is true today, that not a single journalist in Poland was allowed to mention the names of the real Nazi war criminals who had found sanctuary in the Arab states and enjoyed the protection of their governments.

The Church was accused of making a demagogic appeal to the most reactionary sections of Polish society. But the party did not hesitate to throw a man like Piasecki and his PAX Movement into the fight against the Church.

The bishops were accused of wanting to divide the Polish people into believers and unbelievers. But the party had been trying to do this very thing for years. Indeed, they were trying to divide not only the people but even the Polish episcopate by attempting to stir up a number of the bishops against Cardinal Wyszynski.

The Church was accused of not obeying the law. But the party organized groups of rowdies, for example as in spring 1966, when Puchalla, the secretary of the party organization for central Warsaw led a mob which stoned the windows of Warsaw Cathedral.

The party leadership claimed that the Church had compromised itself with the public. But the communists did not dare make a frontal attack for they knew the real feelings of the people. So the communists used salami tactics: first they shut a few seminaries, then they put moral pressure on the priests. They used blackmail here and intrigue there.

However, the party leadership was forced to call off its attacks on the bishops' message. Early in 1966 the text of the letter as printed in *Forum* was published in book form by the Polonia publishing house, complete with all my corrections, although with the addition of many commentaries and opinions taken from the Polish press. Still, any attentive readers could tell from this new publication who had been telling the truth throughout the entire affair and who had been lying.

All the party leaders in the Eastern bloc countries find the Church a knotty problem and they often exchange experiences and ideas about how best to deal with priests, bishops and religious orders. When Ulbricht was in Warsaw in 1963 Gomulka told him that he had twice met Cardinal Wyszynski and talked with him. But they had not reached any satisfactory conclusions. Gomulka went on to tell a few tales out of school. He explained how, from time to time, a Church dignitary would be refused a passport. Each time this happened the Church leaders would appeal to him and he would always reply that in this kind of matter he could only act in his function as a member of the Council of Ministers or as a deputy of the Sejm. Gomulka and Ulbricht laughed uproariously at this joke. Then Ulbricht explained to his host in more detail how the Socialist Unity Party organized the campaign against the Church in the German Democratic Republic. He suggested that Gomulka might follow the East German example and introduce into Poland a ceremony of Youth Dedication to act as an atheistic counterpart to Church confirmation. Ulbricht explained: 'Comrade Gomulka, we make all children take part in this Youth Dedication. We make a big thing of it with plenty of ceremony. Some take part because they want to and the rest because they are afraid. This means that we have a counterweight to the activity of the Church. Why don't you do the same!'

'In our country it is not so simple,' said Gomulka sceptically.

A little later, over lunch, the conversation again came round to problems with the Church and the members of the Polish delegation complained about the great difficulties they had with the Catholic hierarchy. Ulbricht answered:

'In our country there is no problem at all. You see, Polish comrades, we manage things like this: When the pastor wanted the farmers to go to church on Sundays our collective farmers would tell him: "Very well, pastor, if you want us to go to church on Sundays you must join us in the fields beforehand and work with us." Naturally the pastors would refuse and in this way they completely isolated themselves and the Church from the people. There is no problem if you know how to manage things properly.' A Polish official sitting next to me smiled ironically. When I translated Ulbricht's suggestion he whispered in my ear: 'Comrade Weit, what kind of training have you given our German friends that they take us for such fools?'

On one hand the communists harassed the Polish Catholic Church, but at the same time they tried to give the impression to foreign visitors from the West that the party and government not only did not hinder the Church's work but that they actually wanted to help it.

When a parliamentary delegation arrived from Austria, led by the President of the National Assembly, Maletta, they were taken by their hosts to visit a newly constructed church in Wroclaw and given a lengthy lecture about the vast amount of help that was given to the Church in Poland. This bombardment of lies was too much for me: I broke off my translation, excused myself on the grounds that I had a headache and went out into the fresh air for ten minutes.

Many years later, when I had left Poland, a well-known Austrian political figure who had been one of the delegates told me that my behaviour on that occasion had been considered very instructive by the visitors.

In the permanent war – sometimes hot, sometimes cold – waged by the Polish communists against the Catholic Church an important role has been taken by the pseudo-Catholic PAX organization, which was active not only after Gomulka's take-over of power in 1956 but also previously during the Stalinist period. During this time many monasteries and convents were closed, priests were imprisoned and Cardinal Wyszynski was held in detention. Many priests and bishops had to defend themselves in show trials.

I had my first (and only) close contact with the PAX organization in 1955 when it was celebrating its tenth anniversary. This ceremony was attended by many guests from both East and West, and took place in the Working Men's Hall in Miodowa Street in Warsaw. All the speeches were translated into English, French and German. At the time I was still unaware of the true nature of the PAX organization and its chairman, Boleslaw Piasecki, and I agreed to act as interpreter at this congress. All the preparations were made by the head of the foreign section of PAX. The guests from abroad included the late East German deputy Prime Minister, Otto Nuschke, who was the leader of the Christian Democractic Union in East Germany. He must have been well aware of the true nature of the PAX organization.

During an interval – I was still sitting in my cubicle with my headphones on but the microphone on the chairman's table had not been switched off – I heard Piasecki saying to one of his closest collaborators, Dominik Horodynski: 'After the interval the Swiss pastor is due to speak. He has got some pretty strong arguments, so get me the Professor so that I can ask him to speak after the Swiss and answer the points he makes.' By the 'Professor' he meant Jan Czuj, at that time Professor of Theology and Dean of the Theology Faculty at the University of Warsaw, and later Rector of the Theological Academy – a man who had cut himself completely off from the Church and who followed the PAX party line. A few minutes later he appeared at the chairman's table and Piasecki gave him detailed instructions about what he should say in his speech and how to present his arguments. We interpreters did not receive all the texts of the speeches in advance although we had made a request to do so to the head of the foreign section of PAX.

After my involuntary eavesdropping on the internal discussions at the chairman's table I went to look for our organizer, whom I eventually found at the buffet in another room. I asked him for the text of the Swiss visitor's speech, explaining that a written version of the speech must exist since Piasecki had given instructions how it was to be answered. He passed me on to another official whom I asked to get me a copy of the text which Piasecki had. He turned pale and stuttered, 'That is impossible. Ask those gentlemen over there.'

'Those gentlemen over there' referred me to 'these gentlemen over here'; every one of the PAX officials looked me up and down suspiciously, and finally I was directed to the chairman's table where Piasecki and his collaborator, Horodynski, were sitting. I explained to them both what I wanted but received no answer. They remained silent. I asked them again for the text of the speech. Still no answer. Only at my third attempt did Piasecki say curtly, 'Hand it over'. Horodynski pulled the text of the speech out of his pocket and gave it to me with an icy expression.

I found this little episode very instructive since it illustrated the strict hierarchical organization of the PAX movement.

Almost a year later, just before the stormy October of 1956, I learned more about the PAX organization.

Before the war Boleslaw Piasecki was the leader of the Fascist youth organization, 'Falanga', which distinguished itself by its anti-communist, anti-democratic and anti-semitic excesses. During the war he collaborated for a time with the Nazis, and with his accomplices committed many political murders.

He and his followers were imprisoned in north-east Poland by the advancing Soviet armies. A Soviet military court condemned him to death because he and his accomplices had murdered Russian partisans. But the death sentence was never carried out.

In prison Piasecki managed to make contact with the notorious Russian Security General, Ivan Serov, and offered to collaborate with him. What followed has remained obscure, but it is an established fact that Piasecki went back to Poland from Moscow in 1945 and started to build up his pseudo-Catholic PAX organization which his masters were able to use in their fight against the Catholic Church. His collaborators were nominated by the Polish party leadership as deputies in the Sejm, and Piasecki himself became a member of the Council of State and was given permission to take part in private enterprise on a large scale. He set up a country-wide chemicals and plastics firm, 'Inco', was granted a state monopoly to sell devotional objects, built up a book and periodical publishing house and published several journals. His businesses have a turnover of billions of zlotys, but it is significant that the tax inspectors, who check the books of every little tailor, give Piasecki's empire a wide berth.

Piasecki has his own 'direct lines' to Moscow, works from time to time with the Polish Security Ministry, and is one of the most reactionary figures on the political scene in Poland – all this under the cloak of Christianity.

Before the imprisonment of Cardinal Wyszynski Piasecki got permission to visit him and hold talks with him. He recorded the conversation on a miniaturized recording device and handed the tape over to the security authorities. It was as a result of his denunciation that Wyszynski was imprisoned. Piasecki and his officials do not hesitate to bribe Catholic priests or to blackmail them into submission. Naturally the Polish bishops are well aware of his machinations. Both the bishops and the Holy See have frequently declared that Piasecki and his PAX group do not form part of the Catholic Church. All priests and catholics are forbidden to collaborate in any way with the PAX organization.

But, of course, this has not prevented Piasecki from continuing to act as the spokesman of the Polish Catholics. He publishes the only 'Catholic' daily paper, *Slowo Powszechne*, and is so sure of the support of his Moscow backers that he has frequently made sharp attacks on Gomulka without being called to account.

Of course, it is not only the Central Committee of the Communist Party and the PAX organization which lead the fight against the Catholic Church in Poland. There is also, for example, the 'Bureau for Religious Questions' which corresponds to a kind of Ministry of Public Worship and has the authority to 'control' (i.e. to harass) the religious communities. Church affairs are also dealt with by the Security Ministry and by a special department of the Prime Minister's office. This is mainly concerned with the task of 'co-ordinating' (i.e. hindering) the building of churches.

After Gomulka took over the party leadership again in 1956 he made a few more concessions to the Catholic Church each month that the political thaw lasted. He released Cardinal Wyszynski from detention, allowed religious instruction in schools and, in short, acted in a most conciliatory way towards the Church. This was not easy for him, for in the first few months after the Polish October every delegation visiting Warsaw from an Eastern bloc country would remonstrate with him for giving the Church too much latitude. The leading East German officials – Ulbricht and Stoph, Honecker and Matern, the trade union boss, Warncke and the party theoretician, Sindermann to name only a few – were particularly outspoken on the subject. And at multilateral summit meetings between East European countries Gomulka was also attacked by the party leaders of Czechoslovakia, the Soviet Union and Bulgaria. When Ulbricht visited Poland with a delegation around the New Year of 1959 he lectured his Polish hosts in no uncertain fashion, saying that the new Polish policy towards the Church was a step away from socialism, an unforgivable compromise with the most reactionary circles which was bound to have the gravest consequences, and was flying in the face of all the principles of Marxism-Leninism.

In a communist country like Poland an exaggerated campaign against the Church can usually be attributed to sharp divisions between different groups in the party leadership, who all want to prove their ideological orthodoxy by outdoing each other in their narrow-minded and militant attitude to the Church.

But all the anti-Church campaigns organized by the party have not succeeded in winning over the overwhelming majority of the Polish people from their beliefs and their faith in the Church. Even government and party officials are often unwilling to forego marrying in church and having their children baptized – though not in their home towns; instead they go to another town where no one knows them.

So, much to their fury, the party leadership has had to accept the fact of the people's faith in the Church. Although the programme and statutes of the Polish Communist Party state that the party represents the materialist philosophy, Christian believers are accepted as members. However, from time to time the leadership makes an example of someone.

In the late autumn of 1962 I was accompanying a Polish party and government delegation to the German Democratic Republic. We were staying in the enclosed government 'village' of Pankow. One lunchtime Gomulka was clearly in a good temper and was joking quite openly with a small group of intimates about the very well-known Polish singer and actress, Kalina Jedrusik, because she had recently appeared on television with a gold cross on a chain round her neck. The viewers had seen it in close-up. 'What was the point? There was no need for it from a dramatic point of view,' said Gomulka. 'If even our own television puts out religious propaganda . . .'. This casual sentence was enough. For many years the popular singer no longer appeared on television. Some party bigwig sitting at that dining table in East Berlin must have passed on the views of the party leader to the right quarters as soon as he returned to Warsaw.

CHAPTER 7

Two Pyramids of Power

In Poland, as in the German Democratic Republic, there is officially a multi-party system. There is the Polish United Workers' Party, the Democratic Party and the United Peasants' Party. According to the constitution these three political groups are completely independent in both their political programmes and in practical politics; they elect their own leaders, put up their own candidates for parliamentary elections, and publish their own newspapers and journals.

From the highest state institutions – the Parliament, the Council of State, the Government – to the most junior levels of the administration, certain posts are distributed strictly on a quota basis between the three parties. The Democratic Party and the United Peasants' Party are officially supposed to represent different sections of the population: the former the intelligentsia, the so-called middle classes and the skilled workers and the latter the agricultural population.

This is the basis of the façade of democracy. While the communist constitutional lawyers categorically reject the theory of the division of state powers attributed to Montesquieu (legislature, executive, judiciary), because 'in our countries the people are sovereign', they still do not want to abandon democratic forms.

So every few years there are general, secret and direct elections. The whole people has the opportunity to elect its representatives in the legislative organs, right down to the local level.

The Parliament appoints the Government and can, of course, dismiss it in whole or in part at any time. The Government is responsible to the representatives of the people. Things are done so democratically that the electors can dismiss a deputy who has lost their confidence at any time, and elect another, even during a parliamentary session.

The Parliament elects a Council of State from among the deputies;

this is a kind of collective head of state. According to the Constitution and other legislation this council ratifies international treaties, has the right to pardon offenders, names and recalls ambassadors, appoints professors and generals and, in certain well-defined conditions, has the right to enact laws in periods between sessions of the Sejm. But any legislation of this kind must be ratified by the deputies in the next parliamentary session. The Government and the junior executive organs are, in theory, strictly controlled by regulations.

This altogether acceptable and democratic system must never be challenged. Even in the schools it is drummed into the children. All the mass media pay homage to the blessings of the political system. It is the subject of academic congresses and numerous publications. Only occasionally does it become obvious that the system does not really function as it is supposed to according to the official propaganda.

At a critical point in the post-war history of Poland, in the autumn of 1956, Gomulka himself explained, in public, how the 'democratic system in Poland' had been eroded from its original conception – the same system that had been as much praised and proclaimed by the propagandists and constitutional lawyers before 1956 as after. Gomulka's actual words at the time were: 'The people began to rebel. The silenced, enslaved spirits began to shake off the poison gas of untruthfulness, falsehood and double-dealing. . . . There were tragic events in our country too, and innocent people lost their lives. Many other innocent men were imprisoned for many years. . . . Others were brutally tortured. Fear and demoralization spread. . . . Events occurred which threatened and even destroyed the true meaning of the exercise of power by the people. *But now, once and for all, we are calling a halt to this system*. . . . We shall have to make many changes in the methods of work our party employs. And among the most crucial of the problems facing us is *the division of power between the party apparatus and the government apparatus*. The principle that the work of government is the business of the state and its administration must be expressed in practice and not only in words, as has been the case until now. . . . In practical terms the Sejm has *not* been carrying out the governmental tasks entrusted to it under the constitution. . . . The elections which are to be introduced on the basis of the new electoral regulations will allow people to make a real choice, not merely to register their votes.' So much for Gomulka's ideas at that time. But how soon he was to change his opinion.

Over the years I often had the opportunity to act as an interpreter at international discussions involving the various parties, the Parliament and the Council of State. This enabled me to see behind the democratic façade in these areas too. I was able to observe how the independence of the parties, the Parliament and the Council of State is controlled. I saw how an insignificant *apparatchik* could treat a member of the Government even after Gomulka had been in power for many years. I witnessed procedures which would not have been out of place in an operetta, and heard what the small circle who held the real power actually thought of this theoretically powerful pyramid. I would like to illustrate this by a few examples.

The theoretically independent Polish Democratic Party naturally has links with similar parties in other socialist countries – with the exception of the Soviet Union, which is a one-party state. From a political point of view, therefore, an excellent impression is given of independent parties voluntarily combining to work for the good of society in fraternal co-operation. Nevertheless, the Polish people do not quite accept the independence of the Democratic Party, or indeed, of the United Peasants' Party. They suspect that it is not all that it seems.

I witnessed a significant illustration of this through a small error in administration in the summer of 1967.

It all began quite harmlessly. In the middle of May I was summoned by an official of the Democratic Party, Mr Stefanski, who asked me if I could accompany a delegation of his party to East Berlin at the end of May. I agreed. A few days later we met for a preliminary briefing. I was told that the entire leadership of the Democratic Party was expected in East Berlin on May 31 for talks with the Liberal Democratic Party of Germany. The delegation was to be headed by the chairman of the party, Dr Stanislaw Kulczynski, who was also deputy Chairman of the Council of State. The group was also to include Jan Karol Wende, the General Secretary of the Democratic Party and Vice President of the Polish Parliament, and various other officials.

As a gesture of courtesy General Secretary Wende also received me after this interview. He knew me well, and was familiar with my dislike for rail travel. So he began by telling me that the delegation would travel by plane. As I sat in his luxurious office and his secretary served us coffee Wende went on to discuss a further organizational detail. Three documents of about twenty pages had to be translated into written German for the visit. I would receive them a few days before our departure. And he also requested me to fly to the German Democratic Republic on the day before the official delegation, together with a leading official of his party, in order to negotiate with the leadership of the Liberal Democratic Party of Germany on the subject of a joint communique. In order to save time this should as far as possible be ready for signature when the delegation arrived. I agreed to this too.

To begin with this visit seemed to be a routine mission. But from the extensive preparations it appeared that this was not so. Both visitors and hosts looked on this visit as an epoch-making event. In Berlin the President of the Volkskammer, Dieckmann, opened the conference with the most pompous phrases, 'The declaration of the Liberal Democratic Party of Germany and the Democratic Party of the People's Republic of Poland concerning the guaranteeing of peace and security in Europe, and the co-operation of both parties in the continuing consolidation and strengthening of collaboration and friendship between the German Democratic Republic and the People's Republic of Poland, which we are discussing together today will, without any doubt, make a further important contribution to the strengthening and consolidation of the friendship between our two socialist states, and will have *a significance far exceeding our parties and even our two peoples*. It will bear witness to the great importance which we attach to our responsibility to humanity and to the cause of peace, the security of Europe and the building of socialism in our countries . . .'

I had asked Wende to let me have the material which was to be translated in plenty of time. I explained to him how I worked, recording my translation of the written text onto a dictaphone, having it typed and then editing the transcript. Wende promised I would receive the documents a few days before our departure. On the afternoon of May 28 Wende telephoned me at home, after I had already asked to be given the documents several times, and explained that they would be rather longer – about thirty-seven to forty pages – but that the final version would only be ready on the morning of the 29th. The prospect of translating forty pages in one day was not exactly appealing, for I was to leave by plane on the 30th, the day before the delegation, but since there was no other alternative I agreed. I asked a secretary in the publishing house where I worked to keep the whole day free for me on the 29th. She was an exceptionally good typist and still had an excellent knowledge of German, which was her mother tongue. However, any contact with her outside working hours was not to be recommended since she would explain in broken Polish to anyone who wanted to listen that she worked for the Security Ministry. She would add spice to this revelation with details of when such and such an official of the Ministry of the Interior had visited her home 'on official business' and had taken the opportunity to spend the night there.

The next morning I went to the Central Committee of the Democratic Party to fetch the documents. I was taken to the antechamber of the General Secretary – Wende himself was absent – and waited while the necessary telephone calls were made. But I still did not get the documents.

On a desk I could see the two texts of the speeches for the conference and the draft of a joint communique, all neatly stacked in several copies – about forty pages in all; but the secretary would not give me the material. She hovered around, telephoned Wende – without any result. Only now did I realize what was holding things up. On the secretary's desk lay the copy of a letter to the Central Committee of the Polish United Workers' Party, addressed to Zenon Kliszko, a member of the Politburo and Gomulka's deputy:

'Dear Comrade Kliszko, We enclose the text of the joint communique to be signed by the Polish Democratic Party and the Liberal Democratic Party of Germany in East Berlin, together with the speeches of Comrades Kulczynski and Wende. Would you kindly *give your approval to these texts*. Yours faithfully, Jan Karol Wende, General Secretary, on behalf of the Central Committee of the Democratic Party.'

Since Kliszko had still not 'approved' the drafts neither the secretary nor Wende himself could give me the texts to translate. The 'censor' had not yet passed them. This short accompanying note dictated by Wende revealed the true facts. So this was the much-vaunted independence, and autonomy, the free scope the party enjoyed in the state and in society . . .

Now I also understood why I had to fly to Berlin the day before the delegation. It seemed likely that the leadership of the equally 'independent' Liberal Democratic Party of Germany would also have to present the draft of the joint communique to the Central

Committee of the Socialist Unity Party in the German Democratic Republic. But the text could not be presented to Ulbricht or his closest collaborators in Polish; so the interpreter had to arrive a day early.

While Wende's secretary was talking to him on the telephone she suddenly handed me the receiver. The General Secretary apologized that the documents were not yet ready and promised to send them to my home in the course of the day. I left the Central Committee of the Democratic Party with mixed feelings; I had acquired an interesting piece of information about the autonomy of political parties in Eastern bloc countries, but I still did not have the texts.

I received them only at five in the afternoon. And early the next morning I had to be at the airport with the documents already translated and typed. That day I established my personal translation record. Forty pages in five hours. At 10 o'clock that night I had finished.

On the morning of May 30 I flew to Berlin. It was obvious that the officials of the Liberal Democratic Party of Germany also had to get approval for the joint communique. For they insisted, for no obvious reason, in studying the draft until noon. Then they demanded the usual corrections with a great deal of political hair-splitting. Instead of 'Kiesinger-Brandt government' the host party wanted to put 'Kiesinger-Strauss government' in accordance with the terminology laid down in East Germany at that time. Instead of the 'population of the German Democratic Republic' they wanted to put the 'people of the German Democratic Republic'. But the Democratic Party official, Stefanski, who accompanied me, had to stand firm for he could not allow amendments to be made over the head of Kliszko and the communist party leadership. In the speeches which Kulczynski and Wende were to make, their hosts in the Liberal Democratic Party of Germany objected to the expression 'Federal Republic of Germany'; instead they wanted 'German Federal Republic'. As time was pressing it was agreed that all the disputed phrases would be sorted out after the arrival of the Polish delegation during the talks with the Liberal Democratic Party leadership.

At the next meeting Kulczynski, Wende and their companions were welcomed at the Schönefeld airport. Shortly afterwards the 'negotiations' began. Both sides made their speeches and no mention was made during the conference of the controversial phrases in the joint communique. This subject was only brought up in private talks during the lunch interval and in the evening. Both sides were conciliatory. Only the speeches made by Kulczynski and Wende and translated by me into German could not be contested by our hosts – this would have been contrary to protocol.

I found it embarrassing to see the self-satisfied way in which both delegations (the Liberal Democratic Party team was headed by Dieckmann and Dr. Gerlach) assured each other how independent their parties really were. I remembered the phrase of a Polish satirist: 'A clear conscience is often the result of a bad memory'.

After the long drawn out 'Declaration by the Liberal Democratic Party of Germany and the Democratic Party of the People's Republic of Poland concerning the guaranteeing of peace and security in Europe and the co-operation of both parties in the continuing consolidation and strengthening of the collaboration and friendship between the German Democratic Republic and the People's Republic of Poland' had been solemnly signed by the leaders of the delegations in the National Council building in Berlin, the Polish delegation set off for home, but not before the usual exchange of expensive presents.

Did Gerlach and Kulczynski really believe their farewell speeches? The former claimed that the 'outcome of the visit' was 'a major political achievement which had aroused great interest at home and abroad'. The latter declared that the visit was 'highly satisfactory in the opinion of the Polish delegation', because it represented 'a contribution to the strengthening of friendship between our two countries'.

The reader can judge for himself how important this visit was as far as international politics were concerned.

I learnt about the role played by parliaments in socialist countries during the visit of a delegation from the East German Volkskammer headed by President of the Assembly Professor Dr Johannes Dieckmann, which came to Poland on May 9, 1964, and stayed until the 26th. The delegation included representatives of all the parties in the Assembly, with deputies such as Anni Reim, Berthold Schmidt, Paul Pflock, Rosemarie Flesch, Heinrich Maier, Leonhard Helmschott, Ute Bräutigam, Irmgard Höhne and Dr Gregor Schirm. During their stay in Poland they held talks with the Marshal of the Sejm (the President of the Polish Parliament), Czeslaw Wycech, the Vice-Marshal, Jan Karol Wende, and also with the chairmen of parliamentary committees and numerous other Polish parliamentarians. The delegation was also received by Prime Minister Cyrankiewicz and by Edward Ochab on behalf of the Council of State. In the talks which, according to the communique, took place in a friendly and cordial atmosphere, both sides agreed to closer collaboration between the Polish Sejm and the East German Volkskammer. The talks also covered a series of internal and external political problems of interest to both sides. In their tour of Poland the East German visitors saw Wroclaw, Cracow, Tarnobrzeg, Opole and other towns. The delegation visited the museum of the former concentration camp of Auschwitz and laid wreaths at the memorial to the victims of the Warsaw Ghetto and at the Tomb of the Unknown Soldier. The ceremonies marking the end of the visit included receptions in the East German embassy in Warsaw and at the Presidium of the Polish Parliament.

Now let us take a look behind the scenes. Even during the preparations for the visit – I was asked to act as interpreter at the conference held on this subject at the Sejm – it was obvious that there would be important differences and that the private attitude of the Polish hosts would be very different from the cordiality towards the East German 'friends' which, according to the final communique, was shown at every stage of the visit.

Even with questions of protocol there were serious difficulties. First, what was the exact significance on this occasion of the 'closer collaboration between the two parliaments'? During all the many visits by delegations of the Volkskammer to Warsaw the same subject always arose – the representation of the interests of the German Democratic Republic at the Interparliamentary Union by the Polish delegates. For Poland was a member of this highly respected international organization, but not the German Democratic Republic. So before each session of the IPU a working group would arrive from East Berlin with a long list of requests and try to get the Polish parliamentarians to carry out their aims. Often they were successful, but sometimes they would fail and, what is more, the East German delegates who were seeking recognition would always feel they were in the position of petitioners at conferences with the Polish comrades which put them at a psychological disadvantage. This was the case with the visit of the delegation led by Dieckmann, whose thirst for prestige and touchiness led to a whole series of unfortunate incidents.

The annoyance of the Polish side even before the beginning of the visit had its reasons: in order to upgrade the visit from the point of view of protocol the East German officials had demanded that the Polish government should order flags to be flown in honour of the East German delegation, supply the delegates with motor-cycle escorts and lay on a solemn ceremony of welcome with a guard of honour for them to inspect.

The Poles found this excessive. They were prepared for the East German delegation to have talks with leading politicians in the party and government and to get the President of the Polish parliament to accompany the visitors on their tour of Poland, but apart from this they did not want any elaborate formalities. And since the hosts got their way, there was ill-feeling brewing below a thin veneer of 'cordial friendship and fraternal relations' from the very first day of the visit.

Dieckmann was in a bad temper throughout the whole trip – not only because of the official honours which the Poles had refused him, but also for very private reasons. Among the unofficial party accompanying him was a Frau W. who had been introduced to his hosts as his secretary but whom the Poles had no difficulty in identifying as his mistress.

When this lady learnt in Warsaw that the delegation was also to visit the southern regions of the country she expressed a private wish to travel to the grave of her parents in Upper Silesia, where she originally came from. The Poles had no objections to this trip but informed Dieckmann that his 'secretary' would have to leave the rest of the delegation to make this private visit, since the route which had been fixed for the tour could not be changed at the last moment for reasons of protocol.

The local authorities in Upper Silesia were instructed to find the grave and to put things in order if it had been neglected. But Dieckmann did not know of his companion's request, and when he was informed of it by the Poles he immediately started to make difficulties. He did not want to let her out of his sight and behaved like a jealous lover. Whenever the lady exchanged a few friendly words with some local official, or smiled at anything in trousers, the respected President of the Volkskammer would fly into a rage. However, it appeared that Frau W. managed to persuade Dieckmann in 'private talks' to grant her request. Accompanied by a few Polish officials she left the delegation for a few hours.

But although he had given his permission Dieckmann was furious, and relieved his feelings at the expense of his hosts.

The climax came during the delegation's stay in Wroclaw. When Dieckmann's girl friend decided to take a short walk through the town after a reception in honour of the German guests and turned down his offer to accompany her, the President of the People's Assembly of the German Democratic Republic sat down in his hotel suite and drafted a note of protest to the Marshal of the Sejm, Wycech,[1] threatening to break off the visit. The list of complaints against the Poles was wide-ranging. But Dieckmann was cunning enough to restrict his protests to subjects where he knew his 'energetic reaction' would make a good impression on the leadership of the Socialist Unity Party in the event of the visit being cut short. With the sure instinct of a skilled and experienced political performer, he managed to dig out all the weak spots on the Polish side and list them in his protest note.

I shall mention only two of the long list of complaints: When the East German delegation landed in their special plane to make a tour of the sulphur processing plant in Tarnobrzeg there were flags on the airfield but, in their ignorance of the changes introduced in the German Democratic Republic, the local officials had committed a cardinal sin. The black, red and gold flags on the flagpoles did not show the East German coat of arms. Dieckmann blew this up into an affair of national importance and complained that they were West German flags and that the Poles had greeted their East German guests with the emblem of the arch-enemy of both their countries, with the banners of the West German militarists and monopoly capitalists.

He also included in his protest note a complaint about an incident which had occurred at an evening reception in Wroclaw. The Presidium of the local regional people's council was headed by an old *apparatchik* named Ostapczuk. In Western parlance this veteran party official could be called the Prime Minister of Lower Silesia, and as a result of internal power struggles in which he was an eager participant, he could afford to take more liberties than his official position might suggest.

During the reception in honour of the German delegation Ostapczuk did not attempt to hide his contempt for the Polish Parliament, the Sejm, of which he was himself a member. When

[1] Dismissed in 1971

Dieckmann, leader of the delegation, had made an official toast and Marshal Wycech rose to make an official reply, Ostapczuk persisted in interrupting his own Parliamentary President with derogatory remarks about the Sejm. Now the *hosts* should not have stood for these interruptions, but they did not attempt to put the trouble-maker in his place but acted as though they had not heard his remarks. Faced with the powerful hierarchy of the Polish Communist Party the best reaction seemed no reaction. In his protest note Dieckmann made the most of his host Wycech's humiliation with the furious remark that he, as President of the 'supreme organ of power of the German Democratic Republic', would never have permitted an incident of this kind.

When Dieckmann had completed his protest note during the night this official state document of the GDR to the People's Republic of Poland was delivered quite undiplomatically from one hotel suite to another – both parliamentary presidents were staying in the same hotel.

Immediately the wires to Warsaw started to buzz. Telex messages and telephone conversations succeeded each other. The party leadership in the capital was concerned and could not understand this sudden worsening in the situation. Wycech was instructed to calm down Dieckmann at any price and if possible to get him to withdraw the note. In the next few hours the Poles did everything in their power to appease Dieckmann. In this difficult task large numbers of bottles of brandy turned out to be a very effective aid. Finally Dieckmann let himself be persuaded to withdraw the note and to act as though it had never been written.

After this serious diplomatic incident the Poles were extremely careful to give their guest no more cause for complaints or protests. But the tense atmosphere did not improve, for Dieckmann lost no opportunity to take his revenge. In the next few days, whenever he had to make a speech, he would interlard it with malicious remarks: sometimes, like the 'Bonn revanchists' he would describe the GDR as 'Central Germany' in order to give the impression that the East German Parliament regarded the areas beyond the Oder-Neisse line as being part of East Germany, and not as West Poland; or he would pay the Poles a double-edged compliment, saying that 'the German delegation were amazed to see how *clean and well-organized* were the key factories which they visited at the sulphur processing complex in Tarnobrzeg and the biggest Polish mines at Nowa Huta (near Cracow)'. Clearly he was referring to the old jokes about the 'Polish economy'.

When Dieckmann and his retinue finally returned to Warsaw for talks with Josef Cyrankiewicz, the Polish head of government, the latter got his own back when he toasted his German guests with the words: 'I am happy to hear that you have felt at home in Poland, as members of a family.' Then he added in a conciliatory tone, 'You know, with strangers it is different. But between brothers, within the family, there can naturally be disagreements from time to time. But let us agree that such incidents are a sign of cordiality, not of ill-nature.' This time Cyrankiewicz had the laugh on his side. Even Dieckmann smirked reluctantly.

The Polish leadership still had a clear recollection of Dieckmann's rather stormy visit when a new visitor from the GDR announced himself; this man was less in the public view than the President of the Volkskammer but he had – and has – a much greater influence. For Otto Gotsche, the Secretary of the East German Council of State and an old and close friend of Walter Ulbricht was, in reality, one of the most powerful men between the Elbe and the Oder.

Gotsche was officially coming to Warsaw for an exchange of views on the work of the East German and Polish Councils of State. Delegations of the East German Council of State had already visited Poland on several occasions. They would carry out the obligatory tour of the country, the visitors and their hosts would assure each other of their 'deep and lasting friendship' and pull each other to pieces as soon as they were out of earshot.

Among other things, differences of opinion arose from the fact that after Gomulka's return to power the Polish Council of State had ceased to introduce decrees which had the power of law before being ratified by the Sejm.

Comrade Gotsche, who as Secretary of the East German Council of State effectively controlled legislature, executive and judiciary, tried to convince his Polish colleagues that, among other things, the Polish Council of State did not have the right to renounce their power to enact laws.

Clever, well-read, the author of many books and an expert on the works of Goethe, Gotsche is an old communist who enjoyed the complete confidence of Walter Ulbricht. He controlled and led the Council of State according to instructions from Ulbricht who, as chairman, concentrate mainly on the official duties of a head of state.

Over the years Gotsche has managed to work his way up to a key position. He belongs to the small circle of really powerful figures who control the German Democratic Republic. Although he takes great care not to push himself into the limelight he deals unceremoniously with high dignitaries, ministers and deputy prime ministers. He looks like a stern guardian of the law, but in matters of importance he submits to no legal controls.

During his talks in Poland Gotsche made no secret of all this. Since he was speaking frankly with 'friends' his arguments often diverged considerably from the leading articles in *Neues Deutschland* and from official statements. With the support of his friendship with Ulbricht, whom he served loyally, he could take the liberty of speaking in an unorthodox way in Warsaw.

He would happily talk about his many pastimes. He is a passionate hunter, adores playing skat and loves literature. Even during his Polish visit he would not give up his card-playing. His skat parties often lasted until the early hours of the morning, to the despair of his colleagues. Every day the same pattern was repeated. When the boss was absent his colleagues would draw lots to decide who was to be Gotsche's partner at skat that night. But when he was talking about the methods and concepts of the exercise of power the Secretary of the East German Council of State was like a man transformed. He became a brutal, cynical autocrat who set himself above all rules in his own power sphere and dismissed any scruples expressed by his subordinates. The opinions he expressed about the East German Volkskammer and its President ('he is just a man of straw without any real power; his only function is to declare a session open or closed, and even the few words he pronounces on those occasions have to be submitted in writing for my approval beforehand') showed that he could be very outspoken in conversation with his Polish friends.

The talks which Gotsche held with President Ochab, with Horodecki, the Secretary of the Polish Council of State, and with the head of chancellery of the Sejm and the Council of State, who held ministerial rank (I was present at all these meetings as interpreter), gave me a detailed look behind the scenes of the organization of government in a people's democracy.

The East German delegates who had been sent to Poland mistakenly took the statements made by Gomulka which I have quoted earlier at their face value, and were very disturbed by them.

Even journalists and cultural organizers from the German Democratic Republic who were visiting Poland during those years would criticize this attitude. But the Socialist Unity Party leadership was absolutely horrified. Even several years later senior East German representatives would always keep returning to this subject. They were afraid that 'revisionist' concepts of this kind would also set a bad example in other socialist countries.

When Dieckmann and Gotsche came to Poland in 1964 the party leadership in Warsaw explained to them straightforwardly that the German Democratic Republic had no need to worry in this regard. Even Gomulka himself explained to Ulbricht that the Polish Communist Party had been forced to make certain compromises in 1956 because of the situation in the country, and he repeated this explanation not only in 1958 but also in discussions at other times, including the Warsaw summit meeting in July, 1968.

The Poles explained to Dieckmann and his delegation that their newly introduced electoral arrangements – more candidates are put up for election than there are seats for, so that the electors can strike out some names – did not represent any danger to socialism: in the past Poland had even been forced to allow opposition representatives in the Parliament, such as Kisielewski, a lay Catholic journalist. But when the power of the people was once more consolidated it was possible to discontinue this practice. If Poland were to be reproached for allowing a certain degree of spontaneity in important State affairs the answer was that, in the Sejm for example, all the candidates for seats as deputy were minutely vetted by both the party and government apparatus before they were even included on the electoral lists. In Poland there are certain services in the government apparatus which have the job of vetting these people. And 'if we are in a position to vet four hundred and fifty people before the elections, we can just as easily vet six hundred. The people are pleased that they have a choice and even the Western press is full of praise for us. As you see, we can achieve positive results without taking the slightest risk'.

This is one of the most cynical speeches which I have ever had to translate. Incidentally, Dieckmann was advised to see if this example could not be followed in the German Democratic Republic. The President of the Volkskammer promised 'to make a detailed report about the experiences of our Polish friends in this matter on our return'.

As an interpreter, I also found another occasion very informative. A delegation of economists working for the Socialist Unity Party Central Committee were visiting Warsaw. There were talks about industrial problems, the visitors were shown over the Starachowice commercial vehicle works and Janusz Hrynkiewicz, at that time deputy Minister for Heavy Industry and Engineering, received the East German communist comrades for an exchange of views. The visit was organized by an instructor in the economics department of the Polish Central Committee, by the name of Huk. Even during the discussions in the Central Committee and throughout the tour of Poland Huk kept explaining to the East German officials that he was really the actual head of the Ministry for Heavy Industry. He complained about how many problems he had to deal with; for example it was very urgent for him to find a head of the department dealing with investment problems. Moreover he had to pass all the ministry plans before they could be handed on to the Central Committee Secretary responsible for Economic Affairs, Boleslaw Jaszczuk.

At first I thought that this official, who was still quite junior in the party hierarchy, was an upstart who liked to exaggerate his own importance. But I was soon to learn better. During the talks with Hrynkiewicz (who later became Minister for Engineering) the technical questions were quickly followed by the subject of co-operation between the government and the party apparatus. And now there was an embarrassing scene; humbly the deputy Minister showed his complete dependence on the Central Committee instructor, Huk: 'Naturally co-operation with the party is extremely valuable to us. Comrade Huk, who is looking after our affairs, is the party representative and therefore has a wider viewpoint. We value his recommendations very highly. Sometimes I am called to the Central Committee by Comrade Huk. He is not always pleased with us but even when he criticizes us it helps us in our work.' There was more in the same vein. The comrade deputy Minister went on bowing and scraping; he emphasized how useful it was for the ministry to be looked after by Comrade Huk, and so on.

What Huk had been telling his East German colleagues was not boasting but the absolute truth. When he went on to tell us that co-operation with the chairman of the State Planning Commission, Stephen Jedrychowski (later Foreign Minister of the People's Republic of Poland) was excellent, because Jedrychowski consulted him or another Central Committee official before taking any decision, I took Huk at his word. This was a striking illustration of actual power relationships.

So what was left of Gomulka's 1956 speech? Only a sorry comedy. Yet the misgivings felt by the Socialist Unity Party leadership about a possible 'softening' in Poland were clearly still not allayed. At the end of 1967 Walter Ulbricht visited Moscow for negotiations. Both going and coming back he broke his journey at the Danzig station in Warsaw in order to meet a delegation led by Zenon Kliszko, one of Gomulka's right-hand men. The erosion within the communist bloc had already developed so far that virtually no progress was being made in either internal or external politics. Faced with this stagnation, Ulbricht exhorted the Poles passionately,

'The main question is for us to be internally strong and consolidated and to rely on the proven principles of the Marxist-Leninist exercise of power.'

Kliszko's reply was suitably ambiguous: 'An organ has many stops, and it is left to the talent of the organist to choose or reject them, depending on the work he is playing. If he does not use the stops then his audience will not be particularly enthusiastic. In Poland we know our own needs best. We can only assure our comrades from other socialist countries that we are using not only the organ but a whole orchestra with many even louder instruments for the good of our common cause.' It was a sibylline description of actual power relationships in Poland.

CHAPTER 8

The Seventh Party Congress of the Socialist Unity Party

On April 17, 1967, the Werner-Seelenbinder Hall in East Berlin saw the opening of the Seventh Party Congress of the Socialist Unity Party. This was an important event for the world communist movement. Representatives of communist and para-communist parties from around sixty countries came to Berlin. The date fixed for the congress decided the timing of many international conferences of the world communist movement. This was true, for example, of a conference of the so-called editorial commission preparing the international communist conference in Karlovy Vary (Karlsbad) which was held in Warsaw in February 1967. This meeting was much more important than the phrase 'editorial commission' might suggest. For at this preparatory conference basic positions were settled, the communique which was to be published after the Karlovy Vary summit meeting – and which was one of its most important objectives – was discussed, and there was also a long discussion about the date of the East German Party Congress. The communist party representatives who met in Warsaw in February 1967 put forward a few proposed dates which could not be postponed and which clashed with the suggested date of the Karlovy Vary conference. But the most important date was considered to be that of the Seventh Party Congress of the Socialist Unity Party. The importance which the big communist parties throughout the world attached to this congress is illustrated by the fact that they all sent top party leaders to Berlin. These leaders had to allow for the fact that they would be prevented for several weeks from exercising their direct functions in their own countries, for the Party Congress was now to be followed by the summit meeting at Karlovy Vary, and after that would come the May Day celebrations. This consideration may seem unimportant to the Western reader, but it reflects the true political facts in the Eastern bloc countries: The communist system is characterized by a strict centralization of the decision-making processes. (If someone in the West has the money to buy a car he goes into a shop and says, 'I want that car.' But in Poland he has to go through a process which would seem interminable to Western eyes and may even have to show the authorization of the Prime Minister or his head of chancellery.) So there must be really important political reasons for these meetings.

And indeed, there certainly were burning problems in the socialist camp which could no longer be patched up or swept under the table. There was the continuing erosion within the world communist movement; the increasing gravity of the dispute between the Soviet Union and China; internal political developments in Czechoslovakia which were already causing concern to the neo-Stalinists in the Soviet leadership; the persistent efforts of Rumania to free herself at least partially from Soviet tutelage; the mounting preparations for a 'hot' war in the Near East which culminated in the Six Days War and involved the Soviet Union in the provision of large quantities of armaments; there were also internal struggles for power within top party circles in the Eastern bloc countries – disputes about basic political concepts which were concealed not only from the people but even from party members and junior party officials; in Poland the neo-Stalinists were making determined attempts to unseat Gomulka and seize control themselves; in the German Democratic Republic Ulbricht was making alarming claims that the Federal Republic was planning to launch an armed attack in the next few months; and finally, one of the most pressing problems was the economic poverty of the Eastern bloc which was leading to considerable tension between the various countries (each partner was trying to take advantage of the others).

Things did not look good in the 'camp of peace and progress', and this undeniable fact threw its shadow over the Party Congress of the Socialist Unity Party. This was obvious not only from the big speeches but from private discussions between the party leaders in Berlin.

We left for Berlin by air on April 16, 1967, in a special military plane belonging to the 'Government Security Bureau' squadron. The delegation was headed by Gomulka and included Ryszard Strzelecki, a Secretary of the Central Committee and Politburo member who was an old friend of Gomulka's from the days of the underground movement during the war, but who still consented to join the opposition to Gomulka on several occasions so as to protect his career (which he owed to Gomulka); then there was Eugeniusz Szyr, a deputy Prime Minister and Politburo member who was an old communist who had fought in Spain and was already being hounded by the Neo-Stalinists because of his Jewish origins; as is customary in such cases there was also the Polish ambassador to the German Democratic Republic, Feliks Baranowski. The staff accompanying the delegation also flew in the special plane. These were Stanislaw Trepczynski,[1] the head of chancellery of the Central Committee Secretariat, Colonel Gorecki, the director of the Government Security Bureau, with his men, and myself.

After an hour's flight we landed at the East Berlin central airport at Schönefeld. We were welcomed by the entire leadership of the Socialist Unity Party: Walter Ulbricht, Willi Stoph, Friedrich Ebert, Kurt Hager, Erich Honecker, Hermann Matern, Günter Mittag, Albert Norden, Paul Verner, Hermann Axen, Georg Ewald, Werner Jarowinsky, Margarete Müller and Horst Sindermann. Various senior officials of the Socialist Unity Party Central Committee and, of course, many of the Polish Embassy staff in East Berlin were also present. After Gomulka and Ulbricht had embraced in the Russian fashion we drove in Soviet state limousines to the government residence in the special government quarter of Pankow.

That evening Gomulka sent for me through Trepczynski and gave me the Polish transcript of his speech to translate into German.

In spite of the profound disagreements between Ulbricht and Gomulka I noticed as soon as we arrived that the Polish delegation was being accorded special treatment as compared with all the other delegations. The new government hotel in Pankow has a dining-room on the ground floor. An enormous glass door divided a small room from the main area. It was in this more private dining-room that the Polish delegation were served their meals. In this way they were separated from the other guests visiting the Party Congress but had a good view of the whole dining area. According to the strict tenets of communist party protocol this was both a mark of special favour to the Poles and an indication to the representatives of all the fraternal parties that the Polish visitors were regarded as the second most important delegation after the one from Moscow. The top

[1] Appointed Polish deputy foreign minister in 1971

Soviet officials were lodged in a separate building and also took their meals there.

I had quite a lot of work that first evening. I had to translate Gomulka's speech of greeting, which fortunately was quite short – only ten typewritten sheets. Then I had to pass on to the East German officials, who had been detailed to accompany our delegation, our demand that any material or reports concerning the Polish delegation which were to appear in the East German press should first be submitted to me. We had been taught by past experience, for in the past we had already discovered many errors and distortions in the government-controlled East German press on similar occasions. However, I did not manage to get our request accepted even though I had the support of Trepczynski and other delegates. The East German officials explained that a special department had been set up to check in minute detail any material destined for publication, and Gomulka's speech would appear word for word in my translation in the newspapers. So this time there would be no mistakes.

That night I translated Gomulka's speech because I wanted to get it typed at the Polish Embassy on the following day. As I worked I had serious doubts about certain phrases. Of course, I knew that a speech of this importance would have been approved by the Politburo, but I resolved to point out to Gomulka certain passages which seemed to contain errors or ambiguities before he made the speech. I had quite a bit of experience in this area. Since translation involves an exact analysis of every sentence it is easy to discover any errors in logic or of fact. On previous occasions when I had mentioned any doubts about specific points to Gomulka or the other top functionaries in Warsaw they had always accepted my suggestions gratefully. My suggested corrections had always been taken into account in the final manuscript.

The next day we had our first spot of bother with the SUP central organ, *Neues Deutschland*. Before leaving for the Werner-Seelenbinder Hall we discovered that there was not only a picture of Gomulka being welcomed by Ulbricht at Schönefeld on the first page, but also a report describing the arrival of the foreign guests on the second page, which was full of mistakes about the Polish delegation. The position of Eugeniusz Szyr as deputy Prime Minister was omitted. And a man who did not even form part of the official delegation and should never have been publicly named was described as a delegate, and awarded the wrong function: this was the Director of the Government Security Bureau, Colonel Jan Gorecki. In the report he was placed before the Polish ambassador to the GDR, Feliks Baranowski, and described as the 'Director of the Bureau of the Council of Ministers of the People's Republic of Poland'.

When I pointed out this mistake to the SUP officials they were very taken aback at first, apologizing and asking me not to tell Gomulka about their solecism. I took the opportunity to repeat my demand that we be allowed to read any other texts about the Polish delegation which were intended for publication before they were finally released, even at proof stage if necessary.

After breakfast, where Armenian brandy played a large part, we drove in the black state limousines through the East Berlin streets, all decorated with flags, to the Werner-Seelenbinder Hall. The area of the congress was protected by hundreds of police, and everywhere there were East German state security men in plain clothes. Our cars did not stop at the main entrance but drove round the building to a back entrance near a Red Cross train standing in a siding. This entrance was reserved for the more important delegations and individuals. Here everything went like clockwork. The Polish delegation was rather unceremoniously divided into three groups. The first consisted of Gomulka and myself. We were taken to a special salon which was reserved for the leaders of selected delegations and for some members of the SUP Politburo. We were what you might call the first class comrades. The second section of our delegation, including Strzelecki, Szyr and Baranowski, were directed to a room with a large buffet where they could spend the intervals talking and eating at the richly-laden tables with East German Ministers and the leaders of the less important delegations – these were the second class comrades. The accompanying officials – with the exception of Gorecki – were taken to an even bigger dining-room where they could enjoy the company of senior SUP officials. These were the third class comrades. Finally, the party rank and file, the fourth class comrades, were supplied with numerous lounges and dining-rooms in the front wing of the Congress building. When Gomulka and I arrived in the 'VIP' room the SUP Head of Protocol, Streit, immediately pressed a special pass into my hand which enabled me to enter any of the prohibited areas round the building or within the congress hall. In the VIP room, together with a few members of the SUP Politburo, there were the Soviet Party boss, Leonid Brezhnev, the leader of the Czech delegation, Jiri Hendrych, Max Reimann of the banned West German communist party, and, rather surprisingly, Chivu Stoica from Rumania and others.

Gomulka took his place at a table with Brezhnev, Reimann, Stoph, Honecker, Matern and two interpreters, an East German colleague and myself. At the time I was surprised not to see Ulbricht in the room. But Stoph explained to the guests that the SUP party leader was still polishing his opening speech.

Even afterwards, when Ulbricht had delivered a report lasting several hours, I noticed that he always went to a special room in the recesses and did not spend any time with his most important guests, Brezhnev and Gomulka. The Chairman of the East German Council of State was known to be very strict in questions of protocol and so it seemed reasonable to draw the conclusion from his behaviour that he already felt in a strong position *vis-a-vis* the leaders of the most important fraternal parties, for he would never have dared to slight them in this way in the past.

Gomulka asked his German hosts how many foreign delegations had come to the Party Congress, and then added thoughtfully that he intended to invite only a few selected foreign delegations to the Polish Party Congress which was due to take place in eighteen months' time. He explained that if there were sixty or seventy guest delegations and each chief delegate spoke for only ten minutes this would make the congress last an extra day or day and a half quite needlessly.

'Why do we need delegations from mini-parties in Canada, Venezuela, Luxembourg or other small countries?' added Gomulka. 'It's quite enough if they send telegrams. And apart from that, paying their return fares, entertaining them and giving them presents and so on costs a great deal of money.'

Stoph explained that the SUP leadership had also considered this point, but since the Party Congress was being held just before the summit meeting in Karlovy Vary the overseas comrades would be coming in any case, and could call in on their way. What the East German Prime Minister did not say was that the SUP leadership was so full of complexes about the isolation of East Germany in the international community of nations that they would make any effort to make contact with powerful, or at least well-known, foreign politicians, and would then fill the newspapers with descriptions of the proceedings, sometimes in ludicrous detail.

When conversation flagged for a minute I left the room to take another look at the conference hall. Although the congress was not due to open for another half-hour I did not see a single delegate talking informally in the hall or the foyer as they usually did at big party congresses. The sight that greeted me as I entered the Werner-Seelenbinder Hall was quite characteristic, not to say ridiculous.

The hall was full. All the delegates had already taken their places, arranged according to region; on the desks before them, beside the folders containing material about the congress, were red song books from which they were singing revolutionary songs of the labour movement. It was a sight that would have made the heart of any Prussian sergeant beat faster. What discipline!

I returned to the room for the 'best' and 'better' delegates in order to continue interpreting. Gomulka had been given a little note with a sketch of the seating arrangement on the platform. This paper would enable him to find his own place on the platform before entering the hall.

Shortly before ten o'clock, Streit, the SUP head of protocol, gave the sign to leave the table. On our way to the platform we passed through a corridor and into the separate room used by Walter Ulbricht, who now welcomed Brezhnev, Gomulka and the other high-ranking officials from the VIP dining-room for the first time. As Gomulka's companion I was also allowed to enter this Holy of Holies, which contained desks with telephones and a safe. In a small side-room a divan had been set up so that the Comrade Chairman of the Council of State could recover from the exertions of the congress during the intervals between sessions.

The foreign delegations took the seats reserved for them in the first rows of the hall and Ulbricht went to the rostrum. He opened the congress by paying homage to the communist leaders who had died in the last few years, and went on to welcome the three thousand and more delegates and foreign guests. Finally, Hermann Axen, the Secretary of the Central Committee responsible for relations with 'fraternal parties', read out the lists of foreign guest delegates. The congress 'elected' its presidium, secretariat and committees and decided the agenda and order of business.

After these preliminaries Walter Ulbricht returned to the rostrum. I did not have to translate his marathon speech, in which he described the 'magnificent achievements in the building of socialism in the German Democratic Republic' and painted the

West German devil in terrifying colours, covering every area of economic, cultural, political and national life in the GDR. There was no cubicle for a Polish simultaneous translator at the congress. Normally I would have had to sit on a stool behind Gomulka and translate everything in a whisper. But Gomulka decided against this, as he had at the Sixth SUP Congress in 1963, and told me he would follow the speeches and debates in Russian through the headphones which had been placed on his desk. He asked me only to read out his own speech from the German translation cubicle. I found a seat at the side near the front so that I could get to the platform quickly if Gomulka should require my services again. During Ulbricht's long-winded speech I studied the expressions of the delegates, some of whom I knew. I was surprised to see that they seemed to follow with apparent interest the dry principles expounded by Ulbricht, although they must have been quite familiar with them and have chewed them over countless times before. From time to time they interrupted their party boss with loud applause – naturally according to a prearranged plan.

According to the formal statutes and principles of the communist parties, the Party Congress is the party's highest decision-making body. The delegates have to establish the programme for the next few years, and it is they who must also decide which delegates are worthy to be elected to the second highest decision-making body, the Central Committee, which is thus the executive body of the Party Congress. But in practice things are very different. The delegates to the Seventh SUP Congress were nominated at lower level party conferences and the process of election was a farce which the party leadership used to hide its contemptuous treatment of the statutes. The delegates were carefully selected according to whether they were willing tools of the SUP leadership or not.

In the lunch interval Ulbricht interrupted his tedious statement of accounts. In conversation with Brezhnev and Gomulka he expressed in all seriousness the theory that the deeply attentive audience and frequent applause at the beginning of the congress were the clearest proof of the active interchange of ideas between the First Secretary, i.e. himself, and the delegates who had shown their approval of his propositions by applauding. Certainly a very 'logical' theory.

During the lunch interval Ulbricht also explained that the West German Social Democratic Party had sent a letter to the delegates at the Party Congress. Although Gomulka asked to see this document several times, Ulbricht showed no sign of granting his request. Instead he once more served up a theory which I had heard him express in similar words on many previous occasions. The East German government, according to the Comrade Chairman of the Council of State, were in possession of documents which proved that the Federal Republic was planning to make an armed attack on the German Democratic Republic in a few months' time. This story was pretty old hat since Ulbricht had made similar accusations against the West German government at almost every bilateral and multilateral meeting with Gomulka. Usually he would say that the West German army would attack the Democratic Republic in a few months' time, or sometimes the alleged victim would be another socialist country. Naturally a clever tactician like Ulbricht had a definite motive in making these claims, which he never supported with any hard evidence. He was trying to get more help with his own difficulties, and to exert pressure on the 'fraternal parties': he was in fact saying, 'Without our agreement you must not make any contacts with the West German revanchists and revisionists'. That evening when the Polish delegation – this time without their East German escorts – met in the dining-room of the Pankow government guest house Gomulka and the other Warsaw leaders naturally discussed the first day of their visit to East Berlin. From this it appeared that other members of the delegation had also been approached by East German officials about the plans which had supposedly been made in Bonn to commit aggression against the German Democratic Republic. Gomulka's reaction was typical of his whole attitude towards the GDR in general and Ulbricht in particular: 'Of course, it's all nonsense. We are well aware of that and so are the Soviet comrades. But we must try to be understanding towards the SUP. After all, their position is not an easy one.'

Instead of showing Gomulka the letter from the West German Social Democrats Ulbricht had another surprise in store for his VIP visitor from Poland. He passed on to Gomulka a request from the SUP leadership for him to visit Schwedt an der Oder to see the big petroleum processing complex which was supplied by a pipeline from the Soviet Union by way of Poland. Many Polish technicians, engineers and workers were also employed in building the plant. So Ulbricht asked Gomulka to leave the Party Congress for a day and go and make a speech in Schwedt.

Gomulka was taken aback at this request – after all, the East German officials had not said a word about this plan at the time of the preparatory discussions about Gomulka's visit to East Berlin. The Polish Communist Party chief gave Ulbricht an evasive answer: he would consider the suggestion in consultation with his own delegation. When the Warsaw delegation discussed the first day of their visit that evening in the government guest home Gomulka said that he did not understand much about the subjects he would have to cover in a speech at Schwedt and it would really be best if Comrade Szyr represented the Polish delegation at the petroleum plant. So this was decided upon.

Gomulka passed on this decision to Gerhard Grüneberg, the SUP Politburo member, at breakfast next day so that he could inform the SUP leadership. But in the first recess of the second session Grüneberg came up to Gomulka in the Werner-Seelenbinder Hall and gave him Ulbricht's reply. The message said that the SUP leadership requested Comrade Gomulka to go to Schwedt in person since they attached great importance to a meeting between him and the staff of the petro-chemical complex. Unwillingly, Gomulka allowed himself to be persuaded. But when Grüneberg then passed on another request from Ulbricht asking that he should speak mainly about West Germany in his speech at Schwedt, Gomulka burst out: 'For eighteen months I have done nothing but attack the Federal Republic,' he told Grüneberg, but then immediately controlled his feelings once more.

In the evening I was given the text of the Schwedt speech to translate. But then I got quite a shock. I had agreed with Feliks Baranowski, the Polish ambassador to East Berlin, that a secretary from the embassy would type out the texts of both Gomulka's address to the Party Congress and the Schwedt speech. In these cases I usually work with a dictaphone, recording the text by the simultaneous translation method which is then typed out for me to correct. My dictaphone was not very easy to operate. The previous night I had recorded the address Gomulka was to make to the Party Congress and now I wanted to listen to the recording again before dictating the text of the Schwedt speech. But when I tried to do so I realized that part of the translation had been erased. Now with this machine you can wipe out a recording either with a magnet or by switching the microphone to 'Record'. The machine had been in my room in the guest house for the whole day and nobody, apart from the chambermaids, could get in. I had left the magnet-eraser in Warsaw. So someone who had seen the dictaphone in my room must have been trying – unsuccessfully – to listen to what I had recorded. But since the machine was, as I have said, quite complicated to use, my uninvited guests had stupidly pressed the wrong button and recorded their own voices. I could tell from their disappointed conversation that they could not work out which text had been recorded. What a way for a guest of the East German Party leadership to be treated . . .

Furiously I set to work to translate Gomulka's address to the Party Congress once again. I was used to working fast and I dictated the ten pages in thirty-five minutes, went on to translate the speech that Gomulka was to make in Schwedt and then telephoned the Polish Ambassador to tell him that the dictaphone was ready to be collected.

Without my knowledge I had in the meantime become the subject of a dispute in our delegation. Zenon Kliszko, Gomulka's right-hand man, had arrived in Berlin from Warsaw. He was making a stop-over on his way to Karlovy Vary where the communist summit meeting was to take place in a few days' time. It was only at breakfast the next day that I learnt from Trepczynski what a fuss there had been on the previous evening. After a short discussion with Gomulka Kliszko had gone to the SUP Central Committee building where a top secret meeting of some of the top officials responsible for preparing the Karlovy Vary conference was taking place. From there he had telephoned Trepczynski with the request to send me immediately to the Central Committee building since he did not have an interpreter. Trepczynski immediately contacted Gomulka but he decided that I should be left in peace to translate his speeches and that Kliszko should be sent a German and Polish-speaking official from the Embassy. But Kliszko turned down the suggestion and insisted that I should interpret for him since I had attended the preparatory conference on the Karlovy Vary meeting two months previously in Warsaw and therefore was familiar with the subject. And apart from that he did not want a new interpreter. But Gomulka stood firm. As Trepczynski told me over breakfast, the meeting had lasted until the early hours of the morning. Smiling, he slapped me across the shoulders. 'I've saved you from a fascinating job, old man.'

As is usual on such occasions, when our delegation was not attending the congress the delegates would always be surrounded by large numbers of the embassy staff. We were sitting in the foyer of the guest house after breakfast awaiting our departure to the congress. I got into a conversation with some embassy officials which taught me a good deal about the 'private enterprise sidelines' indulged in by the Polish diplomats in Berlin. It was obvious that there was not enough work to give full employment to the hundred and more embassy employees, and it was an open secret that most of them were really working for the Security Ministry. But only now did I realize what lucrative activities they were organizing on the side. Since they saw no reason to hide their transactions from me they were quite willing to explain. 'You see, Comrade Weit, in Warsaw anyone can buy a Soviet-made Zorki camera for 2,000 zlotys in a state shop. But the cheapest car on the market, an East German "Trabant" with a two-stroke engine and 23 horse power, costs at least 85,000 zlotys on the black market. Since we have the right to travel freely between East and West Berlin we can take the cameras into West Berlin at any time. We have a buyer there who will give us 70 dollars for them. At a rough estimate if you convert 70 dollars into West German marks they are worth about 800 East German marks. And a Trabant car costs 7,200 East German marks. In Warsaw we can buy nine Zorki cameras for 18,000 zlotys. And in exchange for these 18,000 zlotys we make 85,000 zlotys when we sell the car in Poland. So we make a clear profit of nearly 70,000 zlotys.'

I made a few calculations in my head. Since the average wage in Poland is about 2,000 zlotys per month they could make as much from a single transaction of this kind as an ordinary Polish worker would earn in two and a half years. But one thing puzzled me.

'But you can't travel from Warsaw to East Berlin hung round with a dozen cameras and looking like a Christmas tree', I said.

'Of course we can't. But since East Berlin isn't very far away from Warsaw we try to go home to Poland as often as possible. Sometimes we use an excuse like a sick mother-in-law we have to go and see, or we say we have to report to headquarters, and the next time there may be a burst pipe in our home in Warsaw which means that the wife has to go home to see to it. And then there is our normal leave which we naturally want to spend in Poland since we're so homesick, and of course the Christmas and Easter holidays. As you see, it's not so difficult to bring back a few ordinary cameras. Anyway, what we've been telling you is only a simplified version. We don't stick to cameras and cars. It would be too obvious. We can't take a car back to Poland and sell it every six months. But there are plenty of other products in Poland. Handicrafts, amber, silver, cut-glass and so on. And it's the same in West Berlin and here – we don't have to stick to Trabant cars. Just think about how much gold costs in West Berlin and how much jewellery costs in Poland'.

This short course in 'socialist' economics was interrupted by the appearance of Gomulka. We got into the government cars and drove to the congress building.

This was the day Gomulka was to make his speech. I had been sent it from the embassy, neatly typed, that morning.

When we arrived at the Werner-Seelenbinder Hall the security officials took me to the translation cubicles so that, according to Gomulka's wishes, I could translate his address into German, or rather read out my translation. The interpreters in the other cubicles would then tune in to mine and translate my text. Gomulka's speech was not only rather anaemic, it also included many phrases which were not quite logical or even wrong. Previously in similar cases I had approached the speaker beforehand and agreed on possible corrections with him.

On the basis of my many years of experience I had pointed out to a few members of the delegation on the previous day that there were obvious errors in Gomulka's text. During lunch, as we were all sitting at our special separate table, Strzelecki turned to Gomulka with the remark that I had discovered some ambiguities in the phrasing of his speech.

Altogether I had noted seventeen points. I was sitting opposite Gomulka for there were often SUP representatives present during mealtimes. When Gomulka heard Strzelecki's words he immediately asked me to sit beside him and show him what it was all about. As soon as I started to make my comments Gomulka flew into a rage. In the text of his speech there frequently appeared the phrase, 'The people of the German Democratic Republic.' My objection was that, although there were two German states, there was only one German people and previously we had always used the expression 'population of the German Democratic Republic'.

'Of course it's quite correct, it should be "people of the GDR",' Gomulka roared at me. The other members of the delegation sitting at the table who had earlier agreed with me now loudly supported Gomulka. My argument that there was a contradiction in his speech in that he went on to declare the SUP and the GDR had 'saved a section of the German people from the sphere of influence of West German militarism', made no impression on him.

I remarked drily that I was only the translator and could easily translate his speech word for word into German without raising any queries.

'Well, what else have you got to say?' he asked. I showed him a passage which said that the existence and *development* of the German Democratic Republic had become *an essential factor* in a lasting peace and security in Europe, but he got even angrier. 'That is perfectly all right. What have you got to say about that?' he asked.

'Isn't it going too far to say that the "development of the GDR" not to mention its very existence, "is an essential factor for security in Europe"? Not even Ulbricht would use such a far-reaching expression.'

Gomulka was getting more and more furious. I covered all my seventeen points but he was so angry that he did not finish his lunch. Apart from a few small corrections which he allowed me to make he did not agree to any of my suggestions. And at every point Szyr, Strzelecki, Baranowski and the others at the table naturally supported him.

On the morning of the day he was due to make his speech Gomulka was quite friendly once more, and as we were driving to the congress he told me in a conciliatory tone that he had crossed out the phrase 'existence and development' from his speech. He asked me to pay close attention as I was making the simultaneous translation, because he might add sentences which were not included in the transcript.

He gave me his Polish transcript and I added his corrections and then translated the speech word for word.

Warned by the errors which we had found in the report about the arrival of the Polish delegation in *Neues Deutschland*, I waited until the interval after Gomulka's speech and went to Hermann Axen[1] with the request that nothing should be altered in my transcript since this translation had been approved by Gomulka. I also asked him either to have the galley proofs sent to me at the guest house that evening, or to arrange for me to go to the editorial department of

[1] Secretary of the Central Committee of the SUP and member of the Politburo since 1971

Neues Deutschland during the evening or night so that I could check the German text.

When evening arrived there was a disagreement between me and the SUP officials. They came to the guest house to try to persuade me to change the text myself.

'Comrade Weit, these are errors of style, not of fact. Of course, they are only details. In your translation you have written "the Federal Republic of Germany". That is wrong. We always say the West German Federal Republic, the West German State, the Bonn government etc. You have a wide range of terms to choose from. But if you use the expression "Federal Republic of Germany" our readers will be offended. It is never used either in the press or in speeches. You can check that from the speech made by Comrade Walter Ulbricht.'

The argument about the expression 'Federal Republic of Germany' or 'West German Federal Republic' had been a thorn in the flesh of our hosts for quite a time. It was not the first time that the attempt had been made to persuade me to follow the East German terminology. But each time I had refused. And I did so again this time. So now my opponents admitted after all that it was not a question of style but of politics pure and simple. 'We are Germany too; the description "Federal Republic of Germany" is an expression of the Bonn revanchists who use it to back their insolent claims to be the only true representatives of Germany.'

But I still did not give in and so it was that the expression 'Federal Republic of Germany' actually appeared twice in the report of Gomulka's speech printed next day in *Neues Deutschland*. I could be just as stubborn as the most stubborn official.

This expression, 'Federal Republic of Germany' had given rise to dissent on several previous occasions, in both East Berlin and Warsaw. In the foreign language publishing house where I worked there had been complaints about it from many different quarters; the East German Embassy in Warsaw let it be known that we had committed a political *faux pas*; the Polish Foreign Ministry appealed to my superiors on several occasions, and once even ended up by claiming that I would be supporting West German militarism if I went on using the expression. Other institutions, such as the *Zachodnia Agencja Prasowa* (ZAP, or Press Agency West) also made complaints. But it was the East German officials in particular who became more and more angry with me for using the expression. But

I stuck to my opinion, in spite of the argument that the Polish expression '*Niemecka Republika Federalna*' translates directly as 'German Federal Republic'. But after I left Poland there was no more of this independence as I could tell, for example, from the German edition of the monthly journal, *Poland*, for which I used to be responsible. Now the editor has gone over to the East German line, there is no more mention of the 'Federal Republic of Germany'.

Still, I had the satisfaction of seeing an expression which was prohibited by the highest authorities in the GDR appear in *Neues Deutschland* during the Seventh SUP Congress. For years before and after there was not a single edition of the newspaper where the Federal Republic was given its official name.

But I did not get anywhere with my other request. In spite of my appeal to Hermann Axen and, later that evening, to Gerhard Grüneberg and Erich Honecker, I was not allowed to see the proofs or to visit the editorial offices of *Neues Deutschland*.

The next day we saw the inevitable results. Apart from the expression 'Federal Republic of Germany', Gomulka's speech had been quite shamelessly altered. Some passages had been missed out altogether, others had been changed, and the published text contained phrases that Gomulka had not even said. Naturally I compared the *Neues Deutschland* report with the text on the next day, and was able to establish these mistakes. Apart from errors like a phrase saying that seven million people had lost their lives in Auschwitz, whereas Gomulka had spoken of four million, the sub-editors had tailored the speech to suit the East German home market. In one long-winded sentence containing more than sixty words Gomulka had praised the SUP to the skies and said, amongst other things, that the party was 'greatly developing the system of social achievement'. But in the *Neues Deutschland* of April 20, 1967, the report said that the SUP were 'developing the system of social achievements to an unprecedented extent'.

I found many other errors of this kind that infuriated me. Other members of the Polish delegation to whom I showed the copy of *Neues Deutschland* were also furious about the distortions in the central organ of the SUP. Since people tend to be sensitive about this kind of thing in the Eastern bloc, the matter was raised with Ulbricht.

On the evening of the fourth day one of the top SUP functionaries apologized on behalf of the party leadership for the – in his words –

'irresponsible action by one of the *Neues Deutschland* editorial staff' and promised that nothing of the kind would happen again. Gomulka was not present at this conversation. I found it very significant that the other delegates were concealing the distortions in the SUP paper from Gomulka, just as they had three days earlier.

I found another fact very interesting too: when Gomulka made a long speech a week later in Karlovy Vary and I, on my return to Warsaw, checked the phrases with those he had used in the speech to the Seventh SUP Congress, I found that my suggestions, to which Gomulka had reacted so angrily, had nearly all been followed. There was no more mention of the 'people of the German Democratic Republic'. On the contrary, he now spoke of the German Democratic Republic as being 'an alternative for the whole German people'; the GDR was no longer an 'essential factor for security and peace' in Europe, but her 'achievements and development (have) great significance from the viewpoint of the power relationship between socialism and imperialism'. But Ulbricht did not seem very pleased with his honorary propagandist, Wladyslaw Gomulka: Gomulka's speech in Karlovy Vary was only published in *Neues Deutschland* after a delay of two days, and then in an abridged version. Although the SUP leadership were quite aware of these distortions and had given a formal assurance that such a thing would never happen again, we soon had a new reason to complain about this kind of intriguing.

I have already mentioned that Ulbricht pressed Gomulka so much that he let himself be persuaded to go to Schwedt to visit the petroleum complex. So on the morning of Thursday, April 20, 1967, we set out in a shining black Zil limousine to drive to Schwedt, accompanied by the SUP Politburo member, Erich Mückenberger. It was a fine day and in Schwedt there was the usual ritual. Gomulka was welcomed by the works management and the local notables, young pioneers from the East German youth organization presented him with the red neckerchief customary on such occasions, and then we visited the factory. It was arranged that we should meet a section of the staff – in spite of Ulbricht's assurances Gomulka's visit was not so important to the East German leadership that they would have allowed the whole of the staff to attend the meeting.

Then we were taken round the works and saw various different plants – for example the measuring installation, the gas separation plant, and a fertilizer plant; everywhere we were greeted by handshakes, were asked to write a few words in the distinguished visitors' book and heard the same words about the 'great joy of the workers over Gomulka's visit'.

Time went quickly by, and the hour appointed for the meeting with the works employees had already passed. But still we were not taken to the hall where Gomulka was to make his speech. From the odd sentence which our hosts let drop I gathered that there were still too few joyful workers present in the hall. When we finally arrived, half an hour late, it was still half empty. Gomulka's expression was eloquent. He must naturally have been thinking how Ulbricht had personally persuaded him to go to Schwedt, and now the half empty hall made him furious.

Disconcerted, the works director explained that it was the end of a shift and this was the reason why not all the workers had managed to get to the hall yet, although they had been looking forward to meeting Gomulka for days.

Originally Gomulka had intended to make his speech in Polish and to let me read it through in German afterwards. I sat next to him on the platform. The works director was standing at the rostrum and making a short speech of welcome to the Polish delegation through the microphone which I was translating for Gomulka in a whisper. But he interrupted me abruptly, 'No need for that; it doesn't interest me.'

He took out his manuscript, drew a line under the third paragraph on the first page and said: 'I will just read the beginning. After these three paragraphs you will read the whole speech until half-way down the last page. Then I shall read the last half page in Polish and you will translate it after me.'

I quickly took out my German translation and marked the paragraph where Gomulka wanted to stop speaking. There was no more time. 'And now I should like to introduce the First Secretary of the Polish United Workers' Party, our honoured guest, Wladyslaw Gomulka.'

Gomulka stepped to the rostrum and I stood beside him. While he was reading the first three paragraphs I looked at the audience. The first few rows were full of the well-known faces of the Polish and East German security men, the watchful, melancholy troop of bodyguards who never left us.

In the back rows I could see hardly a single worker or engineer – only waiters, cooks, cleaning women and a few young boys.

Gomulka seemed to have noticed this too, as I could tell from his tone of voice as he read his speech. Usually he would try to show his audience that he was personally involved in the contents of his speech. He would make gestures, raise his voice . . . But not today. He drawled out his three paragraphs and took a half-step backwards so that I could read out the speech.

After scanty applause we were taken on a tour of the city. This was much better organized. When we stopped at a new housing estate the last two hundred yards, which we covered on foot, was lined with children with paper flags. They waved and clapped as we passed and sang '*Hoch soll er leben*' (Long may he live).

Gomulka asked me about the song. When I explained that it corresponded roughly to the Polish song '*Sto lat*' he was suddenly transformed; his bad temper disappeared and he seemed in the best of moods.

I could understand why: The Polish song '*Sto lat*' had been sung for centuries on family occasions in honour of the central characters in the festivities, such as newly-weds or couples celebrating anniversaries. In 1956, when Gomulka had re-emerged from years of imprisonment during the Stalinist period to take over the leadership of the Polish Communist Party, he was looked on as a liberator and the personification of all their hopes by the entire Polish people. A few days after the Eighth Plenum of the Polish United Workers' Party there was a rally in the biggest square in Warsaw, when Gomulka appeared for the first time as party chief before the people of the capital.

On that cool autumn day in 1956, when Gomulka, their idol, had finished his speech, the audience did not break into the usual applause and choruses of slogans. Instead someone in the crowd suddenly began to sing the words of the song '*Sto lat*' (May he live for a hundred years). In a few seconds tens of thousands of voices had joined in and the song rose to a crescendo. The crowd wanted to tell their idol, 'We do not look on you only as a politician, a statesman and party leader; for us you are a friend and brother, you are one of us.' That day I was standing quite near the reviewing stand in that Warsaw square and I could see how surprised and touched Gomulka was by this spontaneous ovation. The tears came into his eyes.

Now in Schwedt, Gomulka, who was already a very different man, could still be put in a good mood by children singing, not even spontaneously, the German song '*Hoch soll er leben*'.

After we had visited the housing estate the directors of the factory took us and the SUP officials accompanying us out to lunch in a little restaurant. Gomulka ate hardly anything; he had thrown off his usual stiffness and talked excitedly with the local officials sharing his table. Undoctrinaire and eloquent, he abandoned the usual party phraseology; he made no mention of the friendship between Poland and the GDR, nor did he attack the Federal Republic. Instead he spoke on his favourite topic, economic co-operation between socialist countries. He did not hesitate to set up the EEC as an example, and he explained to his listeners, as if it were their responsibility, that the most urgent task was to develop specialization and co-ordinate production in the socialist camp in the same way as the EEC. His table companions were visibly surprised by Gomulka's arguments: All the talk of friendship and unity in the socialist bloc was meaningless, he declared, if we made no progress at all in the economic field. All the party and government leaders in our countries paid lip-service to the idea, but when it came to putting the plans into practice what were wrongly thought to be the special interests of the individual countries took precedence and nothing was achieved.

Gomulka grew more heated. Even the GDR was not faultless in this respect. But he took the sting out of this reproach straightaway. Nor were we Poles. It was a common error in all our countries that we did not want to work together. That every country wanted to lay claim to the best industries and to reduce the others to the level of suppliers of raw materials and agricultural produce. But this agreement to bring petroleum to Schwedt was a good example of successful co-operation that had brought advantages to all the participants.

As our hosts were preparing to leave the restaurant, Gomulka expressed his attitude to this problem in one final sentence which, to my mind, was characteristic of him: 'There can be no lasting political alliance without economic links. If we do not want to run the danger of being demolished by the West then we must strengthen these economic links. *As a rule of thumb you can take it that it takes at least as long to break down an economic alliance as it did to set it up and make it work. This petroleum pipeline is a good example of that.*'

A year later this argument was used to support the armed attack by the five Eastern powers on Czechoslovakia.

During the whole of our return trip Gomulka explained his theory to Erich Mückenberger, the SUP Politburo member who was sitting in the same compartment with him.

When we arrived back in Berlin in the evening we discovered that Kliszko had rung several times from Prague, where the preparatory discussions for the Karlovy Vary meeting were taking place, and that he wanted to speak to Gomulka urgently. The party leader went to his suite to telephone Kliszko and angrily told us at dinner what Kliszko had told him. The representatives of the Swiss Workers' Party or the British Communist Party had made an open attempt to sabotage this World Communist Conference; 'Now, at the last moment, when all the documents have been prepared, the representatives of this party have put forward the suggestion that we publish a one or two-page pamphlet instead of our joint communique. They say that this sort of document would go down better with the workers and the people in the West. They are just fools. We need a programme, not a pamphlet. Let them print and distribute their own pamphlet. Maybe they can build socialism in their own countries with pamphlets!' Here was another example of how little 'proletarian internationalism' really means – that phrase that was never out of the mouths of the communist leaders when they spoke in public.

I had two more important jobs waiting for me that evening. First I had to accompany Gomulka to a discussion with the chief delegate from Rumania, Chivu Stoica, and then, after our previous experiences with *Neues Deutschland*, I had to persuade the SUP central organ to publish Gomulka's speech without making any 'improvements'.

I had given a copy of the German translation of Gomulka's speech in Schwedt to a journalist from the East German news agency, ADN, immediately he had finished speaking, that is around midday. I told Erich Mückenberger, the SUP Politburo representative who was accompanying us, about the behaviour of *Neues Deutschland* in the last few days and asked him to ensure that at least this speech by Gomulka was published accurately. Mückenberger promised to do so.

Back in Berlin the same evening I repeated this request with the support of the whole Polish delegation – with the exception of Gomulka who was not told anything about the matter – to two other SUP leaders, Hermann Matern and Hermann Axen, the Central Committee Secretary responsible for contacts with 'fraternal parties'.

Our hosts insisted that it would be impossible for technical reasons to send me the proofs to check during the night but they assured me that, after all the previous mistakes made by *Neues Deutschland*, special arrangements would be made to see that nothing was altered in Gomulka's speech.

Early next morning I looked through my copy of *Neues Deutschland* for the report of our Schwedt visit – naturally all the delegates were given a copy each day. On the first page was an announcement that Gomulka had taken part in a friendship meeting the previous day with the workers of the Schwedt petroleum complex; a detailed report would be found on page two. I read it through in amazement. This time the *Neues Deutschland* staff had surpassed all their previous efforts. Decorated with lofty sentiments about 'a meaningful demonstration of German-Polish friendship, a most heartfelt welcome' etc. was a dismembered section of Gomulka's speech amounting to less than fifty lines in all. As a transcript of the speech, or even of Gomulka's main themes, it was worthless. The senior SUP comrades were not to be seen at breakfast, perhaps plagued by their guilty consciences. Only the technical staff assisting us showed their consternation. One young girl working in the foreign section of the SUP had been looking after us from the beginning and, as I could tell from her behaviour, had taken all the talk about 'fraternal socialist parties' and similar flowery phrases quite seriously. She was completely taken aback when I showed her *Neues Deutschland*.

At the suggestion of Trepczynski I raised the matter with the top SUP officials at the Werner-Seelenbinder Hall. They promised to inquire into the whole matter immediately. During the lunch interval they told me that the journalists responsible would be severely reprimanded, and that on the next day, Saturday, the paper would go against all the conventions of journalism and reprint the full text.

On Saturday, the last day of the congress, Gomulka's Schwedt speech was indeed published in *Neues Deutschland*, although only on the last page. But when I compared it with the original I realized that once more, in spite of the official assurances of the party leadership, the editorial staff of the party central organ had changed the text on their own initiative. Gomulka's speech had already been dull, long-winded and anaemic, but now the additions made by *Neues Deutschland* made the Polish communist leader look like a political idiot. Here is just one example:

Gomulka had said, 'You Germans and we Poles and all the peoples of Europe owe *a great deal* to the German Democratic Republic.' The *Neues Deutschland* sub-editors had made their Polish visitor look like a complete fool by adding a phrase of their own to this sentence so that, in their issue dated April 22, 1967, page two, it now read '. . . a great deal more than we can say to the GDR'. Any comment on that would be superfluous.

I shall not trouble to quote all the additions made by *Neues Deutschland*. Naturally any attentive reader would only have had to compare the *Neues Deutschland* text with the Polish paper, *Trybuna Ludu* dated Thursday, April 20, 1967 to see that words had been put into Gomulka's mouth which he had never said. But who would take the trouble to do this? There were not many reporters from the national and foreign press in Warsaw at the time. Instead the papers were relying on press reports released by the SUP Congress press bureau. *Neues Deutschland* had not only made additions to Gomulka's speech. It had also suppressed about 350 lines of the text published in *Trybuna Ludu*. Yet the *Neues Deutschland* report was presented in such a way as to give the impression that it was the complete text of Gomulka's speech.

Naturally these cuts were not made haphazardly. In one section of his speech Gomulka had reached out the hand of reconciliation to the entire German people and had at least partly absolved them from the blame of total responsibility for the unleashing of the Second World War. The German people, he had declared, were responsible only in so far as the majority of them had not realized the true nature of the Nazi system. He supported this theory by another sentence in his speech: The communists had never put the blame on the whole German people.

Several times Gomulka had used the phrase 'population of the GDR' instead of 'people of the GDR' and he had spoken in practical terms of how necessary it was to have fruitful co-operation between their two countries. He had mentioned that highly qualified Polish specialists and workers were active in other parts of the GDR as well as in Schwedt, and had emphasized that economic co-operation must be organized on a practical basis at factory level. He had openly criticized the political and economic leadership of the GDR with the sentence, 'We will not hide the fact that there are still contradictions between objective needs and the objective possibilities of co-ordinating the economies of socialist countries on the one hand and the present state of development of subjective factors, especially the planning and administrative mechanisms in the various countries, on the other.'

Any politically experienced reader accustomed to understanding the true meaning hidden behind the elaborate communist phraseology would have had no trouble in seeing what was meant by the phrase, 'the present state of development of subjective factors.'

These, and many other statements, were cut for the benefit of *Neues Deutschland* readers.

After four scandalous examples of distortions and falsifications in *Neues Deutschland* in six days I would have had to be blind not to see political motives behind these incidents.

It was obvious that the East German leadership looked on Gomulka as a spent force in political terms and believed that his removal from office was only a question of time, and equally clear that Ulbricht's intention was to use these means to give 'international' assistance to Gomulka's Polish opponents within the party leadership. I was shocked to see how isolated Gomulka had become even within the circle of his closest collaborators and 'friends'. When, in Gomulka's absence, I expressed my opinion to the members of the Polish delegation that they should at least inform Gomulka in general terms of the way he had been treated in the last few days, one of the top officials told me coldly: 'Stop interfering in political matters. And don't breathe a word to Gomulka. Otherwise you'll get one on the chin that you won't forget in a hurry.'

The man who spoke these edifying words was no less than Gomulka's close colleague, Trepczynski, who by this time had obviously moved completely into the camp of Moczar, Gomulka's opponent.

In communist countries the little court surrounding the leaders, the party apparatus and the *apparatchiks* constitute a power factor that should not be underestimated.

The second task that awaited me on my return to East Berlin from Schwedt was the discussion between Gomulka and the chief Rumanian delegate, Chivu Stoica. Strictly speaking there were three participants in these talks. Since the subject of the discussion was the Rumanian attitude to the approaching summit meeting in Karlovy Vary, and both the French and Polish communist parties were concerned with the administrative preparations for this conference, George Marchais was also present on behalf of the French Communist Party.

Even at that time Rumania was regarded as something of a black sheep by the other 'fraternal parties' in the Eastern bloc since it was already, to some extent, making efforts to act as a sovereign party and sovereign state. This attitude was confirmed by the exchange of views with Stoica. The word 'exchange of views' was not a very accurate description of the meeting, for Gomulka shouted at the Chairman of the Rumanian Council of State in a tone more suited to a sergeant of the old school faced with a new recruit. Furiously Gomulka accused the Rumanians of doing their best to destroy the unity and harmony of the socialist community of nations and claimed that the behaviour of the Rumanian party leadership bordered on treachery. Through their contacts with the Federal Republic they had, whether intentionally or not, stabbed the socialist countries in the back. But the socialist camp, added Gomulka threateningly, had a whole arsenal of methods of silencing or destroying renegades. There were more threats of the same type. The less sound his arguments the louder he shouted. Gomulka was happy to let himself be used by his colleagues and the party leaders of other countries as a tool to attack the Rumanian party, and it was easy for them to goad him on. He believed that he had their full backing and did not realize what a ridiculous figure he cut when he deliberately lost his temper in this way. I had the impression that even Georges Marchais, the French Communist Party representative, was shocked by Gomulka's violent attacks, for he confined himself to trying to persuade the Rumanians to change their attitude, whereas Gomulka made one wild accusation after another against Stoica: 'We have sent Starewicz, the Secretary of our Central Committee, to Bucharest, we have sent you quantities of documents through the Rumanian Ambassador in Warsaw. But you refuse both to collaborate on the preparation of the documents to be adopted in Karlovy Vary and even to make a constructive contribution to the summit meeting itself.'

The paradox was that Stoica, who was himself said to be an old Stalinist, had obviously received instructions from his Central Committee to defend the Rumanian position.

It did not take long to understand the motives for this disagreement. On the evening of Saturday, April 22, after the end of the congress there was a musical gala performance at the German State Opera in honour of selected delegates and foreign guests. In the foyer a table was reserved at one side for Gomulka, Brezhnev and

Ulbricht. The three party leaders took their places there together with Honecker, Ulbricht's heir apparent, the Russian interpreter of the East German leader and myself. The discussions lasted almost three-quarters of an hour so that the interval had to be extended and the second part of the performance postponed.

The conversation started with unimportant matters, but soon turned to more fundamental subjects. The reactions of the three party bosses were especially interesting since Honecker and Stoph, who joined us later, did not join in the discussion.

Gomulka, Ulbricht and Brezhnev seemed to be in agreement on every topic – seemed, because there was no argument during this exchange of views – but on various topics one or other of the speakers would not express an opinion, preferring not to reveal his position. From this one could tell that he did not agree with the ideas of the other speakers.

The remarks of the three party bosses seemed to me to be characteristic of their attitudes, since in this circle they could speak openly to each other and did not need to hold anything back. Naturally all the other East German officials and foreign guests made a wide detour round this table or withdrew respectfully into the background.

The conversation started with a complaint from Brezhnev. The Soviet delegation he said, valued the results of the Party Congress very highly and looked on it as another step in the consolidation of the GDR and the SUP. Ulbricht did not seem very impressed by this praise; naturally he agreed, but went straight on to attack the Federal Republic.

Of course, he said, the significance of the Party Congress far transcended the frontiers of the German Democratic Republic and even of the socialist camp. In his opinion it was useful to know that SUP policies were exerting an ever greater appeal in certain West German circles, particularly among young people. But he also realized that scoundrels of the type of Kiesinger and Strauss, with the support of the most dangerous West German politician, Brandt, would now set themselves a double task. First they would try to drive a wedge between the different socialist countries by means of their so-called new *Ostpolitik*, in order to gain the upper hand more easily. And secondly the East German leadership now had information that they were planning an armed attack on the national frontier in a few months' time in order to convert the cold war into a hot one. This would involve not only the GDR but all socialist countries in certain obligations.

This favourite topic of Ulbricht's did not meet with a response from the other speakers. Then Gomulka reported on his meeting with Chivu Stoica, maintaining that the destructive role of Ceausescu and of a section of the Rumanian leadership was inflicting great harm on the unity of the socialist community of nations.

'The Rumanians,' he claimed, 'keep trying to get out of things by saying that they had not understood some matter or other, but when we then send them a letter they say that they have never received it. Something of the sort cropped up in the talks with Chivu Stoica. We handed the letter about Karlovy Vary to the Rumanian ambassador in Warsaw at the Central Committee building with the request that he communicate it immediately to his party leadership, but Stoica denies receiving it. So as soon as I return to Warsaw I shall have the Rumanian ambassador summoned to the Central Committee and we shall ask him why he has suppressed the letter. Of course, we know that he really did pass on the letter and that it's all just a trick on the part of the Rumanians. And since I do not think that the Rumanian leadership will inform their ambassador in Warsaw of my meeting with Chivu Stoica, he will probably be taken off his guard and admit that he did in fact pass on the letter. Then we can expose the Rumanians' lies.'

On the subject of Rumania Ulbricht supported Gomulka up to the hilt. But Brezhnev kept silent. At that moment I thought that the already rather tipsy Soviet leader did not want to play any more part in the discussions. But I was mistaken. After Gomulka and Ulbricht had discussed the Rumanians and the consequences of their policies for about another ten minutes Brezhnev suddenly cut in with another subject. He was very worried about the attitude of the Western communist parties. In Karlovy Vary there were bound to be certain difficulties. First of all, communist parties who had no influence in their own countries and were even financed by the socialist camp always found new difficulties in the simplest political matter just so as to be able to torpedo our plans. Things were now getting to such a state that we could find a common language to discuss various questions of international politics with social democratic and even bourgeois regimes in Western countries, whereas our communist parties and party leaders were always finding different pretexts to swim against the tide. Brezhnev took yet another drink and continued: Many comrades in our country hold the opinion that a harder line should be taken against these party leaderships and that pressure should be put on them to conform. Other leading comrades hold the view that we should look the danger of the disintegration of the world communist movement straight in the eye and not adopt an ostrich-like attitude. They are of the opinion that this would be the better course to take if we do not succeed in winning over a section of these party leaderships and building up their influence within the Western communist parties until they can take control. Mathematically (a favourite word of Brezhnev's) this might represent a weakening of our movement but we would then be in a position to use the unity of our movement to extend our ranks once more, slowly but on a sound basis.

Brezhnev spoke quite loudly and gesticulated violently; he was clearly experiencing some difficulty in bringing his sentences to a logical conclusion. Although he was already drunk he swallowed a few more brandies. The contradictions and changes that had occurred in Soviet internal and external policy had already made it obvious that there were disagreements between different party factions in the Soviet leadership. But I would not have believed it possible that the leader of the Communist Party of the Soviet Union would discuss such a taboo subject in the presence of five witnesses.

Gomulka supported Brezhnev in this description of the differences of opinion in the Kremlin; indeed, he interrupted him several times to express his agreement. On the other hand Ulbricht did not say a word on this subject. But there was more to come.

Brezhnev admitted there had been negative results within the communist movement – meaning among the different parties – but he went on to claim that great progress had been made in other areas. According to him, this had been achieved by the consistent application of Lenin's principle of seeking temporary allies.

Even our opponents, said Brezhnev, cannot deny that we have achieved major successes in the Near East. We have already partially succeeded in driving the Americans out of this part of the world and we shall soon be in a position to deal them a decisive blow. (What this phrase meant became apparent a few months later in June 1967 when Nasser allowed the Soviets to push him into a war against Israel.)

Nasser, continued Brezhnev, is muddle-headed in ideological matters. But he is a good man (*xhoroshi chelovek*) and has shown that he can be relied on. As politicians responsible for the future of humanity we must naturally make sacrifices in order to achieve progress. One of the sacrifices we have had to accept is that Nasser persecutes the Egyptian communists. But Nasser has the stature to assume the leadership of the Arab liberation movement which makes him invaluable to us at the present stage. This is a creative application of the Leninist principles of alliances with various different political groupings at any given point in time when this can serve the cause of revolution. Once the Arab masses realize what their true interests are we shall not need a Nasser any more.

Or take de Gaulle. Have we not succeeded, at no risk to ourselves, in driving a breach through the imperialist camp? De Gaulle is our enemy and we are well aware of it. The French Communist Party was narrow-minded enough to try to stir us up against de Gaulle for their own particular interests. But look at our achievements! We have weakened the American position in the heart of Europe and this weakening will continue. De Gaulle is a sly old fox. He is aiming for mastery in Europe for himself and in opposition to us. But here we must be flexible. De Gaulle has virtually no chance of realizing his concept of Europe because the other West European countries are too powerful and they would never allow it. But look at the balance-sheet from our point of view, Comrades. Isn't this a success for our policy?

Brezhnev was getting so excited that he slapped his thigh several times. To the Devil (*k chortu*) with those parties that set themselves up as our mentors. What have the Swiss and Dutch parties done to teach their own working classes the true facts? Well, what have they achieved?

Johnson, he continued, is also trying to follow a new policy. We know what he is aiming at with his global strategy. So what kind of Marxist-Leninists are those Britishers with their attempts at bridge-building? They don't even know their own country and their own people. But now we shall confront Mr Johnson with our own global strategy. And we shall see who will win.

Whereas Gomulka expressed complete agreement with Brezhnev's statements, Ulbricht only joined in towards the end. He looked annoyed at Brezhnev's comments about de Gaulle but said nothing. Nor did he join in the criticism directed by Brezhnev, with Gomulka's support, against the various West European communist parties. Only when Brezhnev came to 'Johnson's global strategy' did

Ulbricht join in the conversation once more. Then he immediately tried to guide the conversation towards the Federal Republic.

In West Berlin, said Ulbricht, we have made excellent progress. There is quite strong opposition to Strauss's policies among the youth there. First we tried to win over these students to our side, but the comrades went about it too clumsily. But even if the right-thinking, progressive young people are overshadowed by anarchists and rowdies we must strike the American forces in Europe where they are most sensitive. We should pay much more attention to West Berlin where we can exert pressure not only on the Kiesinger-Strauss government but also on their American backers. If we take the offensive we are sure to get something out of it.

But this suggestion aroused no response from Gomulka or Brezhnev. Both of them listened to Ulbricht – or rather to his Russian interpreter – but did not express any opinion on the thorny question of West Berlin. Ulbricht could not resist the opportunity to take a side-swipe at Gomulka: 'Even some of the most senior of our comrades', he said, 'are sometimes blind to the main characteristics of West Germany. There is no such thing as a Kiesinger-Brandt government, as the West Germans call it. It is a Kiesinger-Strauss government and Strauss is the real master in West Germany. But those comrades who do not know West Germany well enough are unable to understand this.'

I knew in which direction this remark was aimed. The East German officials were constantly trying to put pressure on Polish delegations to replace the usual Polish formula, 'Kiesinger-Brandt government' by the East German version, 'Kiesinger-Strauss government', in official translations, speeches and documents. But the Poles consistently refused to conform.

After Ulbricht had relieved his feelings about West Germany and West Berlin Gomulka tried to get back once more to his old hobby-horse of economic co-operation between Eastern bloc countries within COMECON. But he did not get very far in this company. His companions showed no inclination to take up the subject.

The talks continued. From time to time, Streit, the SUP head of protocol, approached our table and, catching Ulbricht's eye, glanced at the clock. He was trying to indicate that time was getting short. But our host took no notice. From time to time a waiter would approach and serve brandy or fruit juice.

Only after forty-five minutes did Ulbricht give the signal to leave the table. The performance at the German State Opera was able to continue.

This was the end of the Seventh Congress of the Socialist Unity Party. As we returned late that night to the East German government guest house I tried to draw up a personal balance-sheet of what I had learnt behind the scenes at this political parade of the SUP. It was clear the developments in Czechoslovakia were reaching crisis point. And relations between Poland and the GDR, or rather between Gomulka and Ulbricht, were approaching rock-bottom. Both these men were backing different power groups in the Kremlin; they found each other personally unsympathetic, mistrusted each other and represented states with different economic interests.

This mistrust was evident in a significant episode which took place towards the end of the congress. Two days before the official close of the meeting to decidearrangements for the Summit meeting at Karlovy Vary the travel plans for the separate delegations going on to Czechoslovakia had been organized. The special planes and trains, and the departure and arrival times, the questions of protocol all this involved – who was to take leave of whom and who was to greet whom in Prague or Karlovy Vary – the problems of security and transport – all had been decided down to the last detail.

The guests of honour at the congress were laying one final gigantic wreath at the memorial to the Fallen Soviet Soldier in Berlin-Treptow. After the ceremony, as Brezhnev was walking the few hundred yards from the memorial to the waiting limousines with Gomulka, he invited him to travel with him in his special train to Karlovy Vary. When Stoph saw the two most important guests at the congress talking together he immediately joined them and rejected Brezhnev's suggestion quite vehemently. 'It is technically impossible to change things now. The Polish delegation must travel with us.' Either he wanted to prevent Gomulka having a few hours of undisturbed conversation with Brezhnev in the train, or else he was determined to arrive in Karlovy Vary together with Gomulka.

But Brezhnev swept aside Stoph's objections and repeated his invitation to Gomulka, saying that the technical difficulties could easily be overcome by coupling the Polish Pullman carriage on to the Soviet train. Stoph was forced to agree. He beckoned to Streit, the SUP head of protocol, and General Gold, the head of the Government Security Service, and stepped a few paces away from Gomulka.

In a voice of quiet fury, but loud enough for me to hear, he said, 'Fix things so that the Polacks can travel with the Russians.'

It was a significant sentence for anyone who is familiar with communist terminology. For there is no such thing as a 'Russian', only 'Soviet friends' or 'Soviet comrades'. And there is no need to explain the pejorative meaning of the word 'Polack'.

A section of the Polish delegation, including myself, flew back to Warsaw on Sunday, April 23, 1967. In the meantime Gomulka was travelling in Brezhnev's special train to Karlovy Vary, to that 'fraternal allied state of the socialist community' which Brezhnev, Gomulka and Ulbricht were to attack with their tank divisions just sixteen months later.

CHAPTER 9

The Party Officials go Hunting ...

If a traveller from Warsaw to Olsztyn turns right into a beautiful forest about twelve kilometres before his destination, perhaps with the intention of taking a short walk, he will not get far. After a few yards a sign prohibits the entry of vehicles of all kinds. And any curious tourist who continues on foot soon arrives in front of a big placard bearing the words, 'Prohibited military area. Entry strictly forbidden.'

A well-maintained asphalt road, about three yards wide, winds through the thick pine forest and, after a few kilometres, leads to a place whose very existence is shrouded with a veil of secrecy in Poland.

In the middle of the forest lies a big tract of land surrounded by wire fences and closely guarded by troops of the 'Internal Security Corps' (KBW). Administratively this complex comes under the head of the prime minister's office, the Minister Janusz Wieczorek, but in practice it is under the complete control of the local commander, a colonel in the security forces whose authoritarian regime has won him the nickname of 'Mobutu' among his staff.

This complex contains many villas, picturesquely disposed. Many are old, but well-renovated and extremely comfortably furnished. Others have been built according to the latest techniques of modern architecture. The villas are far enough apart for the inhabitants not to disturb each other. The complex also includes administrative and service buildings, quarters for the guards, radio and telephone installations and a club-house.

Lansk, as the complex is called, is uninhabited for most of the year. Even senior government and party officials are usually refused permission to spend their holidays there. Most people do not even know that it exists. This residence surrounded by beautiful woodland acts as a meeting place for unofficial conferences with leading officials from abroad. From time to time a short report appears in the Polish Communist Party paper, *Trybuna Ludu*, saying that an unofficial meeting has taken place 'a few days ago in North-East Poland' between, say, Gomulka, Cyrankiewicz, Brezhnev and Kosygin. The Polish reader is used to this kind of announcement. But what he does not know is that this kind of meeting is just as official as other top-level conferences – but to save time the usual protocol has been avoided and, besides, there is no need for a detailed communique about the course of the meeting, the subjects discussed and decisions taken. These meetings are held in conditions of complete secrecy. The public is only told about the talks with the leaders of a 'fraternal country' when the visitors have already left.

Naturally the leading figures in the socialist camp must also be offered a little rest and recreation. Since the new class of senior and top-level officials have not only acquired material advantages but have also discarded their proletarian consciousness like an old shirt, they are not averse to once-despised bourgeois and even 'aristocratic' leisure pursuits.

So the party leadership decided to develop Lansk as a State hunting ground. The surroundings were ideal for the purpose: magnificent forests, hills dotted with lakes, and not a single village or settlement for miles around, so there would be no intruders. Naturally a considerable amount of investment would be necessary but, after all, it would not do to be miserly either towards important guests or on their own account.

From time to time the communiques about high-level meetings include another short phrase: 'Hosts and visitors also took part in a hunt.' In this way the Warsaw leadership try to give the impression of being 'men of the world' to certain sections of the population at home and to public opinion abroad. In October 1966 Gerhard Grüneberg, a Politburo member and secretary of the Central Committee of the SUP, was a guest of the Polish party leadership in Lansk. Grüneberg had quickly risen to a high position in East Germany. He combined absolute loyalty to the party line with brutality and ruthlessness. With the help of the good relations which he had maintained since the end of the war with the officers of the Soviet army of occupation, with whom he would indulge in endless drinking bouts, he had succeeded in working his way up from junior party official to the post of First Secretary of the SUP for the Frankfurt on Oder district. Since the collectivization of agriculture was going very slowly at that time – the peasants were putting up passive resistance – the Secretary of the SUP Central Committee responsible for agricultural affairs, Erich Mückenberger, the Politburo member, was sent to Moscow, ostensibly on a retraining course. During his absence Ulbricht entrusted his functions to Gerhard Grüneberg. When it turned out that this narrow-minded official had more success in forcing through collectivization in a few months than the less ruthless and more considerate Mückenberger, Grüneberg was immediately kept on in the Central Committee and appointed Secretary and candidate member of the Politburo. Shortly afterwards he was made a full member of this highest centre of power of the Socialist Unity Party. On the other hand Mückenberger, an old communist from before the war, was demoted to the post of First Secretary of the SUP for the Frankfurt on Oder district on the grounds of his obvious incompetence.

When I got to know him Grüneberg was not particularly able, either technically or politically, and had even surprised himself with his meteoric rise (which was achieved through certain traits of his character, rather than through merit) and he suffered permanently from various complexes. Among the leading East German communists he had the reputation of a *parvenu* who stepped into dead men's boots when his own interests, which he slyly linked with the party line, were at stake. The Polish leaders never fully trusted him, for they knew that during the war Grüneberg had been a soldier in the Wehrmacht in Polish Gdynia – that is, he had belonged to the army of occupation – and had only joined the communists after the war.

I often worked as an interpreter with Grüneberg. I got to know him when he headed an SUP delegation to Warsaw in 1961 to negotiate further collaboration between the SUP and the Polish Communist Party. When I came into contact with him I sensed that he was attempting to make up for his inferiority complex by trying hard to impress those around him. He would tell anyone who would listen, including even the chauffeurs, about his good relations with Walter Ulbricht and the Soviet generals. He boasted that he owned a *dacha* and bragged about every conceivable thing. Grüneberg was always extremely careful, though, to avoid committing any political errors and never to depart from his allotted task by a hair's breadth.

Once, at an entertainment held in his honour in the Congress Hall of the Warsaw Palace of Culture, he happened to remark that the GDR was having great difficulty with its potato supplies. His Polish opposite numbers immediately pointed out that Poland had had a good potato harvest that year. They offered to send a few million tons of potatoes to the GDR. But Grüneberg immediately retreated. He cleverly turned the tables and declared he would be quite willing to pass on the Polish offer to Comrade Ulbricht. If the GDR was interested in the Polish offer negotiations could be set up then. In fact the potato deal was eventually negotiated.

On another visit Grüneberg was shown round a radio factory in Warsaw. He talked animatedly to some of the girl workers, questioned them about the position of women in Poland and then added, in passing 'You must fight for more influence in national affairs. In our country a session of the Politburo has just passed a resolution about the improvement of the role of women in the building of socialism.'

Grüneberg's entourage included the Warsaw correspondent of the East German news agency, ADN, a man named Olivier. He diligently noted down every word spoken by this important visitor from his country and then sent a report about Grüneberg's statements back to the GDR. Although the quotations were quite correct Grüneberg immediately smelt trouble. This sentence could be taken as an indirect criticism of the Polish state and party leadership. And Walter Ulbricht had only instructed Grüneberg to criticize the competent Polish authorities about their negative attitude to the collectivization of agriculture. Grüneberg gave the ADN correspondent a real dressing down. He apologized profusely and cancelled the report but he could not appease the important guest. In his characteristic, not very grammatical, way, Grüneberg roared at him; 'If a member of the Politburo and Secretary of the Central Committee like me wants to make a joke there's no call for a journalist to go making a report about it. I'm not a nobody from nowhere. Anything like that must be agreed with me beforehand.' Shortly afterwards Olivier was recalled from Warsaw but he seems to have learnt his lesson from this incident for, as I later learnt, he was subsequently sent abroad to a Western country.

The phrase 'A member of the Politburo and Secretary of the Central Committee' was one that Grüneberg used constantly even in the most inappropriate circumstances. And it was this man, unattractive in human terms but one of the most influential party officials in the GDR, who was coming to Warsaw in 1966 with his wife and his security man. After a short stay in the capital when talks took place we drove to Lansk. Grüneberg had already expressed the wish to shoot a deer in Lansk. So this time the Polish hosts organized a rough programme for the hunt; the details were to be worked out on the spot.

We drove to Lansk in two giant black limousines. As their interpreter I was lodged in the same villa as Grüneberg and his wife. The Polish side in the political discussions was made up of Jozef Tejchma,[1] the Central Committee Secretary, Eugeniusz Mazurkiewicz, the head of the Agriculture Department of the Central Committee and, for part of the time, the first secretary of the party for the Olsztyn district. On the very first day a detailed programme for the hunt was worked out with the local organizers of the hunting complex. Naturally Grüneberg was to get his deer, but only on the last day of his visit. Our visitor's 'bag' was to start with wild duck and to increase progressively in importance. According to the experience of the local organizers this was the best way to keep our guest permanently in a good mood.

Each villa had its own kitchen and staff and, most important, an ample supply of selected spirits and tobacco. Since our important guest, as is usual on hunting trips, drank a few glasses of brandy with his breakfast and was not averse to consuming alcohol throughout the day, I had my doubts about the accuracy of his shooting – in spite of the exceptional hunting guns with telescopic sights and infra-red equipment which were always put at the visitors' disposal.

But my doubts were banished when I learnt about the detailed programme in talks which were held without Grüneberg's knowledge. The expert gamekeeper on the staff of the complex explained that it would really be impossible for him to miss. I was reminded of the jokes that I had heard as a child about the state hunts under the Austro-Hungarian monarchy. According to these stories Emperor Franz Josef had two ways of shooting his quarry. Either the animal was tied to a tree or a second hunter would shoot at the same moment as the Emperor and kill the animal. The Poles had developed a slightly different system.

The gamekeeper explained that a wide area round the hunting ground had been declared a prohibited zone, and the game was bred there. Since there is a shortage of food for game in winter the right

[1] Later appointed a member of the Polish Politburo

kind of food for each species is put out at the same time and same place every day during the cold weather. This practice is even continued in summer when the animals can find enough food in the forest. 'We have to make sure', explained the gamekeeper, 'that the animals get used to finding food each day at a certain time and in a certain place. Then when we have to organize a hunt we know where to look for the game. And incidentally, they get very tame. After years of daily feeding the animals' mouths start to water when they hear the motor of the jeep that brings the food or smell its exhaust. To the animals we're like God sending manna from heaven. When we arrive in the van we are surrounded by expectant animals. We really have to take care not to bump into them.'

According to the programme Grüneberg was due to shoot wild duck on the second day of his stay at Lansk. They were bred on an island in a lake that formed part of the hunting ground. As the motor-boat with Huntsman Grüneberg and his wife aboard approached the island the sky was black with flying ducks. All he had to do was raise his gun and shoot for a few birds to be hit and fall into the water. After a few minutes the 'duck shoot' was over; the quarry was collected out of the water and the 'huntsman' could return to the shore.

Grüneberg was obviously pleased with his bag and seemed in a generous mood. He handed out cigarettes that did not belong to him to all and sundry, and used the liberal supplies of alcohol in the villa to stand one round of drinks after another to the beaters.

In the afternoon we took a walk through the whole complex. One of the things we were shown was a little cage containing a wolf. The director of the hunting ground was trying to develop an improved hunting dog by crossing the wolf with Alsatian bitches. But so far he had had no success.

As we came to the landing stage for the boats I could see why Lansk was known to the initiates as a paradise for anglers. We went to the end of the jetty, which was twenty to thirty yards long, and saw that there were thousands upon thousands of fish in the crystal clear water. Although the water was only a yard to a yard and a half deep it was impossible to see the bottom because of these shoals of fish. Among the countless small fry there would be a bigger fish, about the size of herring, about every half yard. Then there were even bigger ones, up to eighteen inches long. The medium and large-sized fish swam lazily around. They were too well fed and idle to open their mouths and swallow one of the smaller fish which were their food. Our companion explained that the lake was also guarded by security troops to prevent tourists or water sports fans wandering into the inner sanctum of Lansk.

After supper our guest from Berlin, already fairly tipsy, began to tell us about himself.

His villa in the VIP estate, he told us, was directly opposite Walter Ulbricht's house. The SUP leader practised several sports and played tennis early every day, but for a long time he had had no interest in shooting. Ulbricht had only been won round when he, Grüneberg, an enthusiastic clay pigeon-shooter, had persuaded the East German head of State to take part in a clay pigeon shoot. Whereupon he had immediately had a clay pigeon shooting stand put up near his villa.

Grüneberg was quite communicative about his private life. Apart from the Zil limousine, he confided to us, he had his own Trabant car, but he usually left this for his wife. As Secretary of the SUP Central Committee he made about 4,000 Marks a month. He often went to Moscow and had quite a big bank account there. When I asked him how he had come by large amounts of Soviet money he explained willingly. Every member of an SUP delegation visiting the Soviet Union used to get the usual pocket money. But the Soviet comrades were very generous and wanted to supply their guests with extra cash. So they would always offer delegates the chance of publishing an article in a Soviet journal which would be paid for at quite a high rate – about 800 to 1,000 roubles. 'Don't they do the same with your comrades?' asked Grüneberg. Of course, I could not answer this question, but I could only wonder how many months' average income of an ordinary Soviet citizen this fee would represent.

In the evening Grüneberg played cards with his wife and his security man, drank far into the night, and tried to initiate me into the mysteries of the game of skat.

The next day a tour of the forest was organized. Great stretches of woodland were proudly shown off to Grüneberg. When he kept asking if he would be able to shoot a deer that day his hosts answered him shortly that it was hard to tell, perhaps he would manage it. Of course, I knew that the deer was not planned for that day. In fact there was to be no game killed that day. It was not until the next day that Grüneberg was to bag a wild boar. The local staff drove the jeep all over the forest taking great care to avoid all the places where game was to be found.

That afternoon the political discussions were continued in Grüneberg's villa. The visitor immediately made a strong attack on Tejchma and Mazurkiewicz concerning Polish agricultural policy. In a lecturing tone he tried to tell them that the building of socialism must be carried out in every sphere, and that an important sector like agriculture could not be omitted from the programme. Without socialist reorganization in the villages there could be no socialism in the towns and in industry.

Tejchma and Mazurkiewicz countered this argument by saying that Poland had too few tractors and artificial fertilizers to build up really productive collective farms. So the Polish party leadership had chosen a different way. The individual farmers could keep their land and so could aim at higher and higher yields every year. But naturally the socialist sector of agriculture was not neglected. The State-owned agricultural enterprises received generous support and had two particularly important tasks – cattle breeding and the production of high quality seed corn for the whole agricultural sector. But Grüneberg was not happy with this statement and insisted. Tejchma and Mazurkiewicz had to admit, in answer to his direct question, that the major part of the usable agricultural land in Poland was in the possession of individual farmers. Grüneberg laughed contemptuously. His hosts went on to explain the basic principles of Polish agricultural policy. The peasants were, of course, a 'capitalist element', so to prevent their private property becoming too large the so-called 'Agricultural Circles' were set up in Poland; these were co-operative groups which owned and supplied the larger types of agricultural machinery.

In Poland there is a system of compulsory purchase of agricultural produce. Every farmer must deliver a certain amount of produce to the state at very low prices. A proportion of the difference between the purchasing price and the market price is then paid back to the village into a special account belonging to the so-called Agricultural Development Fund. This cash can be used by the village to buy tractors and other machinery which is owned co-operatively by the Agricultural Circle. In this way, Tejchma pointed out, the peasants were gradually accustomed to work and think collectively. Only at the next stage, when the material basis for collective farms existed, and the peasants had learnt from their own experience to accept the principle of agricultural co-operatives, would collective farms be established in Poland too.

The discussion became quite heated. Grüneberg made no secret of his opinions. But everyone present could see that he was saying one thing and meaning another. He was not really concerned with Polish agriculture but was criticizing the Polish party leadership for rejecting the collectivization of agriculture on economic rather than ideological grounds.

When Grüneberg had had his say he became more reasonable, since he obviously did not want the atmosphere to get too strained. 'Yes, there are differences between us,' he said. 'We must uphold the agricultural co-operatives because we are responsible for the whole of Germany and the West German farmers are putting their hopes in our agricultural policy. They do not have the opportunity to unite together to form collective farms and we cannot disappoint them. For them we are a model and an example. It is an enormous political responsibility for us.'

After this argument Grüneberg expressed a wish to visit an agricultural machinery factory near Poznan. He had heard that a machine for drying potatoes for animal fodder had been developed in Poland. The GDR might be interested in buying this equipment. Also he would like to see a few food processing plants in Poznan. Tejchma and Mazurkiewicz agreed and promised to take the necessary steps.

The next day Grüneberg bagged his wild boar. We drove in the jeep through the forest for hours. But only when it was getting dark did the driver stop and switch off the lights. We waited for a few minutes. All around we could hear the grunting of wild boar. Grüneberg's passion for the hunt – helped on by alcohol – was so great that he was too excited to fire his gun at the first attempt. The gamekeeper switched on the headlamps and pointed out a boar standing in the beam of light about three yards from the car, saying 'Please shoot now – that's a boar over a year old', but even then Grüneberg could not manage to shoot the defenceless and trusting animal. After four or five seconds the gamekeeper switched off the headlamps although the boar made no attempt to move. In the darkness he explained to the visitor, 'As soon as another boar appears I will switch on the headlamps. Then you must quickly take aim and fire.' The grunting all around us grew louder. Obviously the animals were hungry and had heard the jeep arriving. After about two minutes the gamekeeper switched the headlamps on again. Now there was a herd of seven or eight wild boar in front of the jeep, all looking in our direction. Grüneberg stood up in the back of the jeep, took aim and fired.

An enormous boar, weighing about 400 pounds, was shot in the head and fell. The gamekeeper turned on all the lights in the jeep, jumped down and cut a green twig from a tree with his hunting knife, which he handed to Grünberg. Grünberg stuck it in his hat and someone blew a special hunting call that meant a boar had been shot. The quarry was loaded on the jeep and we drove home.

Grüneberg's shot must have disturbed the animals, but even so, several times on the way back we had to stop because whole herds of wild boar were standing in our path and only trotted to one side as the jeep slowly advanced and pushed them. Grüneberg did not take any of this in. By now completely drunk he just kept on muttering, 'The very first shot and I got him in the head – isn't that fantastic?'

The whole affair left an unpleasant taste in my mouth – it reminded me of a massacre rather than a hunting expedition. But there was more to come.

The next day Grüneberg was presented with the boar's tusks as a memento of the hunt. For the next three days, until a deer was put in front of his car, he never stopped bragging that he had killed a boar at his very first shot. He even insisted that I should translate the story for the chauffeur who was driving us on a day's excursion to Gdynia.

During the next political talks in Lansk, which covered the Federal Republic, Grüneberg announced, to the astonishment of his Polish partners, that, in the opinion of the Politburo of the SUP, Ludwig Erhard, the Federal Chancellor at that time, was 'fundamentally the best man for our interests'. Any alternative to Erhard, said Grüneberg, 'would be worse for us.'

I was not surprised by this statement for I had already translated a similar remark made by the leader of the SUP at discussions between Gomulka and Ulbricht. But I was surprised by something else Grüneberg said. He told us that, in autumn 1964, he had gone to Budapest with an SUP delegation and was informed by Soviet comrades there that Krushchev was to be dismissed on the following day. 'Since I realized how important this news was I got straight into my car, drove to the airport where my plane was standing ready, and flew to Berlin to inform Comrade Ulbricht.'

Clearly Gomulka had not had such good informants in the Kremlin. For when Krushchev was overthrown in 1964 the Polish communist leader was holding discussions with a Hungarian party and government delegation at the mining combine of Nowa Huta in Cracow. During a mass meeting where Gomulka and Kadar were the main speakers Colonel Gorecki, the head of the Government Security Bureau, suddenly approached the platform and took Gomulka to the telephone. The caller was Brezhnev, who informed Gomulka that Krushchev had just been deposed. He promised to come to Poland in a few days' time to explain the affair to the Polish party leadership. Gomulka returned to the factory hall in a very excited state, whispered something to Kadar, and then took the microphone and addressed the workers in these terms, 'You know more or less what else we were going to say. Now we must leave on very important business.' The delegation's visit to Nowa Huta and Cracow was interrupted and we returned to Warsaw.

What Grüneberg told us about those dramatic days interested me particularly because I had often noticed that the senior SUP officials were much better informed about changes planned in the Soviet leadership than Gomulka was. I remembered the visit of a senior cultural official of the SUP who drank too much during a banquet given in his honour at a state farm in the Lublin district. In his tipsy state he declared that Anastas Mikoyan, at that time still a member of the Soviet Presidium and deputy Prime Minister of the USSR, would be fired in six months. This remark was heard by thirty people, including some of the employees of the state farm. At the time I thought he was showing off. But a few months later his prediction came true. Obviously the East German party leadership was collaborating closely with a faction in the deeply divided and warring Kremlin leadership, was regarded as an ally by this group and kept well informed – better than Gomulka.

But to return to our famous huntsman, Grüneberg. For the next two days he was kept in suspense. His hosts drove him through the forest carefully avoiding the places where deer could be found. He did not get his deer until the third day – and in the same fashion as the boar.

After our guest's hunting ambitions were satisfied we drove to Poznan where the First Secretary of the party for the district, Jan Szydlak, joined in the discussions with Grüneberg. The East German visitor was shown the potato drying equipment at a State farm but it soon turned out that his information was inaccurate. The machinery was not made or assembled in Poland. It was a Dutch installation which was only partly supplied with Polish-made parts. When his hosts tried to demonstrate the equipment for Grüneberg it would not work because it had been badly serviced. It was explained to Grüneberg that Poland possessed only a few installations of this kind. But he stubbornly continued to repeat his wish to buy potato drying machinery in Poland. Naturally nothing came of the proposed deal.

In Poznan Grüneberg was shown over a meat canning factory working for the export trade and then over the Winiary food processing plant. There he was shown the freeze-drying department. He saw, for example, a pork chop being quick-frozen and completely dehydrated in a vacuum container. The treated pork chop felt rather like cork and was similar in weight. The head of the department explained to Grüneberg that this new method of preserving food was very practical since freeze-dried products did not have to be kept in refrigerated storage, they were easy to transport because of their light weight, and foods processed in this way were very easy to reconstitute. All you had to do was to dip the pork chop in water for a few minutes to get a normal fresh piece of meat. However, the head of the department added, this process was not used for food aimed at the retail market because it was too expensive. The plant only supplied the army.

His Polish hosts had prepared a final treat for Grüneberg. We drove to a nearby state farm where guinea fowl and pheasants were bred. After a welcoming ceremony for Grüneberg and the Polish officials accompanying him we climbed into half a dozen horse-drawn hunting wagons and were taken to see the guinea fowl breeding area. The birds were kept in cages piled on top of each other in five or six 'storeys'. These cages were grouped round a horseshoe-shaped area about a hundred yards square. As we got down agricultural workers opened the grilles of the cages and drove thousands of guinea fowl out of the cages. Soon the whole area was covered with screeching birds. Grüneberg shot wildly in all directions, hitting a bird at every attempt. It was like shooting at a chicken run. But our guest was delighted. When he managed to kill about sixty guinea fowl in a few minutes he was bursting with pride. Once more the hunting horns were blown, we got back into the carriages and drove on to the pheasantry. Hundreds of pheasants were sitting in the bushes. Before our arrival a bus full of agricultural workers had been sent on ahead. They used wooden clappers that made a terrific noise and startled the birds. Grüneberg had no difficulty in shooting a good dozen pheasants.

Since he was shooting wildly in every direction, forgetting his surroundings in his enthusiasm for the hunt, Jozef Tejchma, the Central Committee Secretary, and I hid behind a car to save ourselves from inadvertently sharing the fate of the birds.

The grand finale of the 'shoot' consisted in a ceremonial banquet in the Grünebergs' honour at the state farm. The main dish was made up of the pheasants and guinea fowl he had shot. Then we accompanied him and his two sons, who had joined him, to the frontier.

. . . and Travelling

In Poland there is a special service to handle the security of the government, the senior party officials and important guests, the so-called 'Bureau for Government Security' (*Biuro Ochrony Rzadu*). This organization is a kind of state within a state. Administratively it is a department of the Ministry of the Interior but in practice it works on the principle of divided responsibility. The director of the bureau, Colonel Jan Gorecki, his deputy, Glanc, and all his staff are also under the instructions of the party leadership, the men whom it is their job to protect. Colonel Gorecki, clever, urbane, highly-trained and always elegantly dressed, corresponds more or less to one's idea of James Bond.

His East German counterpart, General Gold, was completely different. When I saw him for the first time, big and fat with a red face, I had to take a second look. From a distance he looked confusingly like the German actor, Fröbe. Only when I was closer to him did I see the difference. General Franz Gold has had a much more adventurous life than Colonel Gorecki. According to reliable sources he joined the Nazi party on November 1, 1938, when he was young and politically uncommitted, and fought for his Führer in the war with great self-sacrifice until he defected to the Russians and was re-indoctrinated by them.

The security men appointed to guard important figures have a very broad area of responsibility; certainly they have many duties which, as far as I could see, have little to do with their actual job. They can hardly be said to ensure effective security for the national leaders. And this does not apply only to Poland; tragic experiences such as the deaths of the two Kennedy brothers in America, for example, show clearly that security guards can never guarantee safety. In Poland their duties correspond basically to those of an *aide-de-camp* or even of a valet.

Gomulka's security guard was Lieutenant Colonel Tomczak. Gomulka appeared fairly often in public. On May Day hundreds of thousands of people often filed past the saluting base only a few yards away from the leaders. On other occasions he attended meeting with the thousand-strong staff of a big factory. When the former Chairman of the Council of State, Aleksander Zawadzki, died, a solemn funeral was held in Warsaw. A few days previously the route of the funeral procession was printed in the press. The whole party and state leadership followed the coffin on foot from the Sejm building to the square in front of the Great Theatre in Warsaw. The route, several kilometres long, covered some of the busiest streets of the capital. All the windows overlooking the route were full of people, and many of them were aiming cameras and telescopic lenses at the public figures as they passed. The procession passed by my home and the houses of several of my acquaintances. But I never heard of anyone being checked on by security officers beforehand. Unlike their counterparts in the German Democratic Republic, the Polish leaders do not need the company of their security men and can safely dispense with their services. In the Ujazdowski Avenue in Warsaw you can often see party and national leaders taking a walk without any security protection. It is well known that Prime Minister Cyrankiewicz often drinks a coffee in the Warsaw coffee-houses of Europa or Nowy-Swiat. And without his shadow.

So in general the life of a security officer is not very interesting or varied. They have to wait for their client, accompany him to meetings, to work or to his home, and do all kinds of little tasks for him. But it is different when there are state visits from abroad or when Polish delegations travel to other countries. The security men work out a detailed plan in collaboration with the diplomats in charge of protocol and the officials organizing the visit. They go over the whole route beforehand and check all the places where the delegates are to stop, and take the appropriate security precautions. Every stage of the journey is simulated and checked, in co-operation, of course, with their opposite numbers from the corresponding foreign security service.

The security organization naturally also receives a full list of everyone who has access to the delegates. I was often surprised what an excellent memory the security officials had. During the discussions which preceded the arrival of a delegation I was once presented to one of the security guards; afterwards I found on many occasions that when the delegation was crowded together by a great mass of people a way would be cleared for me by an unseen hand so that I could rejoin the leaders of the delegation.

At meetings and other events the security guards always sit in the first and second rows of the hall together with the local dignitaries. They look very bored during the hour-long speeches and only react at times when the speaker is being applauded. Then they naturally join in the clapping. When the meeting is over the security guards go straight to the cloakroom to collect their masters' hats and coats for them so that there is no delay.

When there are visitors from abroad it is the custom to present the delegates with flowers at every opportunity. A single member of a delegation may receive five or six bouquets in the space of ten minutes. But the person who has made the presentation is hardly out of sight before a helpful shadow appears behind his master and takes the flowers. Then his hands are free to accept the next bouquet. The same thing happens with presents of all kinds. The security guard takes them and hands them on to someone else.

In Poland these 'shadows' are called *Smutni* (the sad men), probably in reference to their expressions. They have to carry out all kinds of formalities in addition to protecting their masters from the crowds. When a delegation travels abroad in a Pullman train no frontier policemen or customs men are allowed to enter the train. Instead the 'sad men' collect the passports before the departure, see to all the formalities at the frontier, and then hand them back to the delegates and staff early the next day.

The same thing happens with customs and passport formalities on air trips. Near the civil airport in Warsaw is a government airport where the government squadron is stationed. All special flights take off and land here. Although it comes officially under the Air Force authorities, this squadron, like the government car fleet, is administered by the Bureau for Government Security.

In this way the life of a security officer follows a normal, clearly defined path.

In East Berlin there is a residential area in the suburb of Pankow which is surrounded by walls and closely guarded. It is here that important state visitors are entertained. This place is approached through Ossietzky Street. Suddenly you arrive at a barrier controlled by special guards. There is an involved system of passes for people and cars to prevent any strangers getting in. The residential area itself was christened the 'village' by the people, and the *apparatchiks* themselves have adopted the name. It is surrounded by the Majkowski Ring and includes many attractive, luxuriously furnished villas with their own staff, their own services, kitchens etc. To begin with the 'village' was the home of East German party and government leaders, hence the use of the word 'Pankow' to describe the East German Government. In later years when Ulbricht had a new modern quarter built for these leaders the 'village' was used to house foreign delegations. Even today there are still some high-ups living in these villas, but they rate below the most important leaders. The old castle that adjoins the park of Pankow also forms part of the 'village' when there are inter-governmental discussions.

Although most of the villas usually stand empty, the decision was taken in East Berlin to build a huge new building in the latest style as a government guest house. The design is a great glass box and it has the latest automated and mechanized equipment. The guest house was then furnished in the height of luxury. So this quiet district of old-fashioned but well-maintained villas, formerly the homes of doctors, lawyers, senior officials, merchants and industrialists, has now acquired a building in the most modern style.

Gomulka had the honour of being the first guest to stay in this residence when he headed the Polish party delegation to the Seventh Congress of the SUP in 1967. Ulbricht himself, bursting with pride, accompanied Gomulka to his suite. During the next few days his host questioned him constantly, 'Well, how do you like it, how are you getting on there?' Gomulka did have a few problems. For example, the noise of the fountain prevented him from sleeping. But this was all sorted out in a few days. Only one thing still gave him difficulty and he even managed to work that out too. When we were sitting in the hall on the fourth or fifth day and waiting for the cars he said ironically, 'The flushing mechanism in the lavatory is really something special. But I've worked out the technique. First of all you have to press the button gently down and then try to push your finger slightly upwards so that the button is at an angle. Then one final sharp push and it works.'

There are also villas for foreign delegations in Warsaw. Depending on how high a visitor rates he is allocated a suitable residence. The assortment is very comprehensive. The best visitors stay either at the Wilanow Palace near Warsaw or in the Belvedere Castle (usually the seat of the Chairman of the Council of State of the People's Republic of Poland). Of course, at multilateral meetings things get more complicated because it is not possible to lodge all the heads of delegations at these two palaces, and some may feel slighted if their residence is less palatial. So a row of modern, luxuriously furnished villas are kept for this purpose in Ladowa Street in Warsaw. Naturally they are also surrounded by walls and gates and guarded by soldiers. There are other government villas at the corner of Narbuta and Pulawska Streets and in Bacciareli Street. The rank and file are put up in hotels.

All degrees of rank are scrupulously observed and protocol is very strict. There are also special villas for state visitors in other Polish cities. In Katowice there is the Stelmach Villa, in Rzeszow the Baranowice Castle and in Lodz there is a villa in Nalkowska Street. The only exceptions are Cracow and Gdansk. In Cracow the most important visitors are put up in the Wawel Castle and the others in hotels, while in Gdansk state visitors are usually entertained in the Grand Hotel Sopot, the former casino.

Naturally a state delegation does not only consist of those persons who are mentioned in the official communique. In addition to the five to ten delegates there are usually about twelve accompanying staff – security guards, secretaries, experts, journalists, interpreters etc.

It is the usual custom for all members of foreign delegations and their staffs to be given a plain envelope containing pocket money. Then at the end of the visit presents are exchanged. The gifts made to the visitors by their hosts and by the visitors to their hosts are carried by lorry.

A special staff draws up the lists, organizes the packing and presentation of the gifts, and not even the chauffeurs must be missed out.

One interesting thing which I have noticed is that the complete present list is submitted to the head of the delegation for his approval. All kinds of things are included: valuable gifts of precious metals, costly tapestries, porcelain and crystal; tape recorders, cameras, radios, down to little packets of cigarettes and spirits for the charwomen in the state residences.

Streit, the SUP head of protocol, once asked me during a visit what kind of thing would appeal to Comrade Gomulka because, as he said, 'we have a filing system where we make a note of all the presents we give so that we never give the same thing twice. But now we really can't think of anything else that Comrade Gomulka would particularly like.' I passed on the question to the secretary of the delegation and the next day I received the answer which I was to give to Streit. Since Comrade Gomulka travelled a great deal he would very much like a set of travelling cases in assorted sizes.

During a state visit the pocket money must be spent. This is not so easy since the programme for the visit is always calculated down to the last minute. So it was interesting to see how the comrades managed to use their money. During a visit to East Berlin all the delegates bought accordions in large quantities. When you consider that these instruments are relatively cheap in the GDR, but very expensive in Poland, it becomes obvious that there are many hidden commercial talents around with an instinctive knowledge of the laws of supply and demand, even though Polish foreign trade goes from bad to worse.

A study of the way national delegations are looked after shows that, on this level at least, the communist aim of heaven on earth has been achieved. Even at breakfast innumerable courses are served: cold meat, fish, caviar, sausages, ham, smoked ham, poultry and game; then comes a wide selection of hot dishes and, to end up with, fruit, cheese and confectionery, all of the highest quality and in accordance with the well-known publicity slogan, 'Only the best is good enough.'

Meals of this type are served for several days. And then there are various snacks in between the main meals. There is no shortage of drink either: French brandy, Russian brandy, Bulgarian brandy, vodka, wines, beer and all kinds of spirits. I was surprised that senior officials, who are not usually very young, could manage to get it all down. But the guests always did justice to the groaning tables. Only Gomulka would refuse canned foods, allegedly on the advice of his doctor.

I think it was Metternich who once said, 'Talented diplomats must have not only good backsides but, even more important, healthy stomachs.' From this point of view the leaders of Eastern bloc countries are exceptionally good diplomats.

The officials who look after protocol have an amazing capacity for sensing delicate situations. With their special knowledge they hit the nail on the head every time. When East German delegations come to Poland even the government car fleet has to be reorganized. Normally all the Polish party and government leaders have Mercedes cars. And when foreign delegations come to Poland they are also supplied with this make of car. But not when the visitors are from the GDR. Who would dare to suggest to Ulbricht that he should get into a German car that came from the revanchist imperialist Bonn regime? No – he is given a Soviet Zil limousine, and, so as not to be out of step, all the Polish comrades change to Russian cars too.

Every country has its famous sights: castles, waterfalls, memorials, the latest modern architecture. Courteous hosts always do their utmost to show an honoured guest everything that is most attractive and admired. During a visit to East Berlin one of the SUP officials looking after our delegation approached me and asked me to translate something for Gomulka. It concerned a matter that was not covered in the written programme: 'Comrade Gomulka, we should like to show you the anti-fascist defence wall.' I translated the phrase word for word. Gomulka remained silent and uncomprehending. When the silence became embarrassing after a few seconds I added softly in Polish. 'The Berlin Wall'. Then the Polish delegates realized what he had meant and naturally agreed to the suggestion. We drove to the Brandenburg Gate where we were received by an officer and taken to a little house where this socialist achievement was described to us in every technical detail. Then we were shown a film and taken to a platform where we could admire this masterpiece of socialist construction. Finally the delegation were invited to sign their names in the distinguished visitors' book. Every country is proud of its achievements. The East German leadership could not resist showing the Berlin Wall to every delegation which I accompanied to East Berlin. There's no accounting for tastes.

On the occasion of Ulbricht's seventieth birthday communist leaders from all over the world flocked to Berlin to join in the celebrations. This was also the occasion when I made the only error in translation that I know of. The festivities were transmitted direct by Polish television and I went to the studio in the top storey of the Warsaw Palace of Culture to make a simultaneous translation of the talks between Ulbricht and Krushchev.

Since the translators on Polish television usually acted as commentators rather than translators during direct transmissions – that is, they could not keep up with the speaker and would just stammer out about one sentence in four – I was left to work alone for a few hours. I had a screen in front of me showing the Berlin celebrations, a microphone on the table in front of me, and wore earphones. After the broadcast was completed I left the studio bathed in sweat, but I was congratulated by all the TV people, including the technicians, and told that I had translated well and smoothly and, most important, without missing a single sentence. But the pay-off came the next day. Andrzej Czalbowski, the producer responsible for the programme, told me that there had been an enormous row after the transmission. A telephone call had come from the Central Committee saying that in one reference I had used the Polish abbreviation NRD (for German Democratic Republic) instead of the initials NRF (for Federal Republic of Germany). As a result the sense of Ulbricht's speech had been completely altered. Millions of Polish viewers who were hearing my translation of Ulbricht's words had been told, 'By that time, I am firmly convinced, the peace-loving population of the GDR will have got rid of their present masters and their political parties.' Of course, Ulbricht was really referring to the Federal Republic.

But the leader of the Socialist Unity Party does not seem to have learnt of this howler, for when he came to Warsaw a few months later to take part in a summit meeting he was still correct and even friendly in his behaviour to me. And Ulbricht is not a man to forgive a slight, so it was obvious that he knew nothing of the affair.

In December 1958 Anastas Mikoyan was heading a Soviet delegation to Poland on the occasion of the anniversary celebrations of the founding of the Polish Communist Party. During his visit he was taken on the usual tour of the country, and we spent a few hours in Cracow. I was present as one of the interpreters since it was a multilateral meeting.

During our stay in Cracow the foreign delegates were shown the old market-place. An enormous crowd of people was pressing in on the delegates so that the security guards and local officials had great difficulty in preventing the crush barriers being broken down. In the market-place in Cracow there is one of the most famous buildings in Poland, the Church of Our Lady. As we passed the church one of the local dignitaries gave a few details of its history and described the Veit Stoss altarpiece which it contains. Mikoyan hesitated for a moment, and said he would like to visit it. Immediately a narrow path appeared between the surging crowds of people, and Mikoyan and the other foreign delegates spent a few minutes in the church together with the Polish party leaders.

Later, over lunch at the Francuzki Hotel in Cracow, the 'opinion researchers' who had mingled with the crowd told us that this had caused great excitement among the people of Cracow; 'Will he go in or not?' And when Mikoyan did go into the church he had immediately won over many of the citizens of Cracow.

In this case, of course, it was essential to fall in with the wishes of the foreign visitor, especially since he had a senior position in the Soviet leadership. But on other occasions attempts were also often made to show guests from abroad how much help and care the communist state devoted to the Church.

CHAPTER 10

'In my opinion you should lock them all up!'

Of all the party and government leaders of the Warsaw Pact countries who have remained faithful to Moscow, Walter Ulbricht remained in power for the longest period. His personality represents the pledge that every change in Soviet policy towards Germany, every ideological somersault in internal policy recommended by the Kremlin, will be followed faithfully and exactly.

Ulbricht, as I saw and observed him, was not only obsessed by power – that alone would not explain the 'irresistible rise of Walter U.' His most noticeable character traits were cunning, cynicism and unscrupulousness, carried to a level which is rare even among present-day communist leaders.

This may be a hard judgement but I believe it is a legitimate one, for I have observed Walter Ulbricht often enough at very close quarters. In this chapter I will try to make a character sketch of the leader of the Socialist Unity Party and to describe his relationship with Wladyslaw Gomulka.

My verdict that Walter Ulbricht was an unscrupulous politician is based partly on an incident which took place during a summit meeting in Warsaw.

It was the autumn of 1963. During September an East German party and government delegation, headed by Walter Ulbricht, was visiting Poland. The delegation from East Berlin included the deputy Prime Minister and economic expert on the SUP Politburo, Bruno Leuschner, who has since died. On the very first day of the visit he had a heart attack and was flown straight back to Berlin in a special plane, although this fact was hushed up and never made public The delegation also included Hermann Matern who was officially 'only' a Politburo member but, according to senior East German officials, really ranked second in the East German hierarchy, a fact that was supported by the seating arrangements during Politburo sessions (Matern used to sit on Ulbricht's right but slightly apart from the other members of the Politburo, the highest governing organ of the Socialist Unity Party). Ulbricht had also brought along his Foreign Minister, Dr Lothar Bolz, and two SUP officials, Georg Ewald and Günther Wischkowsky.

The Polish government and party leadership was represented by the party leader, Gomulka, Aleksander Zawadzki, at that time President of Poland, Prime Minister Cyrankiewicz, Central Committee Secretary, Zenon Kliszko, the Foreign Minister, Adam Rapacki, the Chairman of the Polish Planning Commission, Jedrychowski, Central Committee Secretary, Edward Ochab, Central Committee Secretary, Bolewlaw Jasczuk and finally Eugeniusz Szyr, at that time deputy Prime Minister.

I have listed the names of delegates of both countries in order to stress that decisions made at this level were absolutely binding on both sides.

As always on such occasions discussions were held at two levels. For example, the Foreign Minister, Dr Bolz, who was a member of the National Democratic Party, did not take part in the party talks. But all the members of both delegations participated in the discussions at government level.

At these high-level discussions the only problems dealt with were ones which had been carefully selected beforehand by the Politburos of the Socialist Unity Party and the Polish Communist Party. I knew from the preparatory conferences where the agenda for the negotiations with the East German delegation had been worked out, how important one particular question was for the Polish party and government leadership in general and for Gomulka himself in particular. This was a problem inherited from the Second World War – the German minority in Poland.

Since the end of the war Gomulka had striven persistently to achieve a homogeneous Polish state without any other national minorities; he believed that it was only in this way that Poland could be made internally strong and resistant. In accordance with this policy all the means of propaganda available were used to drum into the Polish people the idea that Poland had fallen such an easy victim to Hitler in 1939 because the country had been weakened by the many non-Polish national minorities and the tensions they created, so that the will to defend the country was crippled.

So Gomulka was aiming to get rid of what he termed 'foreign national groupings' from Poland. According to party propaganda, these groups had consisted of Germans, Jews and Ukrainians before the war. As far as the Jewish minority was concerned Hitler's 'final solution' had decimated them to such an extent that they no longer constituted a national problem for Poland. And as for the Ukrainians who had settled in Eastern Poland before the war, after the shifting of the Soviet-Polish frontier further westwards the great majority of them had now come under the rule of the Kremlin. Yet still the Polish leadership stuck stubbornly to the principle that even the remnants of these two groups should leave Poland. Gomulka made attempts to encourage the Jews to emigrate in the years immediately following the war, again in 1956, and finally in 1968/69. The Ukrainians, on the other hand, were uprooted from the Polish part of Galicia and resettled in various other Polish regions in some cases where the Soviet Union was not ready to accept them.

The problem of the German minority was more complicated. Many of them had fled to the West during the war as the fighting approached, and a larger number were expelled in the years following the end of the war. But a fairly large section of this minority still remained in the areas to the east of the Oder and Neisse and in the north of the People's Republic of Poland. Known as '*Volksdeutsche*' (ethnic Germans) these were people who had had Polish nationality before the war but who declared for Germany during the war and were persecuted after the fighting was over.

In the years immediately after the war Gomulka saw the *Volksdeutsche* from a political rather than a national viewpoint. His propaganda encouraged the idea that a *Volksdeutsch* was automatically a Nazi collaborator. The majority of this ethnic group were shut up in forced labour camps. But there were also some *Volksdeutsche* who were left in peace; they were allowed to keep their homes and find work, and in the course of the years many of them made careers and attained high national and party offices – even in the Central Committee of the Polish Communist Party.

But Gomulka still held the opinion that the former citizens of the German Reich, who had not fled or emigrated in the first post-war years and who lived within the frontiers of the new Polish state, represented a serious nationality problem.

In 1963 Gomulka considered that the time had come to expel this ethnic group, most of whom were, in any case, unhappy at being forced to stay in the People's Republic of Poland and had family links with citizens of the GDR and the Federal Republic. He considered this question so important that he put it on the agenda for the party and government discussions with the East German delegation.

During these negotiations, in which all members of both delegations took part, Gomulka broached the subject. He turned to Ulbricht, gave a brief account of his view of the correct policy to take in relation to minority nationalities, and then declared that he would be happy to discuss the solution of the problem – that is the resettling of this national group – with the German side.

But Gomulka had hardly finished his last sentence, which I translated, when Ulbricht gave him an answer that struck all his hearers dumb: 'In my opinion you should lock them all up!'

The two delegations were seated opposite each other at a long, highly-polished table in the building of the Polish Council of Ministers. Behind the principals sat the interpreters, then a third row of experts and advisers and, seated at little tables in the corners of the room, were the experts in protocol and representatives of the Foreign Ministry and of the chancelleries of both Central Committees. Altogether there were at least thirty people present.

Ulbricht's cold, cynical answer took the Poles aback. His words rang through the room. And naturally no other members of the East German delegation protested against this brutal piece of advice.

Disconcerted, I translated the reply made by the Chairman of the East German Council of State. This was the same Ulbricht who claimed to represent the forces of progress in Germany, who took every opportunity to complain about the fall in the population of the GDR and the shortage of labour; Ulbricht, who was well aware that his word is law in the GDR, who claimed to represent the interests of the whole German people – this was the man who was writing off several hundred thousand of his own people with a single sentence.

But what did he mean by his suggestion that these people should be locked up? Was Ulbricht referring to the policy followed by the Poles in the immediate post-war years? What was behind it all? This attitude of Ulbricht's was clearly contrary to the interests of the German Democratic Republic. In autumn 1962, when Gomulka headed a Polish party and government delegation to East Berlin, and also during the present negotiations in Warsaw, Ulbricht himself had explained to the Polish leaders that, before the building of the Berlin Wall, the East German economy had lost the equivalent of thirty billion marks – according to detailed estimates by economic experts – through 'enticement and abduction'. These were the words he used to describe the flight of several million East German citizens to West Germany. So the immigration of the Germans still living in Poland, who included many skilled workers and technicians, would obviously have been in the economic interests of the German Democratic Republic.

After the close of the morning session the East Berlin delegation left the building of the Council of Ministers for internal consultations. The Poles and Germans were to meet again over lunch in an hour's time. Ulbricht and his men had hardly left the room when their hosts began to discuss the problem between themselves. They paid no attention to the fact that the experts, the protocol organizers and I myself, the interpreter, were still in the room. The only man present who did not seem displeased by the turn in events was Aleksander Zawadzki, who at that time was President of Poland.

The general opinion held by the Polish delegation was that Ulbricht had been trying to set a trap for Gomulka. The Polish Communist Party boss – who also seemed quite irritated – finally said, 'There's nothing we can do about it. These people will have to stay here and we can only give them permission to emigrate in specially hard cases. But we cannot solve the problem.'

During the next few days I got into conversation with an East German official. He seemed at first sight to be narrow-minded and orthodox, but during our conversation he gradually opened up and even gave the impression that he felt doubts and a certain scepticism with regard to the internal policies of the East German leadership. It seemed to me that this official was impressed by the personality of Gomulka and admired the trend towards liberalization which the Polish party leadership had set in motion after 1956. He told me that Ulbricht was motivated by a deep personal dislike for Gomulka; the roots of this antipathy lay in a policy speech which the Polish Communist Party leader had made on October 1956. Ulbricht had felt that he was being personally attacked and could not forgive Gomulka for this assault on his character.

I knew that the East German leadership had raised many objections to the new course initiated by Gomulka after the 'Polish October' of 1956 – on occasions the East Berlin party bosses had clearly interfered in Polish internal affairs. This was true, for example, of Gomulka's new agricultural policy when all the collective farms which had been forcibly introduced in Poland were broken up again. The German Democratic Republic was also displeased by Polish policy towards the Church and, of course, even more so by the willingness of the Warsaw leadership to accept American loans to help stabilize the economy. But I had never heard of Gomulka making a personal attack on Ulbricht. On the contrary, I knew that in 1958 both parties and governments had agreed to avoid giving publicity to any disagreements that might arise. In both countries the mass media were to make only 'positive' reports. And Gomulka had even made an ironic reference to this to Ulbricht himself, '*We* have kept strictly to this agreement. Apart from a few small blunders made by journalists who were immediately silenced there have been no attacks on the German Democratic Republic in *our* country.'

Gomulka was right. I had sometimes witnessed quite stormy disagreements between Gomulka and Ulbricht, but I had never seen or heard of any public attack on Ulbricht by the Polish leader. On the contrary, Gomulka always presented the leader of the Socialist Unity Party as a tried and trusty friend of the Polish people.

After my conversation with the East German official I checked in my library at home and had another look at the text of Gomulka's speech in October 1956 in order to discover what my friend from East Berlin had been referring to.

I did not need to look for long. At the Eighth Plenum of the Polish Communist Party Gomulka, who had just been returned to power, had talked of the mistakes and distortions of the Stalinist period and had not confined himself to discussing internal political errors.

Gomulka's actual words on that occasion were as follows: 'In order to govern a country it is essential for the working class and the workers to put their confidence in their representatives who control the power of the state. . . . To lose the confidence of the working class is to lose the ethical basis for the exercise of power. It is possible to govern a country in such conditions. But it will be a bad government. For it must be based on bureaucracy, on the violation of legality and on force. . . . The essence of the cult of the personality rested on the fact that a hierarchical ladder of cults was created.

Each of these cults covered a certain area in which it operated. In the bloc of socialist states Stalin stood on the top rung of this hierarchical ladder. All the leaders who came below him bowed their heads before him. And those to bow their heads included not only the other leaders of the Soviet Communist Party and of the Soviet Union but also the leaders of the communist and workers' parties in the other countries of the socialist camp. They, that is to say the First Secretaries of the Central Committees of the parties in the various countries, were on the second rung of the ladder of the cult of personality. They wore the garments of infallibility and wisdom. But their cult was practised only within the area of their own countries where they stood at the top of the ladder of their own internal cult. . . . The object of the cult of personality was an expert in everything, knew everything, decided everything, controlled everything and organized everything in his area of activity. He was always the cleverest man, irrespective of what knowledge, what abilities and what personal qualifications he possessed. . . . It was bad enough when a reasonable and modest man wore the robes of the cult. . . . But it was worse, much worse when the privilege of exercising power and thus the right to the cult was seized by a narrow man, a man who would carry out orders undeviatingly, or a corrupted careerist. Unthinkingly, and yet efficiently, these men dug a grave for socialism.'

These were the words for which Ulbricht could not forgive Gomulka. The Polish leader referred specifically in this speech to the 'First Secretaries of communist parties in Eastern bloc countries'. This could not be aimed at some countries where the death of the leader had meant that power had passed into other hands, as in the case of Czechoslovakia. And in other socialist countries like Hungary and Bulgaria the First Secretaries had been dismissed at the instigation of the Kremlin. So, apart from Jugoslavia, the only remaining countries were Albania and the German Democratic Republic. Although Gomulka had not mentioned Ulbricht's name in his speech his meaning was obvious to anyone reading or hearing the speech, which was diffused widely through the mass media. Since that time many of Gomulka's speeches have been published in the German Democratic Republic, but never this one.

But to return to the negotiations between Ulbricht and Gomulka. The East German leader had put the fate of the Germans living in Poland in doubt for a considerable time to come. But naturally

Gomulka and the Polish party leadership did not fall into Ulbricht's trap; the German minority was not locked up.

I have observed Walter Ulbricht at close quarters on many occasions. But never before had he revealed himself in his true colours as he did on that morning in September 1963 as he sat at the long negotiating table in the building of the Polish Council of Ministers, and dismissed hundreds of thousands of Germans with a single sentence. Needless to say, the subject was never raised again at any negotiations between East German and Polish leaders. These two neighbouring countries with many interests and problems in common would discuss developments in the Federal Republic, in Greece, in the Near East and in distant Vietnam; they would talk of the people of Asia and Africa and cover every possible subject but one – the question of the Germans in Poland was taboo.

During the twelve years and more that I spent as an interpreter for the Polish party leadership I often had the opportunity to make personal contact with the top leaders and to get to know their opinions. But it was probably even more important for my judgement of political developments that I was able to analyse changes in the behaviour and attitudes of these men. In the ten years between 1958 and 1968 party leaders like Ulbricht and Gomulka changed considerably. Gomulka's personality altered too, but, even more striking were the changes in political methods and the style with which he exercised power.

I first observed Ulbricht at close quarters towards the end of 1958 when he came to Warsaw at the head of a party and government delegation to a summit meeting with the Polish leadership. At that time he was still the undeviating *apparatchik* and supreme dogmatist who never allowed his attitude to be influenced by anything or anyone, but kept strictly to every detail of the political line of the Kremlin. Later, as the GDR grew stronger and as her economic importance for the Eastern bloc increased, he showed more political and personal self-confidence *vis-a-vis* the Soviet leaders. Gomulka, on the other hand, had still not entirely abandoned his ideas of a 'Socialism with a human face' by 1958 – his concept was very similar to that of the Prague Spring; the description current in Poland at the time was 'a socialism that you can enjoy'. To some extent he still felt himself to be the representative of his own country and not yet as the executor of a neo-Stalinist policy directed against the people.

He knew that he had support in many influential circles in Poland and, to a certain extent, from public opinion abroad and from some very important representatives of the World Communist Movement. But on the other hand he had already started to prepare his own political bankruptcy. Yet Gomulka still had an instinct for the mood of the people. He had not yet forgotten his experiences in the previous few years – isolation, dismissal, imprisonment, preparations for a show trial that could only end with a sentence of death, release, a second rise to power. He still felt that his political rehabilitation and appointment as First Secretary of the Polish Communist Party imposed on him a certain obligation to the people. Ulbricht, on the other hand, would hand out slogans and speeches right and left and was obviously delighted when reports piled up on his desk in which he was 'informed' that his slogans for the 'building of socialism' had been converted into facts.

I remember very clearly one dialogue between Ulbricht and Gomulka which showed how different were their political temperaments. After a reception in honour of the East German visitors which took place in the Polish government residence in Krakowskie Przedmiesce Street in Warsaw, the two party leaders were talking in a side-room while the other guests were enjoying the wide range of alcohol supplied in the big reception rooms.

Ulbricht was telling Gomulka that the GDR had had exceptionally good results in the field of polytechnical education. In view of the technological revolution all over the world, he said, it was necessary to familiarize children with the problems of work at a very early age. 'There is one method which we have now adopted. We try to show the children all kinds of different jobs and types of work so as to establish which particular talents are inherent in each child. And we think it is absolutely necessary to instil a respect for work in everyone from earliest childhood.' The SUP leader paused, sipped his drink and continued. 'In practice we organize things like this. Starting in the elementary schools the normal lessons are interrupted for one day a week. On that day the whole class is taken by the teacher to visit a factory – perhaps a metal-working plant, a chemical works or something of the kind. For example, the children may be taken to a mechanical engineering works, to a metal-working shop. Then they are shown all the machine tools and taught how to use a lathe. We have been very successful with this scheme,' he added proudly.

Gomulka was still sceptical, 'You must have a lot of machines that are not needed for production, Comrade Ulbricht.'

'How do you mean?'

'Well, if hundreds of thousands of children and young people are sent into the factories to operate the machines then the machines can't be used for ordinary production at the same time.'

'Oh, that's no problem with us,' claimed Ulbricht, 'that's all organized by the comrades on the spot.'

But Gomulka did not seem satisfied by this reply. 'Then you must have quite a number of surplus skilled workers and foremen in the German Democratic Republic.'

'What makes you think that – in fact we have a serious shortage.'

'Then how is it possible to introduce so many children to practical production? A schoolteacher isn't qualified to do this. After all, he couldn't even specialize in a single industry. If the children are to visit a different factory or workshop every week then a large number of skilled craftsmen must be released to teach production methods to them all.'

'Oh, the comrades sort that out between themselves on the spot,' repeated Ulbricht.

'And what do you do about working clothes?'

'About working clothes?'

'Yes, when the children visit a factory and work on the machines it's unavoidable that they will dirty their clothes with oil and grease. If that happens week after week the parents can't be very happy about it.'

'Comrade Gomulka, that sort of problem can't carry much weight with us when we're organizing polytechnical education.' Ulbricht repeated his favourite phrase, 'When we are building socialism we must be prepared to pay the price; the main thing is that we have achieved excellent results with this method.'

'Perhaps,' replied Gomulka, thoughtfully and with a touch of irony, 'But optimism is not enough on its own.'

This discussion between an *apparatchik* and a politician who was still capable of sensing the mood of the people took place at a time when Gomulka was still liable suddenly to open his briefcase during journeys by plane or train, take out a few sandwiches made up for him by his wife Zofia, and eat them. At that time, if protocol permitted, the Polish leader preferred to dispense with the army of waiters and servants who would swarm around him in later years.

Gomulka was always the victim of his own complexes – always hesitating, putting off decisions and always worrying about the consequences of his actions. Ulbricht, on the other hand, struck me as a cold, calculating functionary who cared only about his own position. He would make decisions, and then always be ready to reverse them the following day and give orders that were completely the opposite. He was not concerned about the effects this might have on the people.

Unlike Gomulka, Ulbricht was never the 'unyielding fighter' of heroic stature as described in the constant flow of SUP propaganda. He would always avoid meeting his opponents face to face. When the situation in Germany became dangerous for him after the Nazi takeover he simply disappeared. During his time in exile in the West and in the Spanish Civil War, he always took care to stay well away from the firing line. And in the Soviet Union he survived all Stalin's bloody purges whole in body and mind. When Stalin's axe fell he was always there, ready to put his comrades' heads on the block and save his own skin. And he came out of it all very well.

These long years of political opportunism must have had an influence on his personality. Ulbricht secretly despises people who stand up for their convictions and who are ready to fight and to die. In this respect too, he and Gomulka are worlds apart.

As a young communist before the war the Polish party leader was imprisoned for his political activities. During the war he fought actively in the Resistance movement at the risk of his own life. At the beginning of the fifties he preferred imprisonment to changing his political attitudes to fit in with the party line. And when he returned to power in 1956 he reacted like a clerk who has suddenly won a million and is always afraid of losing his emotional equilibrium, although he is determined not to give the money up.

Gomulka always tried to live modestly and avoided any personality cult. But he combined this way of life with an exaggerated sense of mission – a psychological combination which sometimes produced very comical results.

Basically a lonely man, Gomulka never tried to hide his own inner insecurity from the men closest to him. He always tried to win the love of his people or, when this was not successful, to compel it. When he was confronted with a big, cheering crowd his heart melted like hailstones in the sun. During one so-called friendship visit to the GDR by a Polish party and government delegation we were driving through the Halle/Saale district one evening. The column of black government limousines was a hundred yards long and the street was naturally closed to other traffic.

In one of the first cars, behind the television and newspaper reporters and the police and security cars, was the car with Gomulka sitting in front beside the chauffeur with Ulbricht and Comrade König, representing the local authorities, in the back seat.

It was already dark and quite cold. But our German hosts had carried out their preparations efficiently. For miles the road was lined on both sides with thousands and thousands of children waving little paper flags. And every ten or fifteen yards stood a teacher or official, checking that the applause was 'genuine' enough.

The poor children's faces were quite blue with cold. But as our car approached they waved their flags and shouted 'Ulbricht, Gomulka, friendship'. I ducked down in the back seat so as not to confuse the crowd. Who's that gentleman we don't know sitting next to Ulbricht?

Of course, Gomulka knew that this kind of 'spontaneous' demonstration of enthusiasm was organized and could work out how many hours beforehand the children had been collected, how many hours they had been standing waiting in the street, in the cold and damp. He knew perfectly well that on this kind of occasion lists are drawn up of everyone who is to take part so that no one gets a chance to slip away. Yet after the first quarter of an hour of the drive Gomulka was genuinely deeply moved.

He opened the front right-hand window of the car, waved and called to the crowd, '*Moi kochani*, *moi kochani*!' (my darlings, my darlings).

I had observed similar sentimental reactions in him in Poland, especially after 1956 when there was a genuine sympathy for him. At that time the people were ready to forgive his crimes between 1944 and 1948 when thousands of former members of the Home Army (AK), the opposition Polish Peasants' Party (PSL) and liberal Social Democrats were imprisoned and executed without trial. After all, thought most people, he himself had suffered under the system for years, and must have changed completely.

At this time he was the only communist leader in any communist country, to have a chance of being accepted by the whole people. But he threw away that chance, finally and irrevocably, through his later policies.

As Chairman of the Council of State Ulbricht tried to take on the appearance of the father of his country, eager to win the affection of his subordinates, but this attitude always seemed strained. At the numerous conferences and visits where I observed him he gave me the impression of a mixture of an upstart and a cunning and brutal sergeant who, through a fortunate combination of circumstances, has risen to the rank of general but who cannot and will not throw off his old tricks and habits. For him, the men surrounding him were always only pawns and he despised the 'great masses'. Gomulka, on the other hand, was only too often made the puppet of opponents from within his own ranks.

A communist party leader in the Eastern bloc must use every means available to build up his own position at all times; he must eliminate both actual and potential opponents, critics and personal enemies. Stalin had developed this policy to a fine art. He started by killing off his opponents and then went on to his faithful followers. Anyone who survived the massacre had understood: there was only one master and apart from him no one could be sure of his position, his freedom or even his life.

After Stalin's death all this altered. When Krushchev had climbed to the top of the ladder of power he sent his opponents, Kaganovich, Malenkov, Bulganin, Voroshilov etc. (with the exception of the executed Beria) into political exile, but did not take their lives. His successor as party leader, Leonid Brezhnev, had to be even more circumspect. The various factions in the Kremlin leadership did not permit him to take too much power into his own hands. He always had to play one group off against another in order to save himself from falling victim to them.

Depending on the current situation, Ulbricht would follow Stalin's methods or Krushchev's recipe in turn. During the period of Stalin's rule he had succeeded in eliminating all the communist leaders who might have been dangerous to him in a future communist state on German territory. After the war he gradually consolidated his position with foresight and energy, built up his personal following, banished his opponents and consistently based his policies on the faction in the Kremlin which seemed, according to his careful analysis, to have the best 'prospects'.

Once he could be sure of sufficient support from Moscow, his way was clear to becoming the nominal head of state and effective sole ruler of the German Democratic Republic. Ulbricht was, and is, a connoisseur in intrigue and plotting, and he by no means confines his efforts to the area of the GDR.

But it is underestimating the East German leader to call him simply a 'creature of the Kremlin'. Ulbricht could play an independent role *vis-a-vis* the various factions in the Kremlin because these groups were anxious to find allies among the party leaders in other eastern countries, because the GDR had become steadily more important, both economically and politically, to the Soviet Union in recent years and – perhaps the most important reason – because Ulbricht's personality and policies seemed to the Moscow leadership to offer the best chance of the maximum political and ideological stability in the GDR.

This aspect became very clear to me when I acted as interpreter at a meeting in Warsaw early in 1967 when leading representatives of the different communist parties were preparing the Karlovy Vary conference. These talks, or more accurately, these ideological battles, lasted for several days. Finally, the Polish hosts gave a reception at the official residence of Prime Minister Cyrankiewicz. On this occasion Gomulka had a long conversation with Hermann Matern, the leader of the East German delegation. I translated for them and stayed close to Gomulka when our East German visitor was led away by the East German Ambassador in Warsaw, Karl Mewis, to be introduced to a fellow guest. A few minutes later the leader of the Soviet delegation – as far as I remember it was Ponomarev, the Central Committee Secretary, approached Gomulka and discussed various problems connected with the Karlovy Vary conference before going on to talk about the German Democratic Republic and the role played by Ulbricht. I got the impression that Ponomarev was not one of Ulbricht's admirers. He told Gomulka that in his opinion there were still many mistakes being made in the German Democratic Republic and that, in certain matters, Comrade Ulbricht took a very 'independent' attitude. On the other hand, continued Ponomarev, it would be a big mistake to abandon Ulbricht – was he referring to policies once considered by Krushchev as party leader of the Soviet Union? – for the SUP leader had succeeded in consolidating a socialist order of society in the German Democratic Republic, not least through his own strong personality. If Ulbricht, continued Ponomarev, were for any reason to fall from power tomorrow then we could expect struggles for power to break out within the SUP leadership which would soon weaken the German Democratic

Republic and the whole socialist camp. So it is clear that Ulbricht was even supported by those men in the Kremlin who regarded his personality and his policies with scepticism.

The East German ex-leader had also used all the well-tried methods usual in dictatorships to corrupt other men and consolidate his own position. The money was of course paid out by the State. In the GDR party officials, scientists, artists, soldiers and security officials have been showered with orders, medals and decorations which are often accompanied by considerable money awards. Gomulka was very different: he tried to impose his own ascetic way of life on the men around him, and this made him many enemies.

It seemed to me that Ulbricht himself did not attach any great value to academic experts. As an interpreter I never heard him say anything on scientific or economic matters that showed a grasp of the subject. Perhaps he did have expert knowledge, but if so he hid it in a very convincing way. Gomulka may not be much of an intellectual but at least he has devoted a considerable amount of time to economic problems and has a detailed knowledge of this subject. He knew the Statistical Yearbook for Poland practically off by heart.

On one occasion when I accompanied a party and government delegation to the German Democratic Republic, Gomulka and his entourage visited an agricultural production co-operative. He caused great confusion among the specialists on the co-operative and the agricultural experts from the Socialist Unity Party and the East German government because he wanted to involve them in a technical discussion on the basis of his detailed knowledge of agricultural economics. In the end he was introduced to a worthy lady cattle breeder. Gomulka was not satisfied with general information but addressed some very precise questions to the young woman, such as 'How many units of grain do you need in your agricultural co-operative to get a kilogram increase in live-weight in a single bullock?' The cattle girl gave a general answer, saying that important progress had been made in this area in the GDR, especially after the last Plenum of the SUP Central Committee that had considered agricultural problems in the GDR. But Gomulka insisted on a more concrete answer. He repeated his question several times but never got a satisfactory reply. So he began to deliver a lecture himself, explaining how much grain was needed in Poland to increase the live-weight of a bullock by one kilogram, and what combination of cattle feeds had given the best results.

When he was visiting a factory and talking to the marketing, technical and political directors of the business he asked them how many rejects there were in the production of semi-conductors. His hosts were not capable of giving him a precise figure for their factory. Whereupon Gomulka admitted to them that in Poland rejected semi-conductors amounted to eighty per cent, so that only a fifth of the entire production was usable. Then there was the same comedy again. He questioned the East German experts, but they would not give him an adequate answer. He asked power technicians how much was the percentage loss of power with overground supplies – without any success. It was the same when he asked the East German deputy Premier, Alexander Abusch, how big was the *per capita* consumption of fish in the GDR. Abusch avoided giving him an exact answer, saying that for a long time results in this area had been disappointing but that, after the latest decisions taken by some authority or other, some progress had at last been made. Whatever economic subject he broached at discussions with German colleagues, Gomulka was very knowledgeable, throwing out figures, dates and indices, showing an accurate knowledge of production figures and problems in every sector.

However, as time went on Gomulka's interest in such economic details waned. In 1967 during the Seventh SUP Congress there was an argument in the East German guest-house between two members of the Polish delegation, both Politburo members, the deputy Prime Minister, Eugeniusz Szyr and the Central Committee Secretary, Ryszard Strzelecki. The disagreement concerned production figures for tractors but to the careful listener, familiar with the background to the quarrel, it was easy to see that the two officials were not really arguing about tractor production but about differences between two opposing factions within the Polish party leadership. Gomulka, who had introduced the new Polish agricultural policy after 1956, did not join in the debate at first but towards the end he interrupted the two fighting cocks, 'Well, how many many tractors do we make each year in Poland? Is it 25,000 or 125,000?' A few years earlier he would not have had to ask the question – he would have named the exact figure himself.

At this time there was another discussion between Szyr and Gomulka, who kept stating the thesis that it was only in the West that goods had to be attractively packaged because otherwise the manufacturers would lose out in the capitalist competition war.

But in Poland the only important thing was for the contents to be of good quality, the packaging was unimportant. Szyr and Gomulka got quite worked up about Polish light industry, whose products the leader was criticizing – in particular he did not like the selection of ladies' lingerie on sale in the shops. Szyr countered quickly, 'It's quite true. The GDR makes much prettier lingerie.' Then he paused for a moment and added, with a triumphant glance at Gomulka, 'So you see, packaging is not so unimportant after all.' Everyone laughed and peace was restored once more.

I found the attitude of the two party leaders to the arts particularly interesting. Ulbricht is very well read and is sufficiently familiar with classical music, the plastic and graphic arts, and classical German literature to conduct an intelligent discussion about them. Of course, his opinions in artistic matters are based on the narrow tenets of socialist realism, but he is well aware of the importance of the arts for forming the political consciousness of the masses. He looks on art as an instrument of his power. Gomulka is more sceptical. He is interested only in literature and the cinema because he believes that these two arts alone can influence the minds of the people. He is indifferent to music and the plastic and graphic arts. As he said soon after 1956, in these two areas 'one can do the most by doing as little as possible'. And the cultural policy of the Polish Communist Party followed this precept for the next few years.

In the beginning there was another character trait where Ulbricht and Gomulka differed profoundly. But with time Gomulka showed that he was a good pupil. I am thinking of the quality of honesty. During an intergovernmental meeting early in the sixties Gomulka was still shocked when Ulbricht explained one of his tactics to him: 'We unleash a big campaign, even if it is completely groundless. We use our whole propaganda machine against our opponent. After three months we let the whole thing blow over and don't waste any more words on it. But some of the mud sticks to the man who has been attacked, and that is very useful for us.'

In later years Gomulka drew his own conclusions from this lesson and perfected the technique for his own use. But in one respect he always acted correctly. If Poland accepted credits from foreign countries Gomulka always insisted on repaying them on time, but at the same time he was always ready to join in the most enormous swindles, either at the expense of his own people or of the West. So long as his conscience was clear he was happy – and that was easy for him. Communist ideology has a justification ready for any doubters: 'Anything which is done for the good of our cause is justified.' If you can believe in that then you can be at peace with yourself and with the world.

So Gomulka was able to trample on all the promises that he had sworn to carry out after 1956 without any crisis of conscience. At that time he had promised to consolidate Poland's sovereignty *vis-a-vis* the Soviet Union, but in reality he chained his country even more firmly to its 'big brother'. The same thing happened with the concept of equal rights between the different communist parties. After twelve years the Polish United Workers' party (the communist party) had simply dropped the demand. On the contrary Gomulka demonstrated how he could 'serve the cause with a clear conscience' in his attitude to the attack on Czechoslovakia. In 1956 the promise was made that Poland would be a country governed with strict legality. And a few years later, when I was translating at a meeting between Ochab and the general secretary of a Scandinavian communist party, Ochab was able to assure him with perfect truth that there was not a single political prisoner in Poland. Yet twelve years later a whole series of political show trials took place virtually behind closed doors. Moczar's men could imprison anyone they liked; prisoners were tortured during interrogation.

I have described in a previous chapter how the methods of government proclaimed in 1956 'developed' in later years, and the role that devolved on the parliament. But whatever the problem – in questions of general economic policy or of worker participation in the running of their factories, in foreign policy or foreign trade, in matters of personal freedom or politics, Gomulka could wash his hands of any guilt because he was convinced that anything that served the cause was justified.

Only occasionally did the Polish Communist Party leader give way to his notorious outbursts of rage – when some eager follower would bring him details of current news reports. Even when he was abroad this ritual would always be carried out. Gomulka would always begin by reaching for the radio bulletins which included a report of the transmissions of Radio Free Europe prepared by a special department of the Polish radio for a small circle of top party officials. On reading these Gomulka would fly into an almost masochistic rage.

Had Radio Free Europe become the voice of Gomulka's uneasy

conscience, or did he regard it as a real and powerful opposition force which could influence the majority of the Polish people (even, paradoxically, including himself)?

Whatever the truth of the matter, as far as the Polish leadership was concerned the concept of honesty was dead. Here too Gomulka had caught up with Ulbricht and in some respects even surpassed him.

Ulbricht was usually reserved in his dealings with me. He seemed not to be able to forgive me for the fact that we had often competed in seeing which of us could shout the louder. As soon as Gomulka had pronounced a few sentences in discussions with Ulbricht I would translate them into German. But if Ulbricht did not agree with the statement Gomulka had made he would try to reply immediately. Since he speaks Russian very well he could also understand most of what Gomulka was saying in Polish. As interpreter I was Gomulka's mouthpiece – he once said to Ulbricht in Polish, 'He is my tongue'. So he expected me to translate each sentence in its entirety. Therefore when Ulbricht interrupted me after the first few words to express his disagreement I did not consider myself merely an interpreter being interrupted by Ulbricht, but as 'Gomulka's tongue'. So I would simply speak louder, whereupon Ulbricht would raise his voice too, and I would shout even louder until I had completed Gomulka's sentence.

Since at official party and government meetings there would always be between fifteen and twenty officials present on each side, including Ulbricht's own advisers, he would always be furious that anyone could dare to shout him down.

But it was a different matter when Ulbricht came to Poland and had to address large crowds of people without preparation, since on these occasions I would only have to translate his own words. At these times he would act in a very friendly way towards me. On the first of Ulbricht's visits where I was present he brought an interpreter with him who did not translate his words with complete accuracy. The East German leader noticed this immediately and turned to me, asking 'Is he translating that right?' As it happened I had 'switched off' mentally, for on such occasions an interpreter gets in the habit of using every free minute for mental relaxation. So I replied, 'Certainly, he's translating very well.' But Ulbricht interrupted his interpreter, told him he would like to repeat his last sentence in such and such a way, and asked me to translate his words into Polish. At times like this he seemed to forget our shouting matches during his talks with Gomulka.

I have already pointed out that Ulbricht was a more skilful tactician in the manipulation of power than Gomulka. An East German communist official once described to me how Ulbricht had managed to explain the Twentieth Congress of the Soviet Communist Party when Krushchev denounced Stalin's crimes in his own country. On his return from Moscow Ulbricht made a speech at the University of Social Sciences in Babelsberg near Berlin in which he immediately adopted the new Krushchev line and strongly condemned Stalin, the man whom he had set up as an idol for decades.

After Ulbricht's speech one of the students taking part in the closing discussion referred to his own notes and said, 'But Comrade Ulbricht, a few years ago you told us something completely different about Stalin.' The East German leader answered without any hesitation, 'What I have said, I have said, but if you have misunderstood my meaning that is your own fault.' This kind of argument is typical of Ulbricht. Whenever I observed him at political talks he was always very quick off the mark and clever at using modified versions of Stalinist theories as a political weapon even after the death of the dictator of the Kremlin. For example, Stalin had declared that, with the building of socialism, the class war in socialist countries would be intensified because the class enemy would make increasingly desperate attempts at disruption. This theory was essential for Stalin to justify the terror in his own country. But Ulbricht borrowed the precept at a time when nobody in the communist movement was still talking about an intensification of the class struggle, reformulated it in a 'creative' way, and then took every opportunity to declare that the power of the party could only be strengthened and socialism only made a reality if due attention was paid to the fact that – in the German Democratic Republic at least – the former Nazis and Neo-Nazis, the revanchists, militarists, fascists and monopoly capitalists, were constantly stepping up their battle to weaken the German Democratic Republic in order to prepare an eventual takeover. The East German party leader also drew a similar conclusion to Stalin: 'So, as we advance towards the building of socialism we must intensify our war against the class enemy.'

In the years immediately following the war it soon became apparent how Ulbricht really waged this class war. The German Democratic Republic had not even been established as a sovereign state before Ulbricht started appointing junior and medium-ranking Nazis and even senior officers in the wartime Wehrmacht to key positions in the state apparatus. At the same time he discarded many German communists who had been thrown into Hitler's concentration camps and had remained true to their convictions, often despite brutal tortures.

I clearly remember one occasion when Gomulka asked Ulbricht if there were any former Nazis in influential positions in the German Democratic Republic. Immediately the East German leader explained that the GDR had always suffered from a severe shortage of cadres, since many comrades from the old German Communist Party had been in prison and in concentration camps during the Nazi period and, as Ulbricht expressed it, had suffered from a twelve-year gap in the formation of their consciousness. During this time they had been completely isolated from the workers' movement and had not been able to share in the development of socialism between 1933 and 1945. Moreover it should not be forgotten, continued Ulbricht, that these comrades had often collaborated closely with the traditional enemies of the German working class, social democrats, Christians and so on, and in this way had adopted some of the ways of thought of their opponents. 'Naturally we cannot rely on this kind of man, Comrade Gomulka, although there are many among them who have made honest and sincere attempts since the war to close this gap in the formation of their consciousness.'

This explanation by Ulbricht in fact represented one of the most important principles of his personal politics. In his opinion it was preferable to fill important posts with former Nazis rather than with convinced communists who had survived Hitler's concentration camps. For he possessed complete dossiers on the Nazis. They were well aware of this fact and so made obedient followers. It was a case of 'do what you're told and be a good boy, or we'll fix you'. But the battle-hardened communists from the old German Communist Party who had really suffered for their beliefs would not have been ready, as Ulbricht realized perfectly well, to accept in silence or to support his constant shifts in policy and limitless opportunism.

Gomulka, on the other hand, never learnt how to strengthen his own position through the use of clever tactics in his personal politics – on the contrary. He was even reluctant to make personal capital out of the fact that he had been overthrown in 1948 and then condemned and imprisoned by the party leadership. When he returned to power in 1956 the Stalinists in Poland immediately tried to frustrate his reform policies with the help of their outworn old catch-phrases. But naturally they did not make much impression on the people with this method. For example, the accusation that Gomulka was selling Poland to the capitalists by accepting deliveries of wheat from the United States did not cut much ice in a country that was literally threatened by famine. So the Polish Stalinists, known as the Natolin Group after the palace near Warsaw where they held their meetings, became an isolated political sect who could evoke no response in the people.

But unlike Ulbricht, Gomulka felt compelled to seek support from his former opponents. In 1956 there was hardly one senior member of the Polish party leadership who had not strongly condemned Gomulka and 'Gomulkaism' at an earlier period. Even the present Polish President, Marshal Spychalski, who was first made Defence Minister and then appointed to the Politburo by Gomulka, had made one of the most outspoken speeches of accusation against him in 1948.

For a long time Gomulka kept all the men who had brought him to power out of the leadership. For example, Ochab, Rapacki, Morawski and others lost their seats on the Politburo. Gomulka also gradually filled the key Central Committee Secretariat with his former opponents. Finally he even agreed to the dismissal of the 'liberals' among the regional secretaries of the party. This meant that there were no more liberals left among a group of party officials who had acquired great influence in recent years because it was they who decided who should be elected to the Central Committee before each party congress. During the period of political ferment in 1955/6 the party secretaries in a few of the most important regions had come out on the side of fundamental reforms, and therefore of Gomulka – including, for example, Staszewski, the Secretary for the Warsaw district, Wojas, the Secretary for Opole, Mrs Tatarkowna, the secretary for Lodz, and many others. Their opponents seem to have passed on incriminating material about them to Gomulka and he made sure that they disappeared from view.

He acted in a similar way as regards the staffing of the mass media. In 1955/6 the press and radio had earned the gratitude of the political reform movement in Poland. But now Gomulka had all the journalists who had fought passionately at his side against Stalinism dismissed or side-tracked into unimportant jobs. And he closed down many of the journals which had helped him on his way to power.

To me from my position outside the party bureaucracy and intrigues Gomulka gave the impression of a man who was systematically preparing his own downfall. In November 1968 his opponents intended to sit in judgement on him at the party congress of the Polish Communist Party. They did not succeed in their purpose only because the right men in the Kremlin, led by the party boss, Brezhnev, demonstrated their support for Gomulka. They had realized that his opponents were forming a strong and unified front. So, according to the old principle of '*Divide et impera*' (divide and rule) – Moscow thought it better for there to be several factions vying for power within the Polish party and government leadership. In this way it would be easier to control things for themselves.

By this time Gomulka was already totally committed to the Russians, for better or worse. He allowed himself to be talked into dismissing his comparatively liberal Interior Minister, Wicha, and replacing him in this particularly vital post in a socialist state by Mieczyslaw Moczar, a man who was later to put himself at the head of his opponents. Moczar lost no time in building his ministry into a highly effective instrument of political power. He knew how to win Gomulka's confidence and then took every opportunity to go behind his back. He and his henchmen filtered all the information that reached Gomulka. They decided what the party leader should be told and what should be hidden from him. Moczar formed alliances with the widest possible range of factions in the party and state apparatus. He allied himself with the Natolin Group of old Stalinists, won over a few cynical writers and journalists to his cause and appointed them to senior posts and allied himself with the pseudo-Catholic PAX movement, which was really subsidized by Moscow. He got himself elected President of the Union of Former Resistance Fighters and tried in this way to win the support of the Poles who had fought in the Home Army during the war. He obtained material advantages for many of these veterans, and honoured them with the highest distinctions.

In all his political intrigues Moczar had an easy time for, unlike Ulbricht, Gomulka was not wily enough to realize what was really happening. He accepted most of the officials proposed by his opponent back in the party leadership. And since they now held key positions they were soon able to get control of almost the whole apparatus of the Polish Communist Party. This made them very valuable partners for Moczar. Gomulka even appointed to his secretariat, which included his closest assistants, officials who were completely under Moczar's control. So now he was absolutely isolated within the party apparatus.

But this was not enough for his opponents. They remembered Krushchev's words about Tito at the Twentieth Party Congress of the Soviet Communist Party: 'Why could even the all-powerful Stalin not manage to destroy his opponent, Josip Tito? Because not only the whole communist party but the whole people stood firm behind the Jugoslav leader'. So, they concluded, the Polish party leader must not only be isolated within the communist party apparatus – that they had already achieved – but in order to complete the process of neutralizing him politically they must also manage to set him, the hero of all Poland in 1956, at odds with the people. And in his naive way Gomulka fell in with their plans.

In the last ten to twelve years not a single unpopular measure has been taken by the Polish party and state leadership without Gomulka being publicly recognized as its initiator. First of all he agreed to brand Imre Nagy, the Hungarian reforming politician who was abducted and later murdered at the end of the revolt in Budapest, as a 'revisionist' in a speech he made to the workers in a Danzig dockyard. Then he made public attacks against progressive Polish writers. And whenever the Government announced an unpopular increase in the price of electricity, rents, public transport, food or other consumer goods, Gomulka would always appear on television and declare that the decision to make the price increases was his. After he had succeeded in this way in setting the party officials, then the writers, journalists and artists, and finally even the workers against him, it was the turn of the Church. The decisive factor in the battle against the Catholic Church in Poland was not only the fact that Gomulka was given misleading information. The cabal surrounding him found their task made easier by a careful study of his own character. He hated the Church because, in the Polish situation, it had the better arguments on its side. For Gomulka was not surrounded by other atheists. His inner insecurity and complexes were heightened by the fact that the Church had the upper hand in the battle to win over the minds of the people. For centuries the Church had set out not only religious but also ethical standards. If Gomulka could not manage to replace the traditional standards, passed down from parents to children, by the new 'socialist' principles, then he was quite prepared to throw out the baby with the bath-water. In a country in the process of industrialization, with millions of young people leaving the villages for the towns who were no longer peasants but not yet used to being industrial workers, and with all the social tensions that this process involved, it would have been only sensible to maintain the old inherited principles of morality. But, influenced by his overriding envy of the Church, Gomulka preferred to cut off his nose to spite his face. Down with the Church, and with the moral standards laid down by religion. He did not realize that this attitude represented a further step towards his own isolation.

Then there were the peasants. They remembered only too well how, during the Stalinist period, they had been forced into collective farms, and all the slogans that had been dinned into them at that time. After Gomulka's return to power in 1956 these compulsory peasants' collectives were almost automatically dissolved. But now Gomulka's 'advisers' were flooding him with analyses of the shortcomings of Polish agriculture. They persuaded him to accept legislation directed against the peasants, and finally they even managed to get Gomulka to discuss the subject before the television cameras. In a speech which was transmitted live he read a text, prepared by one of his secretaries, in which he declared, among other things, that the anachronistic catch-phrase, 'The land belongs to me' must be discarded. When one peasant gets forty hundredweights of grain from a hectare, and another peasant much less, then it is not just his own private affair – the second peasant is acting against the interests of socialism in Poland. The Polish peasants heard these words from the mouth of the man who had once developed a most liberal agricultural policy and were filled with scorn and fury. They knew only too well what statements of this kind could mean for them in the future.

So gradually Gomulka won himself the enmity of all the groups within the Polish people who had once ranged themselves behind him and supported some of his policies with great enthusiasm. On the one hand he was persuaded to make an attack on the Jews and suggest that they represented a Fifth Column within Poland; on the other he waged a war against the Church, and on yet another against the youth of Poland. In this way he lost the sympathy of his own people.

Even after 1956 Gomulka enjoyed considerable popularity among other communist parties. So it was also important to discredit him abroad. The way he fell into the carefully prepared trap and, with the support of his opponents, came out against the communist parties of Jugloslavia, Rumania and other countries, is yet another example of the way he helped to prepare his own downfall. His 'advisers' even managed to destroy his credit in Western countries. They presented him with data and wrote speeches for him which were based on false and hair-splitting theories about the policies of the Western powers and the conditions of life in the West. In this area too he compromised himself, and often the Polish people as well, in the eyes of the world.

During the stormy weeks of October 1956 the leadership of the Chinese Communist Party had interceded in Gomulka's favour in Moscow. When Ulbricht came to Warsaw in 1963 for negotiations with Gomulka, he tried to persuade the Polish party leader to come out against the Chinese party leadership. At that time Gomulka rejected this proposal of Ulbricht's in no uncertain terms. He declared categorically during the official discussions with the East German delegation that Ulbricht was completely wrong in saying that the leadership of the Chinese Communist Party was isolated from the people and from its own party. At that time he also decisively rejected the suggestion of a world conference of communist parties intended by its Soviet initiators to condemn the heretics and dissidents within the world communist movement and restore unrestricted leadership to Moscow. But a few years later Gomulka's political scope was so limited that he had to adopt all the theories of the most orthodox forces in the socialist camp. Now it was already too late for him to develop consistent and well-conceived policies that would enable him to play a similar role to the Rumanian party chief, Ceaucescu, within the Eastern bloc. Instead he was forced personally to condemn the Rumanians. A clever tactician like Walter Ulbricht would never have allowed himself to be manœuvred into a situation where his freedom of political action was limited in this way.

The men in power in the Eastern bloc talk constantly of 'internationalism'; but at the same time they follow their own national interests – apart from a few tactical moves – in economics, foreign trade and even in ideology. No friendly neighbour relationship of the type that has developed since the end of the war between the French and the Germans has ever linked the Poles with the Russians, or the Czechs, or even with the people of the German

Democratic Republic. They have remained strangers to each other – in accordance with the deliberate intention of Gomulka and Ulbricht.

There can be no doubt that both these men will be condemned in the history of their people. The future historian will not be able to get away from the question of why nothing was done for a quarter of a century to reconcile the two peoples. After all, according to the declarations of their leaders there was no frontier problem between Poland and the GDR, no economic competition, no insurmountable national rivalry. Gomulka and Ulbricht obviously do not have enough imagination to foresee what the children of future generations will read about these two politicians in their history books. Otherwise they would surely make every effort to improve the rating of their 'historical' role by a few points.

In both Poland and the GDR, as in other socialist countries, the men in power try, in a few areas at least, to build bridges between themselves and the people, and to find a cause where the broad masses can identify themselves with the regime. I explain in another chapter how a not unsuccessful attempt was made to transform the people's hatred for the Nazis into a 'bridge' of this kind.

Even Stalin realized that traditional patriotism rooted in the popular consciousness could have its uses in this respect. Following his example, the strict Marxist interpretation of the past history of the two peoples was abandoned in Poland and in the GDR. So now kings, army commanders, nobles had to be used in the service of the right kind of patriotic propaganda. Ceremonies commemorating historical events, education programmes for schools, books and articles all played their part in raising the morale of the population.

I cannot judge what effect this campaign had in the GDR. But one discussion between Ulbricht and Gomulka seemed significant to me. The latter asked why the uniforms designed for the army and police in the GDR so closely resembled those of the Third Reich. Ulbricht explained that this problem had been comprehensively discussed both by the SUP leadership and by their Soviet friends. And they had come to the conclusion that the important thing was the political content, not the form. 'We give people *their* uniforms – a compromise perhaps, but in this way we win them over and it is easier to make them into good communists.'

However, in Poland, the emphasis put on patriotism had a completely different result from the one envisaged. Among the less enlightened people patriotism quickly developed into nationalism and, as for the others the Polish leadership had overlooked one important historical phenomenon. In Poland patriotic feelings had always been aroused at times when the people did not identify with those in power over them, and they always represented an opposition force. And therefore, whether they are governed by their own compatriots or whether there is a bigger neighbour breathing down their necks, the Poles have acquired, in the course of history, an unerring instinct for sensing the true state of affairs.

Gomulka preferred not to see all this. And Ulbricht? Ulbricht would really like his German Democratic Republic to be at least a thousand years old. Then he would find it much easier to suppress 'the reconciliation' between the two halves of the German people and would not have to spend so much energy on keeping the Germans of East and West living their separate lives.

The little Saxon carpenter of long ago who came to decide the fate of millions is a man I know well enough to realize how indifferent he is to other people. In the first pages of this chapter I have described what a diabolical solution he proposed to Gomulka for dealing with the Germans in Poland. During the same visit in 1963 he also confided in his hosts his own method of dealing with the Germans to the west of the Elbe. I can still hear his fluting Saxon voice: 'We get a lot of visitors from West Germany. They come to a country that in their eyes does not even exist, whose existence they do not recognize. So we do this: we imprison, say, one in every ten thousand. He simply disappears. Nobody knows where he is and what is happening to him – not even our own ministers. After a certain length of time we let him out again. Eventually these good people will finally realize that we are a sovereign state.'

I don't know how sovereign the GDR actually is when it is a question of real power politics; as an interpreter I have witnessed many scenes which have made me doubt the sovereignty of the GDR. But how sovereign Walter Ulbricht was when he decided the fate of the people in his power – there I have no doubts at all.

CHAPTER II

The Ultimatum to Dubcek

How many nightingales must be a beast of prey eat before it begins to sing? This ironical question posed by a Polish satirist is not just a play on words but the expression of bitter political experience and knowledge. World public opinion was shocked and disconcerted when the news came of the invasion of Czechoslovakia early in the morning of August 21, 1968. Why had it happened? Communism was a wonderful ideal. But in practice, when the ideal was used as a basis for government, the system devoured nightingale after nightingale during the fifty years of its existence without showing any sign of roaring less fiercely. The West, or at least many circles in the West, had gradually allowed themselves to be lulled into a feeling of security. People could watch the successes of Russian athletes in the Olympic Games and of Russian hockey teams on television, they could listen to Russian musicians of the rank of an Oistrakh or a Rostropovich, and they could see that these were people just like themselves. The caricature version of the Bolshevik running round with a knife between his teeth appeared out of date and out of touch with the facts. Stalin was dead, the Soviet Union had evolved, and the example of China had forced the Soviet leaders to start to see reason. So people said to themselves, 'They're not as bad as all that.' Moreover, the Soviet Union had solemnly declared that it would not interfere in the internal affairs of Czechoslovakia.

But it was not difficult for the Western world to work out its own version of the history of the USSR, a version that would differ considerably from the official interpretation put out in the East. One betrayal of trust, one broken promise has followed another. Brutality, cruelty and naked force have held sway, combined with a complete disregard for people, for the individual, for whole nations. When it is a question of preserving the power of the dictators who rule against the will of those they govern, then any means is sanctioned.

In the night of August 20 to 21 I was awakened by the noise of planes flying over Warsaw. It was the same with hundreds of thousands of other citizens of the capital. I was roused from sleep with a start and immediately realized what was happening. The planned invasion had been carried out. Nothing, not even the appeals to reason from among their own ranks, had been able to restrain the rulers of the Soviet Union, Poland, the GDR, Bulgaria and Hungary from risking a military struggle with a fraternal communist state whose only crime had been to try to build a 'socialism with a human face'. All the solemn promises, all the formulas agreed at bilateral and multilateral meetings had been swept away. So you want communism to be human? We'll soon teach you to know better. The beast of prey had planned its revenge and was preparing to swallow yet another nightingale.

The invasion was no surprise for me. Six weeks earlier I had acted as interpreter at a summit meeting between the five participating Warsaw Pact countries when an ultimatum addressed to the Czechoslovak communist leadership under Alexander Dubcek was formulated and disguised in the form of a letter. On that day the solemn declarations of the Soviet leadership that they did not want to interfere in the internal affairs of other socialist countries were forgotten. All the relevant clauses in bilateral and multilateral agreements were worth less than the paper they were written on. So you Czechs and Slovaks want human socialism? We'll show you who's master in your house.

The party leaders of the five invading countries had arranged their Warsaw meeting at very short notice. In the night of July 13 to 14 the telephone rang in my home. It was Trepczynski.

'I'm sorry to disturb you so late, Comrade Weit. Can you be at the Prime Minister's office in the Aleje Ujazdowski at 8 oclock tomorrow morning, Sunday?'

'What's it all about?'

'You'll be given all the details on the spot tomorrow morning. Your pass will be waiting for you with the porter downstairs.'

Before I went back to sleep I set my alarm clock for half past six so as not to oversleep. My plans for Sunday had been wrecked once again. I hoped it would just be a short discussion which I would have to translate. Perhaps Ulbricht or some other East

German official was making a flying visit to Warsaw, or stopping off in the Polish capital on his way to the Soviet Union. I had already been summoned to brief discussions of this kind on several previous occasions and sometimes I had been able to get away within an hour. I had no inkling of a summit conference on that July night because I had not seen any announcement of a top level meeting in the previous few days.

On the Sunday morning I got into my car and drove to the headquarters of the Council of Ministers. Several hundred yards before arriving at the building in the Aleje Ujazdowskie I came upon a great crowd of uniformed and plain-clothes policemen who were guarding the approaches to the building. At this early hour there was little traffic and most people were still sleeping.

I drove past the government building, parked my car in a side-street and walked back the few hundred yards to the main entrance. In these few minutes the guard on the Council of Ministers building had been further strengthened but I was able to pass unchallenged through the enormous entrance doors. On the right of the entrance hall sat a man in civilian clothes at a table specially set up for the purpose, on which were several lists of names. The hall was swarming with security guards. I went up to the table, announced my name, and explained that Trepczynski had summoned me to the ministerial building by telephone. The official asked me what function I was to carry out, leafed through his lists, found my name, made a short telephone call and handed me a pass.

I climbed the splendid staircase to the first floor and immediately saw some familiar faces: staff from Gomulka's office, secretaries, interpreters. I was taken to a large room which had been quickly converted into a conference hall. In the middle stood a big round table with places for at least twenty to thirty people. On the right cubicles had been set up for the interpreters. Electricians were busy testing the leads from the microphones on the table to the translators' cubicles and between their own control panels.

I still had no idea what it was all about but was soon told that a summit conference about developments in Czechoslovakia was to take place in this room. The meeting had been arranged on the previous day and all the extensive preparations had only been begun on the previous evening.

Just before ten o'clock we interpreters were given lists of names of the delegations who had now arrived. The Soviet leadership was represented by Brezhnev, the Secretary General of the Central Committee of the Soviet Communist Party, Podgorny, the President of the Supreme Soviet, Prime Minister Kosygin, Shelest, the First Secretary of the Ukrainian Communist Party and Katushev, the Central Committee Secretary responsible for co-operation with 'fraternal parties'.

I was particularly interested by the names of the East German delegation. The list of participants included only Walter Ulbricht and Prime Minister Willi Stoph. But I was told verbally that it was highly likely that Erich Honecker, the Politburo member responsible for security questions, and Hermann Axen, who held an important post in the SUP leadership, would also be present. However, later it turned out that Honecker had not travelled with the delegation after all.

The Polish delegation consisted of the party leader, Wladyslaw Gomulka, the State President, Marian Spychalski, Prime Minister Cyrankiewicz and Zenon Kliszko, the Central Committee Secretary.

From Hungary there were only the party leader, Janos Kadar, and Prime Minister Fock. Bulgaria was represented by the party leader, Zhivkov, the two Central Committee Secretaries, Todorov and Boris Velchev, and Prime Minister Kubadinski.

When we interpreters asked for the texts of the statements to be made at the conference we were told that no documents were available; the whole of the conference would have to be simultaneously translated.

While the other interpreters were taken into a side room to be served with a generous breakfast, Trepczynski, the head of chancellery of the Central Committee Secretariat, asked me to help the technicians test the headphones and microphones in the five cabins and the separate microphones on the table. All the connections between the delegates' microphones, the translation cubicles and the headphones were in order. But there were no connections between the different cubicles. I wanted to get the technicians to install connections to link up the cubicles but they told me that the shortage of time made it impossible.

I drew Trepczynski's attention to the fact that these cross connections were essential for the smooth running of the conference since, for example, I could not translate a speech by the Hungarian delegates into German unless I could tune in to the Polish-speaking cubicle. And of course, the same was true of the other interpreters.

There was nobody capable of translating direct from Bulgarian into Russian or from German into Bulgarian. Trepczynski, who was a very capable administrator, immediately grasped the point, talked to the technicians for a few minutes, and half an hour later the connections between the cubicles had been installed.

Shortly before ten o'clock the delegations appeared, together with secretariat staff, experts and security men. There were more than a hundred people altogether. Apart from the actual delegates, their closest advisers, interpreters, technicians and staff from Gomulka's secretariat were allowed into the conference room. Since the meeting was to take place at a round table there was no place of honour. The Soviet delegation took up their seats opposite the windows which would have revealed a view of the beautiful Lazienki Park if they had not been covered by heavy curtains. To the right of the Russians sat the Poles, on their left the Bulgarians, and opposite the representatives of the GDR and Hungary.

After all the delegations had taken their places Gomulka, as host, made a speech to open the proceedings. He suggested that no chairman should be elected, but that each delegation should preside in turn after every interval in the talks. This suggestion was accepted, Gomulka then expressed the opinion that, for reasons of principle, no official report of the proceedings should be made. This suggestion was also agreed by the delegates. Only when Gomulka went on to discuss the agenda did the Soviet delegation raise an objection. Gomulka had stated that the discussions would cover the development of the situation in Czeckoslovakia and that this analysis would then serve as a basis for conclusions. He suggested that each delegation should first express its views on Czechoslovakia and then in the second half of the conference each delegation should speak again to make concrete proposals. Brezhnev immediately replied that he was of a different opinion. Each delegation should make their analysis in the first half of their speech and make any proposals for action in the second half. Apart from the Polish delegation, all the delegates agreed with Brezhnev.

Gomulka was unanimously elected to preside over the first round of the conference. The Polish party leader immediately began his address, which lasted about an hour and a half. He confined himself to analysing the situation in Czechoslovakia, but did not make any proposals.

The political situation in the CSSR, said Gomulka in his introduction, had taken such a turn that it had become necessary to call this 'consultation between fraternal parties'. Numerous talks had been held with the Czechoslovak party leadership under Dubcek, and it had been indicated to them that dangerous tendencies were making an appearance in their country. But the Czech communist leaders had always replied that they were in complete control of the situation in their country. Dubcek and his colleagues had promised on numerous occasions to check the anti-Soviet, anti-socialist and counter-revolutionary forces, and had even set themselves time limits to achieve this; but they had so far done nothing in this direction – on the contrary.

Recently, Gomulka stressed, a significant document had been published in Prague, the 'Two Thousand Words' manifesto, in which the counter-revolutionary and imperialist forces had called openly for the overthrow of the communist regime in Czechoslovakia. Even this manifesto, exclaimed Gomulka accusingly, had not provoked appropriate reaction from the Czechoslovak leadership, and therefore the conclusion must be drawn that they were no longer in control of the situation. This development appeared particularly dangerous in view of the fact that even some of the members of the Czechoslovak Party Presidium had publicly approved the 'Two Thousand Words'.

Gomulka's speech was not at all fluent in its delivery. He often paused, searching for a phrase, and looked around as if he was seeking the agreement of the other delegates. From time to time Cyrankiewicz raised his massive head and glanced at the speaker. To begin with the Polish party leader spoke in Brezhnev's direction, but later he also paid attention to the other delegations. What does 'socialism with a human face' mean? Socialism is itself the most human thing possible, said Gomulka, his voice full of emotion. This kind of catch-phrase is used by the Western imperialists to cause confusion in the working classes and within the party so as to weaken the socialist camp and, eventually, to destroy it. Whenever the imperialists want to destroy socialism in a socialist country the first point in their programme is the destruction of the communist party, and they begin by eliminating their cadres.

Gomulka went on to relate this theory to the developments in Czechoslovakia. When deserving officials were dismissed on the pretext that, as Stalinists, they were incapable of carrying out leading functions, or that they had taken part in crimes in the past, then this was nothing else than the first step towards the liquidation of the party. Of course, in order to restore capitalism, the counter-revolutionary forces must also introduce appropriate economic measures. The attempts made by Czechoslovakia to establish economic links with Western countries were the best proof of the fact that the country was about to abandon the socialist camp.

Gomulka's throat was dry. He took a sip of water, moistened his lips with his tongue and continued. Many counter-revolutionary manifestations were naturally also affecting the exercise of state power in Czechoslovakia. So many clubs and organizations had been set up that one could already speak of the establishment of bourgeois political parties. The mass media in the CSSR were controlled by counter-revolutionary forces who were obviously involved in the preparation for a takeover of power. If one studied the Czechoslovak press, radio and television then it was quite clear that the only aim of these institutions had become to cause confusion among the working class and the people and deflect the workers from their true interests.

Gomulka paused for a moment and then raised his voice: The abolition of censorship was equivalent to the renunciation of any claim by the party leadership to exercise the slightest influence on developments. He waited a second and continued in a melancholy voice, saying that in the CSSR they were faced with a new phenomenon in the international communist movement. There could be no doubt that a counter-revolution was taking place, but it was a counter-revolution in a new form. Previously this term had been used to describe an armed uprising against the power established by the revolution of the working class. 'But here,' as Gomulka expressed it in his own words, 'we are dealing with a counter-revolution in which no shots are exchanged. For us it would, of course, be much more simple if there were shooting, for then we could react in a very different way.'

Then he turned to face Brezhnev: 'But in no circumstances can we allow the counter-revolution to be victorious.'

The Polish party leader then illustrated his theories with quotations from the Czechoslovak, West German and American press. Naturally they were chosen in such a way as to support his arguments.

Although at the beginning of the conference Gomulka had given his silent consent (without casting his vote in favour) that each delegation should cover both analysis and proposals in a *single* speech, he deliberately omitted the second half of his speech for he did not want to commit himself on the measures that should be taken before the other delegations had laid their cards on the table.

After Gomulka's speech Brezhnev began his address. He gave full details about why the Czechoslovak party was not represented at this Warsaw conference. Dubcek and his followers had been repeatedly invited but they had always found excuses not to come. Early in July the Czechoslovak Communist Party leadership had been invited to a meeting with the 'fraternal parties' in Warsaw. Appropriate letters had been sent to Dubcek by the central committees of all five countries taking part in the conference. The talks should have taken place on July 7.

However, Brezhnev stated that the last letter had only been handed to the Czechoslovak leadership on July 8. A few days later, the Soviet leader claimed, the Prague leadership was handed a further request from the communist party of the Soviet Union to take part in a summit conference of the Eastern bloc in Warsaw on July 13. Brezhnev referred briefly in passing to a telegram which Alexander Dubcek had sent to the Warsaw Conference as at present constituted. In it Dubcek had claimed that he had not received this invitation from the Soviet Communist Party. But Brezhnev insisted on the fact that the Soviet Ambassador in Prague, Chervonenko, had passed on the invitation to the Czechoslovak Central Committee. So this was just another of the excuses made by the Czechoslovak leadership to avoid multilateral talks with the five 'fraternal parties' in the hope of holding separate bilateral talks with the different party leaderships.

Brezhnev looked round the table and surveyed all those present before sitting down again in his place.

In conclusion Gomulka discussed the procedure of the negotiation once more. He suggested that the aim and purpose of this summit meeting was to compose a letter to the Czechoslovak party leadership. There were two suggested versions: a Polish and a Soviet draft. Both were similar in principle but differed in phraseology. Therefore it would be necessary to form a committee which would present the drafts to all the delegations during a recess and incorporate their suggestions for amendments and additions so that the final text could be approved at a plenary session of the conference. Before this recess, during which the comrades could familiarize themselves with the two drafts under consideration, he would like to ask Comrade Kadar to report on his latest contacts with Dubcek.

The Hungarian party chief told how he had met Alexander Dubcek several times on the Hungarian-Czechoslovak border – on the last occasion only a few days previously. He had attempted to make Dubcek understand why the 'fraternal parties' were so worried about developments in Czechoslavakia. At their last meeting Dubcek had replied that there was no cause for any concern since the leadership of the Czechoslovak Communist Party was in complete control of the situation in their country in every respect.

Kadar went on to say that he completely agreed to the proposal to send a letter to Dubcek and his followers. But he wished to emphasize that any decisions over and above this could lead to serious consequences in the whole world communist movement and also inside Czechoslovakia. Kadar spoke in a noticeably quiet tone of voice.

At this moment, quite uninvited, Walter Ulbricht joined in the debate. One cannot really say that he spoke. In his high voice he shouted across the room in such a way that I could hardly keep up with the translation. 'What is happening in Czechoslovakia, Comrade Kadar, is only a part of the American-West German global strategy for destroying socialism in each separate country. If you think, Comrade Kadar, that you are helping the cause of socialism with your objections and reservations then you are making a big mistake. And you have no idea what will happen next. Once the American-West German imperialists have got Czechoslovakia in their control then you will be the next to go, Comrade Kadar. But that is something you can't or won't understand!'

This was the tone Ulbricht took to abuse Kadar and Fock, his Prime Minister. As the atmosphere in the conference room was growing increasingly tense Brezhnev interrupted Ulbricht's flow of words and proposed that the conference should now go into recess, as planned, so that the delegates could familiarize themselves with the two draft letters.

Each delegation then named its representative on the committee to work on the final draft. The Poles nominated Zenon Kliszko, the East German delegation Hermann Axen, the Soviet delegation Katushev. The task facing the committee was quite difficult. First both draft letters had to be translated into all the languages of the participating countries. Naturally all the delegates had some knowledge of Russian; but they still demanded a translation of the documents into their own languages – no doubt following the example of Walter Ulbricht who had insisted for years on speaking only in German at international conferences.

On the first floor of the Council of Ministers a few rooms had been arranged for the text translators, and they began their work straight away. The rattle of typewriters filled the long corridor. To save time for the committee both letters were translated paragraph by paragraph, and the completed sections were immediately sent to the room where the committee was sitting. While the translators were working on the next paragraphs disagreements were already appearing within the committee. For it turned out not to be so easy to agree on the same formulas. The Polish delegation, for example, insisted on a paragraph stating that the rehabilitation of people in Czechoslovakia who had been unjustly persecuted in the past should be continued. The delegations of the Soviet Union, Bulgaria and the GDR were against such a paragraph. Ulbricht's confidant, Hermann Axen, wanted to include a reference in nearly every sentence to the 'machinations of the Kiesinger–Strauss government' as he expressed it, and this also led to protests from the other delegations.

Meanwhile discussions at the plenary session continued. Ulbricht spoke at great length about the 'enemy forces' which wanted to divert Czechoslovakia from the path of socialism so as to separate the country from the socialist community of nations. The other socialist countries could not allow this attempt to go unchallenged. Willingly or unwillingly, a section of the Czechoslovak leadership had become the servants of world imperialism. The West German imperialists had had time to realize that it was not so easy for them to subjugate the German Democratic Republic; so now they were trying a policy of encirclement so that they could also attack the GDR from its southern flank.

The East German party leader described the plan of the Czechoslovak party leadership to hold their party congress in just over two months as the gravest factor of the situation. If order could not be restored in the CSSR by that time, said Ulbricht, they would be faced with a completely new situation. For then there would be a new Central Committee and a new Presidium of the Central Committee; all the good communists would lose their posts and then what could they do? 'So we must react before this party congress can take place,' he assured the conference.

The toughest speech was made by the head of the Bulgarian delegation, Zhivkov. The socialist countries owed it to the Czechoslovak working class and the people of the CSSR to give their country every assistance in fighting the counter-revolution; he added – these are his actual words – 'military assistance not excluded'. (A few days after the Warsaw conference I heard Western radio broadcasts which said the Bulgarian delegation had taken the most moderate position during the meeting – a crass error.)

Then Kadar once more gave a brief statement of Hungary's attitude, although he confined himself to generalizations. He was obviously glad that no final decision was to be made at the Warsaw summit on measures to be taken against Czechoslovakia, and that Dubcek and his followers were only to be presented with an ultimatum.

Before Brezhnev expressed the attitude of the Kremlin leadership a break for lunch was arranged. I was summoned to a table where Gomulka, Cyrankiewicz, Kliszko and Spychalski had been joined by Ulbricht, Stoph and Axen. Over lunch the lively political discussions continued. For example, Gomulka told of how, during the unrest in Poland in March 1968, only a few students had rebelled against the basic principles of the regime. Their meetings and demonstrations had been filmed with telescopic lenses. These films had shown quite clearly, claimed Gomulka, that many of the demonstrators had only taken part out of hooliganism. 'For instance, we could see that many of them turned round as they were being chased by the People's Militia and thumbed their noses at the policemen. So we should not exaggerate the importance of this kind of event.'

Ulbricht immediately began to criticize Gomulka's relaxed attitude to demonstrations and Stoph backed his party leader eagerly. But when Ulbricht saw that his warnings were having no effect on Gomulka he changed the subject. He told his table companions that the East German authorities were in possession of detailed information about a visit to Czechoslovakia made by Zbigniew Brzezinski, the American political writer of Polish origins. This material also included the text of a speech that Brzezinski was said to have made in Prague. Ulbricht, the able tactician, knew only too well how to decoy Gomulka.

Professor Zbigniew Brzezinski is one of the intellectuals most detested by Gomulka. He has published many works on communism and after the 'Polish October' of 1956 he re-visited his old country. During the last few years Gomulka had frequently attacked Brzezinski's theories in public speeches. For the Polish leader this acute analyst of the communist social order was a promoter of anti-communist ideology, one of Poland's worst enemies and an 'imperialist running dog'. It seems probable that Gomulka had not read all Brzezinski's books or he would have been able to see that many of the ideas presented by the writer were not so very different from various theories developed by Gomulka himself twelve years earlier. But now, when Ulbricht used his information about Brzezinski as a bait, Gomulka immediately rose to it. He asked Ulbricht to pass on the documents which were of the greatest importance for Poland. The East German party leader promised to send him the papers. Although Gomulka could be certain that this time Ulbricht would keep his promise he reminded the East German leader to be sure to send the papers direct to him. Gomulka also took the opportunity to describe how, on one visit to Poland; Brzezinski had met the well-known Polish philosopher, Leszek Kolakowski, who now lives in Canada. On that occasion one of the men had handed written documents to the other, 'But, unfortunately,' said Gomulka in a disappointed tone, 'We were not able to establish what sort of material was involved.' It is easy to see how closely the Polish security authorities watch foreign visitors.

With unconcealed pleasure, Gomulka went on to describe how even the Jugoslav authorities were now having trouble with their students, and how the party and state leadership in Belgrade had been obliged to take energetic action. Now the Jugoslavs, who used to try and give us lectures, were finding that they had to handle trouble of their own making. We had known for a long time that the Jugoslav experiments in reducing the influence of the party and making the state apparatus more independent were doomed to failure. Gomulka was getting in such an excited state that he hesitated, with an 'er, er' after every few words. I knew him well enough to recognize this as a sign of great emotion. He gave his view of the role of the party leadership in the following words, 'Tito is introducing experiments in the economy and thinks that this is the way to, er, er, serve socialism. Of course, er, er, this is wrong. Power is not, er, er, made of elastic to stretch or contract as you like. If you renounce power in any area, then the result is not, er, er, a vacuum; instead the enemy immediately takes it over.'

Gomulka must have felt the personality and policies of Alexander Dubcek as a living reproach. It was clear that he hated the Czech leader because of his popularity within Czechoslovakia, and envied him for it. Naturally these ambivalent feelings were the result of the memory, which he tried in vain to suppress, of the time twelve years earlier in October 1956 when he, like Dubcek, was the hero of his own people. At that time Gomulka had promised the Poles a complete change in policy from the earlier repressive methods. He had promised legality and announced that the activities of the security authorities in the years before 1956 would be closely investigated. He had condemned the cult of the personality and demanded complete equality and non-interference in Poland's internal affairs from the Soviet Government. He had promised to free the economy of its bureaucratic fetters and to re-establish freedom of thought. When he returned to power in October 1956 all the collective farms, the 'agricultural production co-operatives' forcibly established by the state, actually were broken up again. Gomulka dismissed all the Soviet 'advisers' who had been forced on the Polish Government by the Kremlin and sent them back to Russia. Indeed, he did not even hesitate to drop the Soviet Marshal Rokossovski from the post of Polish Defence Minister, and to get him recalled to the Soviet Union. Compared with Gomulka's aims in 1956, which, within the context of the communist system, were truly radical, the Dubcek of 1968 was a moderate reformer. But, since Gomulka had changed in the past twelve years both as a man and as a politician, his attitude to Dubcek was negative from the start. By 1968 Gomulka's position had already been weakened by internal power struggles to such an extent that he had to reckon with the possibility of being overthrown at the Polish Communist Party Congress which was to take place in a few months' time in November 1968. Since he had had to abandon one political position after another inside Poland he was now looking for allies abroad.

Even during the lunch interval at the Warsaw summit meeting Gomulka was using every means to show Ulbricht that only he was the right man for Poland – he was well aware of the influence Ulbricht had with some of the factions within the Kremlin leadership. This search for allies was also illustrated in Gomulka's speech to the plenary session of the conference, described earlier. The

Polish leader ended his speech with the characteristic sentence, 'The Soviet Union holds the leading role in the socialist camp and for this reason it also has the right to certain privileges.'

For the Western reader who does not usually pay close enough attention to the nuances in the phraseology used by communist leaders this remark may seem a political cliché. But there is more to it than meets the eye. Until 1956 phrases like 'the leading role of the Soviet Union' or 'the socialist camp with the Soviet Union at its head' were *de rigueur* throughout the communist sphere of power. One must be familiar with the history of the communist movement to realize what it meant when Gomulka dropped this formula out of hand on taking over power in Poland in 1956. He replaced it by the phrase, 'the Soviet Union, the biggest and first socialist country.'

This political catch-phrase had hardly entered the vocabulary of Polish communists before the shock waves spread through the whole Eastern bloc. In the years immediately following 1956 the fraternal parties took every opportunity to accuse the Polish party leadership of deviating from Marxism-Leninism, betrayal of the communist ideal, the introduction of bourgeois ideology and similar mortal sins – one reason being the fact that Gomulka would not use the formula about the leading role of the Soviet Union. He was once even strongly attacked by a few Stalinists at a meeting of the Central Committee. In 1957 they protested that even a country the size of China accepted the leading role of the Soviet Union. Impulsive as he was, Gomulka answered that he had talked with Chou-En-Lai and knew what the Chinese said – and also what they thought. A few years later Krushchev quietly dropped the 'leading role of the Soviet Union'. But now in 1968, when no one had used the phrase for years, Gomulka revived it in a tone of servility.

After lunch Brezhnev spoke on behalf of the Soviet delegation. He began in a reasonable tone and carefully modulated his voice. One could not avoid the impression that he was not only making a speech but also listening to his own words. He wanted, the Soviet party leader began, to express the view of the USSR as regards the latest developments in Czechoslovakia. The highest organs of the Soviet State, the whole working population of the Soviet Union, were following with growing concern the direction which matters were taking in a fraternal socialist state. Marxist-Leninists had always learned not to avoid responsibility but to fulfil all their international obligations.

The worthy comrades sitting round the table looked bored. Everyone knew what was coming – an hour-long speech with theories, formulas and arguments that had only one thing in common – they were not new. Any 'worthy comrade', especially if he has a senior post in a socialist state, must have a well trained backside. It is an unwritten rule of protocol that everyone should listen with 'great interest' when the representative of a fraternal party speaks. And when one of the most powerful men in the mighty Soviet Union makes a speech then the audience must be all ears. Only occasionally, when the speaker pronounces a sentence in a loud voice and then pauses briefly, do they know that it is their duty to provide 'stormy applause'.

There were, continued Brezhnev, basic rules of socialist society that had been clearly formulated in the classics of Marxism-Leninism and which could never be flouted. That did not, of course, mean that the Soviet Union wished to impose its own opinions, attitudes and methods on any other socialist country. Such an attitude would be contrary to the whole history of the Soviet Union and the Soviet Communist Party. The Soviet Union had always supported the view that every party was in the best position to know conditions in its own country, and would apply the general principles of the socialist development of society creatively, and take account of national characteristics. But when the interests of other socialist countries were involved, when the unity, the power and the whole existence of the socialist countries were endangered, then it was the duty of communists and of leading statesmen to afford every assistance to the Czechoslovak working class and the whole Czechoslovak people.

This was the birth of the awkward attempt at self-justification which later entered the international political vocabulary under the name of the Brezhnev Doctrine. The sentence that had been spoken hung menacingly in the air. The General Secretary of the Soviet Communist Party paused briefly. Nobody clapped, but his listeners thought it wise to nod their heads in agreement, a small gesture that expressed submissiveness and unconditional agreement.

Through the five-foot-high glass window of my cabin I could observe the reactions of the participants very clearly. For the most part they just looked bored.

Only the Hungarian delegation followed Brezhnev's speech with the greatest attention. When it had been announced after the last interval that Comrade Brezhnev was to speak, a senior official – I think it was a Central Committee secretary or a deputy prime minister – accompanied the conference interpreter for the Hungarian delegation to the Hungarian cubicle so that he could translate Brezhnev's speech as accurately as possible. This event showed how much importance the Hungarians attached to the summit meeting in general and the speech of the Soviet party leader in particular. At the same time one could tell from the reactions of the Hungarian delegation that the party leadership in Budapest, which had been acting as a mediator between the other four Warsaw Pact nations and Czechoslovakia in the previous weeks and months, had not been informed by the Soviet authorities of the actual aims of this Warsaw summit meeting. I got the impression that Kadar and Fock were quite prepared to agree to any decision by the conference, even if it contained gross inconsistencies, so long as no military intervention was decided.

But Brezhnev stuck to his guns. He had been unmoved by all the Hungarian warnings that rash measures against Czechoslovakia must result in political and moral damage to the Soviet Union that would outweigh any advantages. He had also disregarded all the reservations of the Western communist parties. And since Brezhnev was dependent on the power structure within the Soviet top leadership he naturally could not permit himself to show the least weakness or uncertainty at this conference.

He gave the impression of an actor practising his role in front of the mirror, always taking care to make the most of his melodious, rather metallic voice; only occasionally, when he used particularly extreme phrases, did he lose his control. He was well aware that he was playing the strong man, the heavyweight of the communist world movement.

It was easy to see how proud he was of speaking 'in the name of 200 million Soviet citizens'. No – more than 200 million Soviet citizens. In the name of all the good communists of the whole world, in the name of all the progressive forces in our planet. He had made this claim so often himself, and heard it quoted so often by others, that he now believed it himself. He was the spokesman of all progressive forces in the world, in the whole of humanity; so every word that he spoke was of historic importance. Louis XIV could say, '*L'état, c'est moi*'. But when the top man in the Soviet Union spoke in a way that amounted to claiming 'The whole of progressive humanity, *c'est moi*', then no party leadership from the Eastern bloc was allowed to challenge him – certainly not the petty troublemakers and 'manipulators of the counter-revolution' in Czechoslovakia.

In a booming voice, which could not conceal the many contradictions in his speech, Brezhnev claimed that the Soviet Union conceded the right to independent development to every socialist state. But almost in the same breath he stressed the determination of the Soviet leadership to use all the might of the Soviet Union to strangle at birth the least sign of independence in a fraternal country.

Brezhnev paused for a moment and then continued by saying that the latest developments in Czechoslovakia indicated clearly that the party leadership was no longer in control of the situation. The Czechoslovak comrades had already been warned several times that they were only a step away from the abyss, and that a strong stand must be made against the forces of international imperialism. Even Comrade Dubcek had admitted this, as was shown at the Dresden meeting and other talks, and he had promised to restore peace and order in his own country with the greatest possible speed. But these had been empty promises. It was true that the Czechoslovak party leadership had immediately dissociated itself from the 'Two Thousand Words' manifesto, but what had happened then? Some of the Prague comrades, members of the highest organs of government, had disregarded all the principles of democratic centralism. In opposition to the principle binding on the whole communist movement that a measure can only be discussed before a decision is taken, but that afterwards the minority must range itself alongside the majority, these comrades had tried publicly to defend the 'Two Thousand Words' in more or less veiled terms. So if counter-revolutionary ideas had taken root even in the highest levels of the party and state apparatus, it was impossible for proletarian internationalism, for the fraternal countries, to take the dishonourable role of inactive spectators. The Czechoslovak comrades, indeed, all the Czechoslovak workers, demanded immediate aid from the working classes in the fraternal countries, and this aid must be given to them. Brezhnev's speech went on and on, flowing like a stream of muddy water; in the general boredom only Walter Ulbricht occasionally threw a hostile and ironically triumphant glance in the direction of the Hungarian comrades, Kadar and Fock.

As the hours dragged on the delegates showed certain physiological symptoms from which even leading statesmen in communist countries are not immune. For instance, Todor Zhivkov, the head of the Bulgarian delegation, was visibly sleepy. First he glanced through the papers on the table in front of him, then he stared round the room, and finally took off his headphones. Perhaps the noise continuously buzzing in his ears disturbed him, or perhaps he only wanted to show that he could follow 'his master's voice' – Brezhnev's words – without a translation. When the Soviet leader raised his eyes from his notes a few minutes later and looked round the circle of delegates he noticed this obvious lack of proper respect. He glared at Zhivkov with an expression that a teacher might use with an inattentive pupil: So you aren't interested in what I've got to say? When the head of the Bulgarian delegation realized his mistake he looked disconcerted and then quickly reached for his headphones and put them on again. After that he was one of Brezhnev's most attentive listeners, along with Kadar and Fock. The Soviet leader went on to say that not only the Soviet people but the peoples of the fraternal countries, as shown by the speeches of the other comrades, were in complete agreement on the analysis of the situation and on the conclusions resulting from it.

Finally the Soviet General Secretary came to the end of his speech and raised his voice: The criticisms of the shortcomings and errors in the pre-January period in Czechoslovakia were fully justified. The Soviet Union was in favour of any constructive criticism. But when this was used to destroy the leading role of the party as a whole and to emasculate it, then all the party leaders could only agree in saying: The counter-revolution will not succeed in Czechoslovakia. This was the united and indisputable view of the working masses in our five countries.

So now I knew a historic decision had been taken. It was interesting to see how Brezhnev insisted on basing his arguments on the agreement of the five Warsaw Pact countries taking part in the meeting. It was the same old story. Anyone planning to put an evil action into effect always tries to implicate his audience in his decision. Clearly the Soviet authorities felt that their *unilateral* action in suppressing the Hungarian uprising of 1956 had been a mistake.

The reactions of the other delegates to Brezhnev's speech varied. Ulbricht was obviously unhappy that no definite decision had yet been made. That is, no decision to put the whole of Dubcek's revisionist gang under lock and key and to sort out the whole situation in Czechoslovakia. The Hungarians, on the other hand, seemed relieved by the same fact that irritated Ulbricht. The Bulgarians, who had gone the farthest with Zhivkov's demand for military assistance, seemed quite satisfied.

However, even within the different delegations opinions were divided about the best response to developments in Czechoslovakia. I could observe this from my cubicle and I also overheard scraps of conversation which suggested that there were disagreements. These were based not on opposing political attitudes but on differences of character.

For example, Brezhnev did not allow himself to be tied down. The many contradictions in his speech would later permit him to come down on one side or another as it appeared necessary. He could claim to have pressed for a tough line, but at the same time to have guaranteed each communist party the right to take its own path. And so far no official decision on military intervention in Czechoslovakia had been made.

Kosygin, on the other hand, gave the impression of a very worried man. The role of judge which he had adopted at this meeting did not seem to suit him. Podgorny, the Soviet head of State, looked, as always, rather self-satisfied. Shelest, short, fat and bald, looked round the table gloomily. Only one of the Soviet delegates looked completely calm: Katushev, the Central Committee Secretary responsible for contacts with the 'fraternal parties', a man whose decisions strike awe in the hearts of many communist leaders throughout the world. Here, surrounded by his powerful superiors, he looked like a petty, insignificant, junior official who is concerned only with the smooth running of his department. Diligently he rushed to and fro – from the conference room to the room occupied by the drafting committee, from there to the translators, always carrying a pile of papers – the typical hard-working assistant.

The two Hungarians, Kadar and Fock, were obviously glad that they had not yet been forced to agree to the kind of 'international assistance' to Czechoslovakia that had caused the deaths of so many of their countrymen twelve years earlier. In the intervals between the talks the other delegates shunned the Hungarians as though they were lepers.

Ulbricht was furious that no definite measures had yet been

decided against the 'revisionists' around Dubcek. 'A chain is only as strong as its weakest link,' he said during a recess, in a tone that was both boastful and hectoring. 'If a few enemies of the people in Czechoslovakia think that they can weaken our whole camp from Prague, then they have made a very big mistake.' During the closing session the East German party leader could not hide his anger. The last round of talks had been delayed for a few hours because, in spite of working flat out, the text translators had not had the time to translate into Russian and duplicate the ultimatum drafted by the committee. And when the technical staff mistakenly announced that the text was ready and all the delegations returned to the round table to sign it, it turned out that the fair copy of the text had not yet been made.

During this final session Ulbricht took the chair. Since the microphones were switched on I could also hear the private conversations within the delegations from my cabin. On Ulbricht's right sat Hermann Axen, a small, round, agile and very clever man. He had been nominated to the drafting committee by the East German delegation. When Ulbricht said quietly to Stoph, who was sitting on his left, that the final session could begin, Axen pointed out to his leader that more time would be needed for a fair copy of the text to be made. So this session, where the only item on the agenda was the signing of the document, could not yet begin.

Normally in this situation Ulbricht should have asked the participants in the meeting what action should be taken. But instead he turned to his right, glared at his subordinate, Axen, as though he were saying, 'Who asked you for your opinion?' but then said in a quiet tone, 'That is nothing to do with us. It's the Poles who should be ashamed that they aren't capable of organizing their bureacratic administration properly. I shall open the session now and then we shall see how they get out of it!'

And this is what happened. Ulbricht declared in a loud voice, 'Dear comrades, we have now come to the end of our work and have assembled together here to sign the letter to the Central Committee of the Czechoslovak Communist Party. I request our hosts, the Polish comrades, to give us the document.'

The 'Polish comrades' were taken aback. Gomulka declared that the final version had indeed been translated but that it had not yet been typed out; after a short whispered exchange with his head of chancellery, whom he had summoned to him, Gomulka informed the conference that it would be at least another half hour before the text would be ready.

Ulbricht tried to look worried, but he could not hide his satisfaction.

To understand his attitude it is important to remember that a top policy meeting like this Warsaw summit conference takes place on three levels. First there were the plenary sessions and then the negotiations by the drafting committee in which the different phrases were composed and polished. At this level, where detailed work was done, there were immediate disagreements between the delegations. During their work the members of the drafting committee remained in constant contact with the leader of their delegations, consulting him about every sentence and asking for instructions. Once the leaders had given their opinion the committee members returned to their room and carried on negotiating. So the final version of the letter to the Czechoslovak Communist Party leadership had already been approved by the leaders of the delegations. The third and most important level of the conference was the unofficial talks which took place during the recesses.

Naturally the plenary negotiations at the Warsaw Conference had to be constantly interrupted to give the drafting committee and the translators time to do their work. In these intervals Brezhnev and Gomulka frequently left the other delegates and held private discussions. Naturally the other delegation leaders knew what this meant: they were excluded from this third, and most important, level of the conference.

Meanwhile the other delegates sat in the room leading off the conference room, devoted themselves to the culinary delights of the cold buffet, discussed matters and waited. Although Ulbricht put a good face on it and talked first to the Bulgarians and then to the members of the Soviet delegation it must have been a hard blow for him that he was not asked to join Brezhnev and Gomulka in their discussions.

During these intervals the Hungarians were still quite isolated. Kadar, the party leaders, and Fock, the Prime Minister, sat alone at a table and talked together.

But Ulbricht was not out of temper only because Brezhnev and Gomulka had not consulted him separately. During the plenary sessions the question had also been raised of the language in which the ultimatum should be expressed. Gomulka had suggested that Russian should be used. He based this suggestion on the fact that translating the document into the other four languages would needlessly prolong the conference. But Ulbricht immediately countered, 'The document must be drafted in all the languages of the participant states, for we are not only party leaders but also the highest representatives of our countries. As party leader I might be able to sign a note addressed to another country in the Russian language, but, as Chairman of the Council of State of the sovereign German Democratic Republic, I cannot be expected to send an official letter to the Czechoslovak leadership in Russian. This would be more grist to the mill of the imperialists who always claim that I follow Russian, not German policies in my country. Moreover, it would be contrary to diplomatic usage. It is completely out of the question. And finally, we cannot subordinate such important political problems to organizational inadequacies.' After this side swipe at his Polish hosts Ulbricht raised his voice and added sarcastically, 'This conference has been badly organized if we are to be at the mercy of technical staff for such fundamental questions.'

Since Ulbricht had rejected Gomulka's suggestion so categorically the conference now discussed whether five identical letters should be addressed in the appropriate languages to Prague on behalf of each of the different Central Committees and governments. In this case each Central Committee of the five parties would act separately in sending the letters. This idea was again rejected since time was short and Dubcek would have received five separate letters. The aim of the conference was a joint letter. So Ulbricht was obliged to give in. The head of state of the German Democratic Republic had to sign an official ultimatum in Russian to another country in the name of his government.

There were other details which led to arguments between the delegations during the summit conference. For instance, the plenary conference discussed for almost an hour the question of when and how the letter to the Czechoslovak leadership should be published in the different countries. To begin with they could only agree on the 'how' – the ultimatum was to be published in the central organs of the communist parties of the five countries involved.

Then the timing was discussed. Ulbricht suggested that the letter be published on the following day, immediately after the end of the discussions. He swept aside the objections of the

Bulgarians and Hungarians who pointed out that they would first have to make an accurate translation of the letter into their own languages. Turning to Hermann Axen he whispered, 'Is the German version ready?' and received the answer 'Certainly'.

'We have made our translation, comrades, so why can't you do the same before tomorrow?'

But on this point too Ulbricht had to climb down. Brezhnev declared that the Czechoslovak leadership must be given at least one or two days to have the letter from the Warsaw meeting translated and to study its contents. Then the Czechoslovak Party Presidium would need at least a day or a day and a half to formulate their reply. Gomulka supported Brezhnev; he pointed out that it would be tactically inadvisable to publish the ultimatum immediately especially in view of public opinion in both West and East. 'If we publish the letter tomorrow then, as Comrade Brezhnev has pointed out, there will be an interval of three to four days before we receive a reply. And how shall we look in the meantime, Comrades? World opinion will be told the contents of our letter immediately but will not understand the reasons for the necessary delay before the Prague leadership answers it, so it will be thought that the Czechoslovak Party Presidium is ignoring our ultimatum. Apart from that there is another point which I do not think we should overlook. Unfortunately there are parties in our international communist movement which are so undisciplined that they do not even agree with us in such an obvious fact as the existence of counter-revolution in the CSSR. If our letter is published tomorrow these parties will also learn of its contents. But this is against our interests. Should we give them time to organize themselves so that they can continue to support the revisionists within the Czechoslovak party leadership and back up their position?'

The other delegates agreed with these tactical considerations expressed by Gomulka. Although Ulbricht maintained his objections the delegations agreed not to publish the letter in the party newspapers of the participating countries until four days after the close of the summit meeting.

The East German leader had some unpleasant surprises at this summit meeting. When the conference discussed the type of 'assistance' which should be given to the Czechoslovak working class he said, in an undertone, 'We could, as has already been suggested, stir up the Slovaks and start everything going in that way, and then . . .'. At this Brezhnev threw him a scathing glance and he did not finish his sentence. Now it was Ulbricht who was being called to order by an unspoken retort from his lord and master, 'Did anyone ask for your opinion, Comrade Ulbricht?'

Even when the East German President insisted that he wanted to maintain bilateral contact with the Czechoslovak leadership after the Warsaw meeting he was voted down by the other delegations. He had wanted to go ahead with a meeting with Dubcek which had already been agreed for the beginning of August. But the other party leaders believed that talks should first be held between the Soviet Union and the Czechoslovaks, and also that they should wait for a reply to the letter from the Warsaw meeting.

It is true that there were other delegations, for instance the Bulgarians, who held the view that the events twelve years earlier in Hungary had shown the best way of dealing with counter-revolutionary forces, and that there was no reason for not using the same methods in Czechoslovakia instead of delaying matters with letters, party contacts and so on. But they did not show their displeasure as openly as Ulbricht. So the East German leader had plenty of reasons to feel resentful during the final round of the talks under his chairmanship.

When the Russian version of the ultimatum was ready at last, one of Gomulka's secretaries brought the document into the conference room and placed it before his chief. But Gomulka did not seem to know what to do with it. Time had been so short that there was only one copy. Should he read it out himself in his broken Russian, or should he ask Brezhnev to do so? He began to stammer, and then waved over a girl interpreter to the table. 'Read this document aloud!'

Since there was only one copy the party and government leaders of the five powers had to sign the ultimatum to the Czechoslovak Party Presidium without having the opportunity to study the text in detail. With this significant episode, the official part of the summit meeting drew to a close.

The end of the meeting was marked by an official reception which Gomulka gave in honour of his guests. Apart from the men who had taken part in the conference about a hundred other people were invited to this event, which was to start at three in the afternoon. These included members of the Polish Government and diplomats from the countries which had taken part in the conference. They all arrived punctually, but since the end of the official conference had been delayed because the text of the ultimatum was still not ready, the guests wandered aimlessly through the long corridors of the Council of Ministers building, or talked together in small groups. Finally they were packed off home like schoolboys and told they would be informed by telephone when the reception was ready to start.

After three hours' delay everything was ready at last. The leaders of the delegations exchanged self-satisfied toasts; only Wladyslaw Gomulka, the host, enlivened the formal exchange of compliments by an unconventional remark. He declared that the conference had certainly gone very well but that the menu he was presenting to his honoured guests at the reception was of scandalously poor quality and he must apologize for it. He forgot to tell his honoured guests that between three and six o'clock several members of the staff of his secretariat had approached him and presented him with an 'ultimatum' from the cooks. 'We were asked to prepare the food for three o'clock. If we are not allowed to serve it straight away we cannot be answerable for the quality of the dishes.'

The tragedy of the Czechoslovak people, the tragedy of the Czech and Slovak communists whose only aim was to imprint more human features on a communist government and party, had now begun. All the hopes of this small country and its people were crushed by the tanks. Apart from the political results this was the prelude to countless personal tragedies which are still having repercussions today and to which no end can be foreseen. At the same time it was an expression of the profound internal crisis in which the communist camp is becoming more and more deeply embroiled.

Index